ONDON

TO BIDE · TILL THEY DECAYD THROU

LEATHER LANE

HATTON GARDEN

CHARTERHOUSE S

SHOE LANE

FARRINGDON ROAD

CENTRAL MAR

SITE OF FURNIVAL'S INN

REVI...

HOLBORN

HOLBORN CIRCUS

VII

HOLBORN

HOLBORN VIA

FARRI

FURNIVAL

12

BARNARD'S INN

BARTLETT'S BUILDINGS

THAVIES INN

S. ANDREW S

SHOE S

PLUMTREE S

29

NORWICH ST

DEAN ST

TOOK'S COURT

URSITOR ST

BEAM'S BUILDINGS

12

28

NEW STREET

HARDING S

36

JOHNSON'S COURT

18

27

CLIFFORD INN

IV

FLEET

ST

STONECUTTER

S REEL

JOEIN

51

32

SALISBURY COURT

17

K

MITRE COURT

SERJEANT'S INN

23

24

BOUVERIE ST

WHITEFRIARS ST

SALISBUR SQUARE

9

PRIMROSE HILL

NUTTON S

MIDDLE TEMPLE LANE

INNER TEMPLE LANE

16

35

MAGPIE ALLEY

NORTHCLIFF HOUSE 22

23

Site of TEMPLE BAR

V

TEMPLE

21

STREET

1670   TEMPLE BAR   1879

THE LAWYERS

Inscribed by the Author

Tyndale Daniell
1971

— for Alexander —

Dedicated to
The Legal Profession

and the members of the A.B.A. in their bi-centennial year.

THE LAWYERS

– The Inns of Court: The home of the Common Law –

by

Timothy Tyndale Daniell
Barrister-at-Law, of Gray's Inn

together with a Bicentennial Essay on
Anglo-American Law in the present day
by J. M. B. Crawford, A.B., M.A., Middle Temple

with illustrations by T. T. D.

Wildy and Sons Ltd
London W.C.2
Oceana Publications, Inc
Dobbs Ferry, New York
1976

Inns of Court
– continuing best seller–

1st Edition 1971

Wildy and Sons Ltd
London
Oceana Publications, Inc
Dobbs Ferry, New York

Oceana ISBN: 0-379-00593-X
Library of Congress Catalog Card Number 76-25744

Printed in Great Britain by
Layston Litho Ltd, Buntingford, Herts, England.

PREFACE

TO THE SECOND EDITION

The Royal Commission on legal services has begun in earnest. No doubt members of both bodies will survive their ordeal.

Much water has flowed under the bridge of Father Thames since the first edition was published in 1971. Whereas the Temple itself has changed imperceptibly; the London Skyline grows ever newer and more daunting, and we 'all' grow perceptibly older. Indeed London Bridge has crossed the Atlantic (to a new mooring at Lake Havasu City, Arizona).

This edition attempts to cover new fields of the law outside the Temple. It is auspicious that moves are afoot, which if successful, will see the restoration of a fine old legal monument, Temple Bar – 'long associated with the Temple' and its return to London. Thus I have included what may seem of disproportionate length.

I wish to thank particularly, Mr. Henry Summerfield, for his masterful contribution to chapters one, two, and three. His goodwill and that of our clerks, Mr Pike and Mr. Hayter, have been much appreciated.

I am very grateful to the Bar Council for providing – in their many pamphlets – much information to Henry and me. Philip Gaudin, Information Officer to the Bar, in providing ideas and information in the writing of this book. I am asked to point out, and gladly do so, that the text as printed is my sole responsibility.

Thanks are more than due unto: Charles Puckett, for his collaborative guidance on the architectural buildings mentioned in the text, and especially Temple Bar, which is an old hobby-horse of his; Sir John Summerson, for his extreme kindness in lending a scholar's ear on the manuscripts; various colleagues in the four Inns, as also the Treasury Offices, who have assisted greatly; the typesetters 'en bloc' whose production staff of Herts Typesetting Services Ltd (under the helm of Mr. Brian McCarthy) have prepared this publication without sleeping for a week; and the unbreakable will of one Bill Palmer, the printer, and his good daughter Judy, without whose toil this book would have remained 'on the shelf'.

It goes without saying that Kenneth Sinkins of Wildy's remains the best publisher in the world.

Perhaps Horace would have said of this all: Numerisque fertur Lege solutis.

T.T.D.

4th July 1976.

CONTENTS OF THE BOOK

THE FOREWORD

by the RIGHT HON. LORD DENNING,
MASTER OF THE ROLLS

I wish that this book had been available when I first started in the law. It tells the story of the Inns of Court. They go back for some 600 years. No one knows who founded them. They have no charters to stamp their beginnings. Nobody endowed them with funds. They just grew. Groups of successful pleaders formed themselves together in 'guilds', just as the tradesmen did. These men practised law in the Courts. They got young men to help them and to learn the profession as apprentices do. Then came the turning point of their fortunes — they were recognised by the Judges as exclusive. The Judges allowed audience only to the members of the Inns of Court. No one could appear as an advocate except a member of these privileged societies. This monopoly ensured their success. Practitioners became rich and influential. Students sought to join the Inns of Court so as to gain likewise. The leading practitioners were appointed by the King to be his serjeants at law — servientes ad legem. On becoming serjeants, they left the Inns of Court and became members of Serjeants' Inn. Many of them were afterwards appointed to be Judges. Such was the structure in the fourteenth and fifteenth centuries. So prosperous did the Societies become that in the time of the first Queen Elizabeth they built splendid halls in which they held magnificent revels. It was their Golden Age. Just think of the great names: Sir Edward Coke of the Inner Temple; Francis Bacon of Gray's Inn; and later Sir William Blackstone of the Middle Temple, and Lord Mansfield of Lincoln's Inn. They were the very makers of English law.

Ever since the Inns of Court have retained their unique place in our island story. They have been the exclusive source from which the advocates have been supplied. They have been the training ground for students of law. But not only for those intending to practice law. The best families always sent one or two of their sons to London to join one of the Inns of Court for the culture and education they dispensed. From these Inns of Court men went forth all the world over. Wherever the English went — whether as settlers to the United States and Canada — or as administrators in the East Indies, or beyond — there went a goodly number of men trained in the Inns of Court. If you should look through the names of the Ministers, Statesmen and Judges of the great countries overseas, you will find time and again that they started at one of the four Inns of Court. These men carried with them the law which they had learned here. They took with them 'the rights of Englishmen' — a watchword throughout the States of America. Their influence on the legal systems of the world has been immeasurable. And, when it came to drawing up Constitutions, they played a leading part. Look at the Declaration of Independence. Look to the Constitutions of Canada, Australia, India, and many others. You will find them drafted by members of the Inns of Court.

Still the good work goes on. If you should visit, as I have, many of the countries of the Commonwealth, you will find many men — including Prime Ministers, Cabinet Ministers and Judges — who started at the Inns of Court.

Today the great countries overseas have their own law schools. They train their own lawyers and judges. But they still return to visit us — to see the places from which their forerunners came. They will find here that we try to keep up the traditions inherited from the past. They may like to look a little more closely into our story. If so, they will find it in this excellent book — written with care, skill and devotion. It should find a place in every lawyer's library.

The Rt. Hon. Lord Denning, P.C.
The Master of the Rolls.

4th July, 1976

ix

INTRODUCTION By LEONARD CAPLAN Q.C.

Of Gray's Inn and the Middle Temple, One of Her Majesty's Counsel Learned in the Law, Master of the Bench of Gray's Inn

All the countries sharing the heritage of the common law are nurturing a living growth which continues to develop not only in its original soil but also where it has taken root elsewhere. What was initially a sturdy plant has been strengthened by a notable process of cross-pollination, enabling it to adapt to the changing circumstances of an ever-changing world. But the character of the stock remains unimpaired, still vigorously embodying a concept of human relationships which succeeds in being both moral and pragmatic, a blend of high principle and common sense.

The motor car with a defect in one of its rear wheels, the ginger beer bottled together with a dead snail, and the harm caused by each to persons having no contractual nexus with the manufacturer, were the elements in a striking instance of this inter-action, adaptability and animating spirit. In 1916 the Court of Appeals of the State of New York found itself able to hold, without direct authority for guidance, that in the circumstances of the case before it the maker of the motor car was liable in tort for the harm so occasioned to such a user; Cardozo, J. observing that 'Precedents drawn from the days of travel by stage coach do not fit the conditions of travel today'. Sixteen years later the House of Lords reached the conclusion that the manufacturer who had bottled ginger beer along with a decomposing snail could be liable in negligence for the injury thereby caused to the health of a consumer. In the course of his speech in that case Lord Atkin referred to the 'illuminating judgment' of Cardozo, J. in the American case, which he said 'states the principles of law as I should desire to state them', and expressed what is as true today as it was then that 'It is always a satisfaction to an English lawyer to be able to test his application of fundamental principles of the common law by the development of the same doctrines by the lawyers of the

Courts of the United States'. The moral rule that you are to love your neighbour, he said, 'becomes, in law, you must not injure your neighbour'; and after posing the question 'Who, then, in law is my neighbour?' proceeded to formulate an answer which in his view made it 'clear that the law in this matter, as in most others, is in accordance with sound common sense'.

Although from time to time divergent trends, in some branches of the law, manifest themselves in various of the common law countries, historical perspective reveals that ultimately the trend is towards uniformity. Thus, nearly fifty years ago, Professor Goodhart could say that 'the present American tendency is strongly away from the strict English doctrine of stare decisis' and that in this regard 'English and American Courts are at the parting of their ways', while a distinguished American academic, Dean McMurray, was writing that 'in most American jurisdictions today a more rational theory as to the binding force of precedent generally obtains than that held by the British House of Lords'. Today those statements are no longer true. The House of Lords moved significantly towards the American position when in 1966 the Lords of Appeal unanimously resolved that, although treating former decisions as normally binding, they proposed to depart from such decisions when it appeared right to do so.

Another gap which had arisen and has now been substantially, although not completely, closed is in the area of liability for negligent statements. The English cases had apparently negatived the existence of any such liability, save in the limited circumstances where there could be held to be a special duty of care. But in the United States this was seen as unduly constraining and it had been decided that the liability existed whenever 'the relationship of the parties, arising out of contract or otherwise' was 'such that in morality and good conscience the one has a right to rely upon the other for information and the other giving the information has a duty to give it with care'. Without adopting this formulation, the House of Lords has now decided that the limitations which were previously thought to exist were too narrow, and that the legal duty to take care when providing information arises in a wider variety of circumstances.

It is not alone the judiciary in the common law countries but also the practitioners of the law who have had, and will continue to have, a vital role to play in the organic process which is at work. Unless the Courts are assisted by adequate citation of relevant cases decided in other common law jurisdictions the full potential of our great shared inheritance will fall short of being realised. But this is not all that has to be. For interpretation is at least as much a matter of the spirit as it is of the word. Happily, confraternity of spirit exists in overflowing measure, extending across oceans and manifesting itself in many forms. There are the occasions when the Bar of one country plays host to that of another; there are the myriad contacts of a more personal nature, in which connection one remembers the glories of that friendship and correspondence, over so many decades, between Mr. Justice Oliver Wendell Holmes and Sir Frederick Pollock; and there are those especial means by which the profession delights to show its brotherhood. Amongst these latter, as a Master of the Bench of Gray's Inn, I cannot forbear to mention that we have numbered among our Honorary Benchers the immediately past Chief Justice of the United States of America and the late Mr. Justice Frankfurter; and that in our historic Hall, which sustained bomb damage in the last World War, there now stands an oriel window marked with a commemorative plaque affording us a constant reminder of the generosity of the American Bar, for which we are abidingly grateful, in the help they gave towards its resurrection.

PENSION CHAMBER,
GRAY'S INN   4th July 1976.

Leonard Caplan

xii

CHAPTER 1

THE LAWYERS

Shadows we are and
Like shadows depart

THE LAWYERS

THE LAWYER

The trench of the Common Law is dug deep into history, through which every unwitting aspirant lawyer sets his compass. One of the first descriptive definitions of 'the lawyer' is recorded by the poetic genius of Geoffrey Chaucer, himself almost certainly a member of the society of the Inner Temple. It is glorious prose set in modular verse and should be recited with a swagger:

> A Sergeant of the Lawe, war and wys
> That often hadde been at the parvys,
> Ther was also, ful riche of excellence.

> Discreet he was, and of greet reverence.
> He semed wich, his wordes weren so wyse.

3

Justyce he was ful often in asseyse
By patente and by pleyn commission:
For his science and for his heigh renoun
Of fees and robes hadde he many oon.

So greet a purchasour was no wher noon.

Al was fee simple to him in effect,
His purchasing mighte not been infect.

No-where so bisy a man as he ther nas,
And yet he seemed bisier than he was.

In termes hadde he caas and domes alle
That from the tyme of King William were falle.

Thereto he could endure and make a thing,
Ther coude no wight pinche at his wryting;
And every statut could he pleyn by rote.

He rood but hoomly in a medlee cote
Girt with a ceint of silk, with barres smale;
Of his array telle I no longer tale.

The text is a significant tombstone: many questions surrounding the historical origins of the law, are hereby answered circumstantially.

Firstly, a glossary of the 'quaint' English:—
Parvys, the portico of St. Paul's where Serjeants held out-door chambers and conference (and referred to in greater explanation elsewhere).
purchasour, a conveyancer,
infect, meaning invalid; thus Chaucer's learned lawyer had the wits to circumvent the restrictions of passing title to property which had been imposed by the statutes De Donis, on feudal tenure.

4

in termes, he knew the cases by the dates of the terms which was their citation.
endyte, compose.
pinche, blame.
ceint, a girdle

The early legal portrait that emerges is of a man engaged in conveyancing (which was and is of major commercial interest for many), but uninvolved in any criminal practice, probably because the then system of surety, by men known to the accused, precluded greater forensic argument in trial. Chaucer's man is clearly a forbear of the profession we all know and love, for he is and seems busier than he actually is, although his spare time is, we are told, spent mugging up the case-law and its distinction even then between statute book and the Common Law precedents. The lawyer is sober-clad, and enjoys the fees which his stature has behoved him to accept.

In the twentieth century, the lawyer is still a mystery to the layman. The lawyer is a generic term used to describe a practitioner who has qualified in his legal training and joined the legal profession. The profession differs according to the historical traditions which a country has inherited.

In England, for example, the profession is divided into two channels: the solicitors and the barristers. Solicitors are general practitioners of the law, appointed to act for members of the public in matters of a legal nature. Barristers are surgeons, or a lawyer's lawyer, who exercise a special function as court advocates on the instruction of solicitors and their clients. They represent the client in a Court of Law, and plead the case commensurate with the skill of their training and expertise. Barristers enjoy the exclusive right of audience in the Superior Courts.

Within the United Kingdom, Scotland (who divide their legal profession into solicitors and advocates), and Wales as also the Republic of Ireland, the legal profession is divided between the two streams of lawyers.

Other countries follow a different practice: In France there are three primary types: *avocats* – the litigous lawyer, *notaires* – the non-contentious conveyancer and drafter, and *conseils juridiques* – or the legal adviser.

In the States of America, the legal profession is not divided: all lawyers are attorneys. The specialisation into advocacy or conveyancing, for example, is however as deep as in Europe. As a matter of fact, public debate in England is giving serious attention to the division of the Legal Profession today, and the Royal Commission of 1976 may recommend a more logical dividing line between advocates (barristers and to include some solicitors) and notaries (conveyancing lawyers). All await the way this cookie will crumble.

From Chaucer's time until now the division of the lawyer into two branches has existed in England. The Ordinance of King Edward I, in 1292, instructed the King's Judges to 'provide and Ordain' a certain number of 'attorneys and apprentices'. The attorneys were the forerunners to the solicitor as he is now known. Apprentices were apprenticed to the law itself – *apprenticii ad legum* – and not to the more senior practitioners. They became the modern barrister. This statute conferred on English lawyers their status and was derived from the Crown 'the Fount of Justice', to quote Professor Dicey. The growth of a body of pleaders trained in the 'Common Law' Courts developed with the *servientis-ad-legem*, or servants of the law. They became the senior advocates of Sergeants-at-Law; from whose august body, Judges were appointed. Then as now The Bench controlled the conduct of the practitioners through the membership of the bodies of the various Inns of Court and Chancery, to be described in Chapter Eight.

THE ORDER OF THE COIF

'Coiffure', a fashion of dressing the hair; headdress. Oxford Dictionary.

The ancient and venerable Order of the Coif was founded in the English Common Law, formed part of the English Common Law, and flourished for 800 years with origins fastened in the closed books 'ere legal memory began.

What was it and who were the members?

The Serjeants are a grateful race,
Their dress and speeches show it,
Their purple robes from Tyre we trace,
Their arguments go to it!

The Order was a small body of eminent men, learned in the law, who administered the realm and from whom the Judiciary was appointed exclusively from their own rank. These gentlemen were titled 'Sergeants-at-Law', and their apparel was dis-

The Ante-Screen by dusk

tinguished by a close-fitting cap of white lawn, which the wearer was never required to remove, even in the presence of royalty.

Sir Edward Coke, himself created a brother of the Order in 1606, referes to his brethren thus: 'Of these serjeants, as of the seminary of Justice, are chosen Judges; for none can be Judge, either of the Court of King's Bench, or of the Common Pleas, or Chief Baron of the Exchequer, unless he be a Serjeant; neither can he be of either of the Serjeants Inns, unless he hath been a Serjeant-at-law; for it is not called Judges' or Justices' Inn, but Serjeants Inn;' Preface to the 10th Report: Commentaries.

ORIGINS

What the Forum was to the wise men of the law of ancient Rome, old St. Paul's Cathedral was to the Serjeants-at-law 'that often hadd been at the parvys' (in the style of Geoffrey Chaucer), and in the thirteenth century alluded to the Order as already an ancient institution. Of early serjeants created, Geoffrey Ridel in 1117, is one of the earliest on record, as also:

William de Warenne (1195),
Reginald de Warenne (1168),
Hugh Murdac (1179),
Simon de Kyme (1191),
Hugh de Gaerst, 1179,
Ranulph de Glanvil, 1179,
John de Cumin, 1174,
William Basset, 1176,
Maurice de Berkely, 1190,

9

Henry de Brayboock, 1199,
Hugh de Cressy, 1177,
William Fitz-Stephen, 1176,

and Richard deHeriet, in 1195, may be included of the twelfth century.

There is hardly any Order more ancient to be found, viz.,

The Order of the Garter, instituted 1330,
Bath, 1399,
Thistle, 1540,

And the oldest title in the English peerage was 1181,
the first Dukedom, 1338,
the first Marquis, 1385,
and the first Viscount, 1440.

The most famous lawyers of every age, from very early times were of this body, and comprised the serjeants-at-law who were promoted from their Inn of Court to the Order and one of the Serjeants' Inns now extinct, by writ under the Great Seal of the Crown on the advice of the Lord Chancellor. As the serjeant took leave of his Inn of Court for higher things, the Inn tolled its bell as if in grief. All Common Law Judges, that is those who presided over the King's Bench and the Courts of Common Pleas, were appointed from their ranks, until the Judicature Act of 1875 abolished the rule that common law Judges were required to be appointed from the Order of the Coif. The close fitting white linen cap was worn until the time of Charles II when wigs came into fashion, and thereafter the coif was fastened or pinned on the top of the wig, which legacy is retained to this day by the dress of the judges of the High

Court. The Order was probably a product of the tenures in sergeantry where feudal land was held of the king by grand or petty sergeanty as a 'servant of the crown', hence the derivation of the name.

When Serjeants' Inn became extinct (after 1875) the Serjeants returned to the Inns of Court in which they had started their careers. Thus it came about that the Inns again included Judges among their senior members.

There is no record of the date of the foundation of any of the four Inns of Court — Lincoln's Inn, Inner Temple, Middle Temple, and Gray's Inn — they were flourishing well before 1400. Their rights and duties rest on no royal charter or statute. They are not bodies corporate but voluntary 'Honourable Societies'. It is a matter of law that these Societies have powers delegated from the Judges to admit persons to practise in the King's Courts. The Inns of Court are colleges to this day.

THE LAW STUDENT

The Law Student — whether he reads for the Bar or takes Articles for Admission to the Roll of Solicitors — may agree with Oliver Wendell Holmes!

'Only when you have worked alone — when you have felt around you a black gulf of solitude more isolating than that which surrounds a dying man, and in hope and despair have trusted your own unshaken will — then only will you have achieved' — from a lecture on the Profession of the Law, Harvard 1888.

12

Legal education in England differs from that of America and some Commonwealth nations. In England, a student may decide (or it may be decided for him), to go up to university and read law before he embarks on a career. However, if he wishes to read for the Bar, either as a fresh young scholar or as a young gentleman with a degree, he will enrol for admittance to an Inn of Court (see Chapter Five), and 'eat his Dinners', and qualify successfully in the Bar Examinations. Thereafter he will be called to the Bar by the Treasurer of his Inn of Court, and commence practice.

Alternatively he may decide to be admitted as a Solicitor of the Supreme Court: in which case, having left school or the university, he will 'do his articles' with a firm of practising solicitors and simultaneously read for the exacting professional examinations held by the Law Society.

In either case, he remains a barrister or solicitor for life, unless he should choose to withdraw from the Rolls of the Supreme Court, or otherwise be disbarred or struck off.

The School of Law is the educational body which administers the legal education of a 'student barrister'. Since its creation in 1852 (as the Council of Legal Education) it has survived a chequered history. It expanded with the proceeds of sale of the Inns of Chancery in the nineteenth Century, on their demise (see Chapter Five). Post-war values have altered those hitherto accepted in education, and young men now have to be taught to become gentlemen, before they are eligible for call.

The Great Screen
of
The Musicians' Gallery
1571.

14

THE BARRISTER

There is no profession in the world seemingly as anomalous as the Bar. The barrister may not advertise his services — even though many may want to hear of him; he does not talk to solicitors direct except where his clerk has permitted him so to do; he does not shake the hands of his colleagues; — these and other niceties cause popular misconceptions. There are old-established reasons and rules for the conduct and etiquette of a barrister.

If he advertised himself, he might compromise the standards expected of him and the duty of honesty he owes to the courts. If he spoke freely with solicitors or clients in his professional capacity, his impartiality might be prejudiced and his position diminished: there is no room for contingency fees in England (where Counsel receive a 'cut' in the costs awarded his client, if his case succeeds). As the system stands, he is on call to whoever requires his advocacy or legal advice.

> From the moment that any advocate can be permitted to say that he will or will not stand between the Crown and the subject arraigned before the Court where he daily sits to practice — from that moment the liberties of England are at an end.

... Fortunately the liberties of England have not ended since the writing of this cardinal rule by Erskine, who was Counsel for a 'political' defendant, and was savagely attacked for accepting the brief to defend. As with Voltaire, a barrister may disagree with the opinions of his client, but true liberty grants all men the right to speak, and the barrister upholds his duty of service to a client. This is known as the taxi-queue or 'cab-rank' principle. In 1975, the Chairman of the Bar Council, Sir Peter Rawlinson, Q.C., expounded its relevance in the modern day:

> Persons accused of crimes, however odious, must be given the service of responsible lawyers and must continue to be tried, as they are being tried, calmly and dispassionately, and afforded all the safeguards against miscarriage of justice. If we fail in this duty, the terrorist's bomb can do worse than maim and kill the innocent; it will destroy the fabric of justice itself and of the free society which it is our desire and our duty to defend.

In all representations that a barrister makes in a Court of Law, and duties he owes thereto, he will present the interests of his client and not allow his private feelings to detract from his client's instructions.

> Sir, a lawyer has no business with the justice or injustice of the cause which he undertakes, unless his client asks his opinion, and then he is bound to give it honestly. The justice or injustice of the cause is to be decided by the judge. Consider, sir, what is the purpose of Courts of Justice. It is that every man may have his cause fairly tried by men appointed to try causes. . . A lawyer is to do for his client all that his client might fairly do for himself if he could.

In 1951, Lord Denning (when he was a Lord Justice) spoke in the Court of Appeal:

The duty of counsel to his client in a civil case — or in defending an accused person — is to make every honest endeavour to succeed. He must not, of course, knowingly mislead the Court, either on the facts or on the law, but, short of that, he may put such matters in evidence or omit such others as in his discretion he thinks will be most to the advantage of his client. So also, when it comes to his speech, he must put every fair argument which appears to him to help his client towards winning his case. The reason is because he is not the judge of the credibility of witnesses or of the validity of the arguments. He is only the advocate employed by the client to speak for him and present his case, and he must do it to the best of his ability, without making himself the judge of its honesty. Cicero makes the distinction that it is the duty of the judge to pursue the truth, but it is permitted to an advocate to urge what has only the semblance of it.

Barristers receive a fee for each and every instruction he fulfills. The fee is customarily marked on the brief *before* the barrister's clerk has accepted it, and thus makes no difference to the outcome, won, lost or settled.

A barrister may not sue for his fees, and this originates with the 'honorarium' of a pleader in Medieval times.

The Bar divides itself into Common Law Bar, and Chancery Bar. The Common Law Bar concerns itself with the more litigous aspects of the legal arena —

Criminal – Divorce – Contract – Negligence et cetera
– whereas Chancery work embodies the proverbial
'deeds and documents' pertaining to, inter alia,
conveyancing, probate and trusts. There are further
specialist Bars: Admiralty, Planning, Patent, Parliamentary, Tax and even the ever-growing 'Capitalist
Transfer' Bar.

Although the historic Assize system was abolished
in 1971, barristers continue to belong to Circuits and
Circuits mess wherever their practice is conducted
outside London. The Circuits originated with the
itinerate Justices holding the 'King's Peace' who
replaced the parochial feudal courts of the barons
throughout the shires and counties. The surviving
Circuits are: South-East, Western, Midland and
Oxford, Northern, North-East, Wales and Chester.

Life on Circuit has its ups and downs but does
much to foster the warmth and friendship shared by
members of the Legal Profession.

At the beginning of their careers most barristers
join one of the six circuits which have existed from
the reign of Henry II (1154-1189). The chief town of
each county, and certain of the other principal cities
of the Kingdom, three times each year, held the
King's Court of Assize there, to hear and determine
civil and criminal cases – and empty the jails! –
'Oyer, terminer and general jail delivery,' as it was
called in a mixture of Norman, French and English.
In early days most criminals were arrested and kept in
prison until their trial, but as the usual punishments
were fines, of branding or maiming, forfeitures and
execution, the itinerant judges found the jails full and

left them empty. Nowadays, most of the accused await their trial on bail, and many of them are punished with imprisonment. So now that the situation is reversed, the Judges fill the prisons instead of emptying them. Groups of Barristers used to travel round with the Judge, to represent those who appeared before him, and gradually, those who followed a particular itinerary formed an association. They dined together in the Assize towns, and their associations became known as Circuit Messes. Each developed its own traditions, customs and discipline, and did much to ensure that members of local Bars, who lived and practised in centres outside and merely came to the capital City, shared the standards and traditions of the rest of the profession.

In 1971 the Courts Act substituted Crown courts for Assizes for Quarter Sessions, as described in Chapter three. and thus the circuits of the Judges. Any Barrister who is a Member of one circuit may now appear without any restriction or extra charge on another circuit, but the professional organisation of the Circuit Messes still continues. Each Mess elects its own Circuit Leader, a Barrister of repute and some seniority, which has its representation on the Bar Council.

When he finishes his pupillage, a Barrister must join, or if he is *very lucky* remain in, a set of Chambers. Once established in Chambers the young Barrister receives work more quickly than used to be the case, but even so, many find it necessary to supplement their income. The lucky ones do this largely by 'devilling', — doing work for more senior

19

Barristers and receiving one half the fee for doing it, — but many also do part-time work, teaching, law reporting, writing on legal and other subjects, and acting as temporary part-time Court clerks. Some find these part-time occupations so congenial that eventually they take them up full time and abandon the Bar altogether. Indeed many people who are called to the Bar enter salaried employment immediately they are called or immediately after their pupillage, without practising at all. Good jobs await them in the Civil Service especially in its legal Departments, in Local Government, in the administration of the Courts, and in commerce and industry generally. These Barristers have their own professional organisations, such as the Civil Service Legal Society, which includes Solicitors. Generally speaking, Barristers in full-time employment have no rights of audience in the Courts, but Barristers employed by Government Departments may and do represent those Departments in prosecuting minor criminal cases in the Magistrates Courts.

As the young Barrister becomes busier he tends to drop the part-time occupations already described, and later perhaps acts from time to time, temporarily, as a Deputy Circuit Judge or a Recorder, whose functions are described in more detail elsewhere.

A land-mark in the Young Barrister's career is the day when he receives his 'Red Bag' from a Queen's Counsel to whom he has acted as junior in an important case, and who is so pleased with the help which the junior has given him that he buys, and through his Clerk, presents to his junior a Red Bag, embroidered on the outside with the junior's initials, and suitable inscribed within. From then on a junior carries his wig and gown in a red bag, instead of using the blue bag to which he was entitled on call.

QUEEN'S COUNSEL

Queen's Counsel – or – Taking Silk. Francis Bacon, the Essayist and later Lord Chancellor, was appointed 'Counsel extra-ordinary' by King James I by Letters Patent at the beginning of the seventeenth century. Not until the eighteenth century did the custom of regularly appointing 'King's' or 'Queen's,' (according to the sex of the reigning Monarch) take hold. Then one or two were appointed each year, but as the Serjeants faded away, and finally disappeared, at the end of the nineteenth century, silks, as they are called, became more numerous. They wear a silk gown instead of the stuff, or cotton, gown worn by junior counsel. They constitute about one-tenth of those in practice at the Bar.

Queen's Counsel are still appointed by Letters Patent, on the recommendation of the Lord Chancellor, to whom any junior may apply (to 'take Silk') who thinks he is sufficiently experienced. Every year there are several times as many unsuccessful applicants for Silk as successful ones, but the unsuccessful may try again thereafter. The list of new Queen's Counsel, usually about 30, of whom a few are Court Officials or Professors or others who do not intend to practice, is announced each Maundy Thursday, and on the first day of Easter Term the new Silks are sworn in by the Lord Chancellor, and go to the Royal Courts of Justice to be welcomed on behalf of the Judges by the head of each division of the Court. The new Silks enter the Courts in order of seniority, and each in turn is called forward and addressed by the Judge as follows: 'Mr. X, Her Majesty the Queen having been pleased to appoint you one of her Counsel learned in the Law, will you take your seat within the Bar.' The Bar of the Court, like the Bar of Parliament, separates that part of the Court room, which represents the old right of representation from the area behind, where suitors and others who had no right of admission to the Court itself, could congregate to watch the proceedings or make their requests to the Court. The new 'Silk' normally answers this question with another silent bow which formally recognises his right to precedence over other barristers to put motions to the Court. It is said, whether truly or not, that one Barrister whose girth was so great that he could hardly fit between the Benches, replied as he bowed 'With difficulty, my Lord.'

A Queen's Counsel cannot appear in most Courts unless he is assisted by, or 'leads', a junior Barrister. The Junior must be adequately remunerated for the case, and the Silk normally receives a larger fee, usually twice as much, as the junior. This makes it expensive to employ him, even if the new Silk's fee is in fact no more than, or even less than, he would have been paid as a very experienced junior. Silks are therefore normally instructed only in weighty cases which justify the payment of such fees. Because of these differences between the type of work which a

Barrister may have done as a junior and that which he must hope for as a Q.C., taking Silk is for some almost like commencing a new career, although for others the transition may be very smooth indeed. Some, of course, earn less than they did as a junior, while some few never succeed in establishing themselves at all. A Q.C. however, cannot revert to being a junior Barrister.

Opponents attack the expense of the system, and argue that the junior is overpayed and under-worked: Supporters of the system urge the desirability of the most skilled and experienced Barristers reserving for themselves the more difficult cases. Furthermore, in many of these cases, the facts are so complex or the law so difficult that even if there were not a 'Two-Counsel rule', Two Counsel would be employed. Indeed it often happens that a junior Barrister may lead a still more junior one, where in some cases the party voluntarily choose, because of the difficulty and complexity and importance of the matter, to brief several juniors.

The rising Barrister may seek, and possibly obtain, an appointment as a Recorder (who is a part time Judge whose functions are described in Chapter Three). A Recorder must agree to sit at least twenty days a year in the Crown Court or County Court and is appointed by the Monarch on the recommendation of the Lord Chancellor. Sitting as a Recorder not only gives the Barrister experience as a Judge, but enables the Lord Chancellor, who is responsible for recommending persons to be appointed as Judges, an opportunity to observe his capacity. Barristers may also obtain judicial experience as arbitrators, as part-time members of other Statutory Tribunals, as Chairmen of Public Enquiries appointed by the Government, e.g. to report on matters of public concern, serious disasters, suspected mal-administration, or the dealings of commercial companies (the unacceptable face of capitalism).

The successful Barrister who is well thought of in his profession will also receive the honour of being appointed a Master of the Bench of his Inn. As such he must play his part in the running of the Inn and the provision it makes for its students. All High Court Judges are always elected Benchers on their appointment as Judges. This accolade is a great distinction at the end of a career.

The Benchers and the Circuit Messes for centuries exercised the only control there was over admission to the profession and its discipline, although a Judge could always rebuke any Barrister who appeared before him. There was little or no co-ordination between the various Inns. There was little between the Inns and the Circuit Messes. The General Council of the Bar of England and Wales, from its institutions in 1895 exercises no disciplinary powers but its rulings are generally accepted on questions of professional conduct and etiquette.

The profession continued to suffer from lack of a common body to speak and act for it: in 1966 the 'Senate of the Four Inns of Court' was created to supply this shortcoming, and to deal especially with discipline and professional education. In 1974 however, following on the recommendations of the

Senate Committee under the Chairmanship of a distinguished retired Judge, Lord Pearce, the old Senate and Bar Council were replaced by a new central governing body, 'the Senate of the Inns of Court and the Bar,' to which are elected representatives. The Law Officers of the Crown, the Attorney-General and Solicitor-General, and also the Chairman of the Council of Legal Education, are ex officio members of the Senate. The Bar Council continues an autonomous existence 'to maintain the standards, honour and independence of the Bar, to promote, preserve and improve the services of the Bar, and to represent and act for the Bar in its relations with others and in all matters affecting the administration of justice'.

THE AMERICAN BAR

Seventeen years before the inception of its English 'sister', the American Bar Association was formed (in 1878) to 'advance the science of jurisprudence, promote the administration of justice, and uniformity of legislation throughout the Union, uphold the honour of the profession of the law, and encourage cordial intercourse among its members'. Anyone who has enjoyed the hospitality and intercourse of the American Bar will vouch wholeheartedly for the successful avowal of the aims of the ABA.

... Of the 14 signatories at the preliminary conference for the Organisation of the ABA ... in 1878, five were Southerners, who have traditionally maintained the warmest links with Britain, from the time of the Cession.

THE BARRISTER'S CLERK

'He is a barrister first sir, a lawyer after'.
'Who says so, sir?'
'His clerk. Good-day.'

The origins of the status of clerk are unclear, but he was known in Dr. Johnson's time. Better known is the fact that Charles Lamb (1775-1834) referred to his father, John: 'I knew this Lovel. He was a man of incorrigible and losing modesty', who died in 1799 having been in the service of the Inner Temple and to Samuel Salt, barrister, for over forty years, which would authenticate that Clerks existed by the middle of the eighteenth century, at least.

Every barrister knows that the most formidable law unto himself is his clerk. A barrister may be made or broken by his clerk, although like his principal good wine, it is hoped, improves with age. Because barristers have no legal status as defined in any enactment, he cannot sue for his fees. If a famous advocate defends an infamous fellow successfully, the latter may in theory send a postcard from his retirement-villa in the sun, declining to pay for his trial defence. The advocate may go 'all pompous and purple' but he may only regret that he was not prosecuting in the case. The barrister's clerk is charged with the duty to collect fees, one among a hundred other duties. Because a barrister may not advertise himself, he may not contact solicitors, the Very Important Persons who hand out their briefs to the Bar: a solicitor who wishes to engage the services of a barrister on behalf of a client — to 'instruct him', as the saying goes, approaches his clerk. The barrister's clerk acts as go-between. Indeed, such is their power behind the throne, that firms of solicitors may associate a set of chambers with the clerk, 'Potts', rather than the head of Chambers — 'Sir Bumble Bee', and thus a young barrister is more fortunate at his outset to be seen walking in the company of the senior clerk than Sir Bumble.

A clerk may be described as the barrister's agent in all matters that affect his principal's activities in the law. The clerk may have upwards of 15 principals, and very often there is a head clerk overseeing one or two others in a set of chambers. The clerk negotiates the fees of his counsel — 'We can go into court on this matter for a fee of £100' — and administers the secretarial nature of a lawyer's life, in paperwork and in appointments. The clerks earn in addition to a salary, a commission on the fees received. But the single aspect which makes the barrister's clerk so profound an influence in the byways of the profession is his special relationship with the practitioners. Old Sir Bumble may have started at the Bar some forty years ago, when Potts was but a junior clerk. As Sir Bumble's practice expanded, young Potts was the ever faithful witness — a travelling companion on circuit for nights on end away from home, or counsellor after countless trials — and those memories are fastened to the past when Sir Bumble is appointed to the bench and offers Potts the appointment of Judge's clerk. (In the old days this happened: Today Judge's clerks are civil servants.) There must have been satisfaction for the two learned souls sitting while younger advocates played their forensic skills before them, and Potts was seen to slip a note to His Lordship which may have read: 'Not like the old days, sir, do you remember how you used your kerchief with such effect on a similar lady in the witness box.'

There we have it, the mutual confidence between the busy lawyer and his clerk. There is the story, kindly brought to my attention by one of the old school (who was told it by his father, also a clerk in The Temple some 80 years ago): A chief Constable of an Assize town called upon the presiding judge after the courts had adjourned for the day. A man was on watch at the judge's door, who intimated that the judge was busy on notes and should not be disturbed. The chief constable went away and later complained to the judge in person, when they met up, of the manner of the man who had turned him away. The judge was sympathetic as he listened to the scraps of the conversation:

> 'And how long did he reprimand you in this abusive way?'
>
> 'He was very rude in the spate of less than a minute, my lord.'
>
> 'Good gracious, how you have suffered; but I've been at the other end for 35 years, Chief Constable.'

For the young barrister embarking on the long haul of experience his clerk is a very good friend, guiding him through the intricacies of his first cases, such advice being in the form of questions but with the force of a colonel, and many a young advocate

28

survives his first ordeals by stint of the patience of his clerk. In the precincts of the courts, the clerks are as well known to the judicial brethren and court officers as are counsel. When a clerk accepts a brief on behalf of 'his' barrister, it is he who estimates the length of the pending action, the hour when a witness is likely to be needed, and a clerk of experience will often tell you the result of the case before it is half-heard. The unofficial duties of the clerk may be even more varied than his official duties. He must continue to hold a persuasive tongue on a disgruntled litigant as well as an aggressive one. The story is told how two, tall, oriental gentlemen recently opposed one another in a High Court trial, and, when the lawyers had had their fill — and gorged on the meat of the case for a fortnight — and the judge had delivered his judgment, still the loser would not accept defeat, and instead, abused the victor on the steps of the High Court as the parties were taking their leave. The victor did not take kindly to the reference of his mother's anatomy (but had learnt enough of English law to realise there could be no libel of the dead). Accordingly he retaliated with all manner of soothsayings about the other gentleman's mother, as passers-by gathered intrepidly. The two gentlemen were, however, saved from a further involvement with the law by one of the barrister's clerks who nimbly came between them.

'In the name of Allah and the Queen', he said, 'now hop it . . . And take yer bleeding family with yer'.

29

Apt quotations so often do more than sound legal argument.

When a solicitor sends instructions to a barrister he attaches all necessary documents and letters (traditionally the bundle is tied round with red tape) and these are returned with the barrister's opinion or other document he has been instructed to prepare, or at the end of the hearing in Court. Clerks have no legal qualifications, but they have their own professional organisation, the Barristers' Clerks' Association, which looks after their joint interests and concerns itself with the training of new entrants, who will aspire to the high standards of this exacting profession.

THE PROFESSION OF SOLICITORS:

The origin of the solicitors' branch of the legal profession is as far back in history as that of the Bar. As previously discussed in Chapter One, in the earliest litigation before the King's Courts the parties had to appear in person, but by the time of Henry II it was already possible for representatives to appear, and the Statute of Merton, 1235, provided that all freemen could 'do suit by attorney'. In the writings of Bracton in the mid-thirteenth century there are many references to attorneys. Edward I ordinance of 1292 regarding 'the appointment of a certain number of attorneys and apprentices-at-law' has been mentioned earlier.

Solicitors in their own right first appeared in the fifteenth century and performed similar functions in the Courts of Equity as the attorneys did in the

Common Law Courts. There was yet a third analogous profession, namely the proctors, who operated in the ecclesiastical Courts in Doctors Commons (see Chapter Four). An Act of Parliament of 1728 for the first time regulated the professions of attorney and solicitor.

Until the end of the eighteenth century attorneys and solicitors were members of the Inns of Court and Chancery. By the end of the seventeenth century the Inns of Chancery were almost exclusively the preserve of attorneys and solicitors. Unfortunately the latter Inns gradually perished. They became little more than dining clubs and never exercised the authority and control over their members, as did the Inns of Court. The final exclusion of solicitors and attorneys from the Inns of Court came about in 1793.

The Act of 1728 made provision for the service under articles by young solicitors and attorneys and, for examinations as to fitness to practise, to be conducted by the Judges. Shortly afterwards, in 1739, came the foundation of the first voluntary association of these practitioners, a body with the delightful name of 'Society of Gentlemen Practisers in the Courts of Law and Equity'. This body was the forerunner of the present governing body of the solicitors' branch of the legal profession, The Law Society, which was founded in 1825.

LEGAL EXECUTIVES

The Lawyer's Best Friend

Unlike the barristers' or magistrates' clerks the

solicitor's clerk has always done much of his master's professional work for him. Indeed solicitors' clerks probably have more contact with lay clients than all the other members of the legal profession. Until recently they possessed no formal legal qualifications or legal education, but many of them nevertheless became experienced and learned in the law, and at least as capable at negotiation, advising, writing letters or preparing other documents as their principals. Many were given their articles by grateful lawyers, and, themselves became eminent solicitors, like W. S. Gilbert's fictitious Sir Joseph Porter, K.C.B. ('H.M.S. Pinafore') who progressed from 'polishing up the knocker on the solicitor's big front door' to 'ruler of the Queen's Navy' (First Lord of the Admiralty) without ever going to sea.

Of recent years solicitor's clerks have renamed themselves 'Legal Executives', and the Institute of Legal Executives has been formed which presents full educational standards and, provides education and training for aspiring solicitor's clerks, examines them, and grants them admission to the profession if they satisfy the stern examiners. It is, however, possible for a youth or girl to start in the humblest position as a solicitor's office boy, girl or typist, and work his or her way up to the very top of the legal tree.

THE LAW SOCIETY

The Law Society early obtained powers under a Royal Charter, and was described as 'The Society of Attorneys, Solicitors, Proctors and Others, not being Barristers, practising in the Courts of Law and Equity in the United Kingdom'. A number of supplementary Charters have been granted since. Rules of Court in 1836 made it obligatory for attorneys to pass the examinations of The Law Society and in the following year the Master of the Rolls supervised examinations in Equity for solicitors. From the mid-nineteenth century onwards Acts of Parliament entrusted The Law Society with ever-widening powers of administration and control. The Solicitors Act 1843, although it empowered the Judges to make regulations for their examinations, subsequent Acts have put complete control over qualifications for solicitors in the hands of The Law Society, subject to the approval of their regulations by the Lord Chancellor, the Lord Chief Justice and the Master of the Rolls. The Supreme Court of Judicature Act 1873 made all solicitors, attorneys, and proctors Solicitors of the Supreme Court of Judicature, and, as such, officers of the Court.

The maintenance of professional standards has always been in the forefront of the duties of The Law Society. The 'Society of Gentlemen Practisers' had, in its opening statement, declared their 'utmost abhorrence of all mal and unfair practice' and resolved to use their utmost endeavours 'to detect and discountenance the same'. The Law Society committed itself, as stated in its 1845 Royal Charter, to 'promoting professional improvement and facilitating the acquisition of legal knowledge'. The Council of The Law Society state:

> These words have always been interpreted as requiring the Society to set, maintain and where

necessary improve professional standards, deal with complaints, and, where appropriate, initiate disciplinary action against offenders. It is in the interests of the profession that the rules of conduct, which are basically designed to govern the behaviour of honourable men and women and thus protect the public, are properly enforced since, otherwise, the repute of the profession as a whole would decline'.

The detailed conduct of these functions is in the hands of the Professional Purposes Committee of The Law Society, who regulate professional conduct, investigate complaints, and, where there appears to have been serious professional misconduct, bring the solicitor concerned before the Solicitors Disciplinary Tribunal. This Tribunal is not itself part of the machinery of The Law Society. It is appointed by the Master of the Rolls from among present or past members of the Council of the Society and it has power to order the name of the solicitor to be struck off the Roll or to suspend him. There is an appeal to a Divisional Court of the Queen's Bench Division. It is also possible for the solicitor who has been struck off to make application, in certain circumstances, to be restored to the Roll.

The Law Society is responsible for the education and training of solicitors. It conducts examinations for admission to the profession and it manages the excellent College of Law which runs training courses at premises in London, Guildford, and Cheshire.

The Society is also responsible for administering the Legal Aid Scheme on behalf of H.M. Government.

34

This is a formidable task, involving the employment of a staff of some 1,250 and the operation of some 40 separate offices throughout the country.

The number of solicitors with practising certificates in England and Wales was about 30,000 in 1976.

Although the Law Society has wide statutory powers to control the whole of the solicitors' branch of the profession, membership of the Society is voluntary. In practice the great majority of solicitors are members. Its governing body is the Council, consisting of 70 members, of whom 56 are elected on a constituency basis; they elect the remaining 14, who possess specialist knowledge on particular aspects of the legal practice and branches of the law. The Council delegates its work to a number of committees, who frequently co-opt non-Council members, dealing with such matters as Non-Contentious Business, Contentious Business, Legal Aid, Education and Training, Professional Purposes, Law Reform, Future of the Profession, International Relations, and various specialist types of practice.

The Society has a staff of more than 200 (exclusive of those working on the Legal Aid Scheme), under a Secretary-General. Its headquarters are at the Law Society's Hall in Chancery Lane. Apart from offices and council chambers, this building provides many facilities for members. There is a large and excellent library, a reading hall common room, members' dining room, grill room, bar, and entertainment rooms.

Apart from The Law Society, there are throughout

the country a number of local law societies which play an important part in the professional and social life of their areas.

CHAPTER 2

THE COMMON LAW

THE COMMON LAW

Introduction — The Broad and Narrower senses — Origins — An Historical Context — Common Law versus Civil Law — Church and State — The Doctrine of Precedent — The Adversary System — The Divine Right of the Common Law — The Rule of Law in England — An American Postscript.

So they shall wash their hands and their feet, that they die not: And it shall be a statute for ever to them,

> ... The Lord spake unto Moses.
> The Book of Exodus, Ch.31 v.21.

Moses was no common Lawyer.

Every system of law is an essay written by the society it upholds.

Moses saw man as created in the image of God, born to follow the path of righteousness laid down by the law as revealed from the Heights of Sinai, but free to succumb to the materialism of the Golden Calf and the corruption of the earthly power.

The Common Law proceeded on the theory that the law is there waiting for the Judges to reveal it. As one Court may correct the views of its predecessors, without waiting for the intervention of the legislature, this apparently rigid doctrine gives the Common Law a flexibility which many think lacking in the Roman Law systems of continental Europe. Yet this very flexibility can be a weakness, and the Continental systems, with their written codes of the rights of man, sometimes give more effective protection against the possible tyranny of the modern state than the more flexible Common Law can provide.

Behind the Iron Curtain the law safeguards only the freedom of the communist state itself. Its subjects live, die, think, behave and vote in the ways their despots decree, and suppresses their freedom from the 'corrupting influence' of Western ideals of the individual liberty.

Many of these ideals originated in the Common Law. The Common Lawyer sees it as his duty to help ensure their survival. The threats to their survival today comes not from tyrannical kings or even, to any great extent, from the fear of foreign invasion, but from the competing need to protect and provide for the poor, the weak and the deprived. *The Common Lawyer is fortunate that in his task he can call on the millenium of legal knowledge which has survived the vicissitudes of fortune, and civilisations' changing standards.*

The Common Law of both America and England is the tradition of laws passed down by generations of Judges, but yet remoulded by each era 'refined and defined in precedent'. The Common Law is an aged tree, with roots going down to the Anglo-Saxon chronicles and beyond, a trunk grown impervious to the slings and arrows of either good or bad husbandry; and inscriptions worn into the bark by famous men etc. Yet from its branches must still be fashioned the shield and spear needed to challenge the threats of tyranny which, however new their shape, are but reproductions of those against which it has fought from time immemorial.

The phrase 'Common Law' has two meanings, one broad — one narrow. In its broad sense it is the whole general body of the law of England and North America, and of all those other countries to which has spread this system of revealed law, defined by precedent, enlarged and regulated by legislation, yet free to grow and change without it.

In its narrow sense it is merely that part of English law which is still not to be found in any statute, but only to be discovered in precedent, in recorded judgments and legal text-books. Common Law, in this sense, is to be contrasted with Statute Law, the laws enacted by Parliament. The English Parliament is the supreme legislator of the kingdom, and can alter and abrogate the Common Law as it will. The Courts are obliged to construe Acts of Parliament in accordance with settled principles, and to give effect to them accordingly, however ridiculous the result may seem. Yet only Parliament can amend a statute, but it is wonderful how its whole effect can be changed by judicial 'interpretation'. There are many instances in which the Judges have felt themselves able so to do. Where the courts are unable to correct faulty drafting

41

(as to enable the true intention of Parliament to prevail), the only remedy is an amending Act, yet Parliament is so busy that these are often long delayed.

The phrase 'Common Law' is also often used to mean the law which traditionally held sway in the 'Common Law' Courts of the Kings Bench, Exchequer, and Common Pleas, as opposed to the more flexible system of 'Equity' by which the Lord Chancellors strove to mitigate the rigidity of the medieval Common Law and to supplement its limitations by grafting on to it such doctrines as those of trusts and such weapons as injunctions, specific performance decrees and equitable execution. Thus equity invented the doctrine of trusts, whereby without disturbing the legal ownership, beneficial ownership was vested in those who were more justly entitled to the property in question. Similarly whereas the Common Law looked upon a mortgage as giving the mortgagee absolute rights against the mortgagor, equity realised that a mortgage was only a security for a debt, and invented the equity of redemption which entitled a borrower who paid his debt to get his property back.

The development of these dual and competing systems of 'Law' and 'Equity', each with its own Courts and its own Practitioners — both usually prey to bitter rivalries and conflicts, led to many anomalies and much wasted efforts. Eventually, by the 1873-1875 Judicature Acts, the two systems of Courts were merged, and so in effect were the two systems of law by an express statutory provision that

42

'in the event of conflict between them the doctrines of Equity shall prevail'. These Acts replaced the old and competing Courts with one Supreme Court of Judicature, consisting of one High Court of Justice, divided into Chancery (in which the Old Courts of Equity found their place), Queen's Bench (which replaced the old Common Law Court), and Probate, Divorce and Admiralty ('Wills, Wives and Wrecks' in which were combined those parts of the law most subject to the influence of the Roman Civil Law). In the current decade this system has been slightly reorganised, by substituting a system of Crown Courts for the old Courts of Assize in which the judges used to sit throughout the country, and by transferring Admiralty work to the Queen's Bench division. Most Probate work has been transferred to the Chancery Division, and the Divorce Division has been renamed the Family Division adding to its work the old Chancery jurisdiction of the Lords Chancellors over wards of Court and infants.

ORIGINS OF THE LAW

The Common Law unfolded over centuries and was evolved before the written word took note. Despite the adage 'it is a good rule to start at the beginning', its origins are thus obscure where precise account is called for. The Anglo-Saxon, like later communities, relied on the motives of its members to behave and co-ordinate peacefully. The clearest motive then and now, perhaps is either the instinct of sexual appetite or the division of territory. (Much as the Common Law juries and lawyers may have enjoyed the permutations of the former over the years, it is the rights and disputes of men concerning land that actually accounted for the early attempts of a 'Common' Law). Ownership of land was a sufficient surety for the good behaviour of its holder. Landless men could have no rights as spake a law of Aethelstan. The feudal system was espoused to the pyramid of lordship, where every male in society was his lord's vassal, except the princes of the realm. The early law and customs required a man to acquit himself well in his dealings, every man according to his station.

'He who seeks to build a bridge across the gulf of the Teutonic conquests between the Roman and the English institutions, still builds it somewhat at a venture' is the oft-quoted remark of a famous historian. At any rate there were two significant effects of the Roman occupation of Britain, though neither were substantive on the Common Law. Firstly, where the Roman courts existed in their far-flung province, they became the model of the ecclesiastical courts, which remained traditionally outside the Common Law. Secondly, the early Roman missionaries caused, with their arrival, the customary 'English' law to be put into written codes, hitherto unknown in the Germanic backdrop of the continent.

Before the Norman Conquest Roman jurisprudence therefore had little influence on the developing Saxon law of England, but the Christianising of the island tribes embedded in the land the influence of Roman law with the Canon law of the Church. Justinian's

Corpus Juris was published too close in time to Augustin's mission to Kent in A.D. 597 to travel with the Saint.

The Normans brought with them their own Norman-French language and law, but gradually each of these absorbed and fused with the existing Saxon language and law, and it is in this fusion which many see the origins of the Common Law. The Norman kings themselves travelled throughout the land, dispensing justice wherever they were seated at the time, building magnificent halls and castles like that of Winchester, the old Saxon capital, in which they could live and sit and do justice. Later the King's justices of 'assize' travelled the country in his stead, preserving the uniformity of the law and the influence of the King, and yet absorbing some of the customs and laws of their Anglo-Saxon predecessors. Soon the decisions of the Judges were recorded in the Year Books, and commented on by writers of legal text books, and so formed precedents for the administration of justice. Each year the Judges came back from their circuits to London, and there discussed and sat in Courts together, and so one unified system of law, one 'Common Law' with its unique doctrine of precedent, held sway throughout the land.

AN HISTORICAL CONTEXT:

Until the Conquest, the law was discharged by men of substance and of rank — very often the men of the church, learned in the law, who some centuries later provided the first professional 'lay' lawyers with their own model.

When it is considered how swiftly William and his Norman barons gave to England a measured administration after their arrival, the best view must still stand that already, in Anglo-Saxon times, the Normans and English were kinsmen, and that Caen — la ville de sapience — was the stronghold of administration to both kingdoms. The Norman Conquest, far from adding to the legal systems existing in England, probably detracted from its development, by the heavy emphasis and revival of administrative dominance, which has since been fastened on by historians, as a convenient date for unwritten laws to become written. This nascent legal profession breathed on and fertilised the older systems which had been represented in England, and the slate was wiped clean of tribal inconsequence. The educational houses of the medieval era were the monasteries, and thus the vestibules of all learning. It was natural therefore that the legal gentlemen of the age were priests and not lawyers — the post-Norman period followed the Anglo-Saxon tradition — for example, Bishop Aethelric and his monks of Abbingdon, with men such as Alfwin, and the brothers Sacol and Godric.

It is in the twelfth century that the King, the overlord of all, was constrained for the first time to be represented by counsel in an action which arose out of his Majesty's summary dismissal of the three Bishops, of Salisbury, Ely and Lincoln. The threat of 'appeal' to Rome by the first-mentioned, Roger,

Bishop of Salisbury — in default of proper justice —
affirmed the part played and the shadow left by
Lanfranc in practice and procedure which not even
Aubrey de Vere, the (first) king's counsel could
hinder.

LANFRANC, Archbishop of Canterbury.

Lanfranc was born about A.D. 1005, and followed
a family career in the law, which he studied perhaps
at Bologna, and there enjoyed at first hand the
benefit of the Papal tribunals, through his father, a
city father of Pavia. In 1070 Lanfranc was appointed
to the see of Canterbury, and began his brilliant
tenure of that distinguished office, exercising
renowned forensic skill. It is of no coincidence that
the case between Lanfranc Cantor v Bishop Odo was
the best reported case of the age (1071); his advocacy
demolished the defence put out by the other side —
helped as he was by St. Dunstan who appeared to him
one night with the message 'go and win'.

Lanfranc was one of the earliest practisers of the
law to give it an individual impetus.

In 1158, the celebrated litigant Richard de Anesty
sued for a divorce and invoked quite freely the
adjudication of Rome on procedural points.

And a few years later, when the Pope was again
appealed to, he is on the record with the following
remarks of his English tormentors; '. . . (Thomas of
Marlborough, on behalf of the Monks of Evesham had
sued the Bishop of Worcester, and the two parties, far
from tiring of the litigation, made off to Pope
Innocent III and his cardinals and there indulged in

47

forensic combat. One side then complained of the other that all the good lawyers had been taken by the other side): "for we stood there entrenched in our advocati, for both sides had hired four, but mine were the better men"... Nobody ever wanted good store of advocati in the Court of Rome, spake the Pontiff with a smile. The winner "fainted with joy" on hearing judgment, but was promptly in risk of arrest by creditors for the costs of the lawyers' bills, and, with no more money, had to defend himself in person in the ensuing battle, at which the tiring Pope spoke up: "... When you and your lawyers learned ... (this) ... you must have drunk a good deal of your English beer".'

This case is of interest in the development of the Common Law because the Pontiff ruled on the procedural technicality between law and fact: the advocati in the case were forbidden to address themselves to the facts, 'they must speak of the law, and that when it is wanted'. As for the procurators, they knew the facts. It is in the reign of Henry II, the king-father of the English Common Law, that it emerges further.

RANULF De GLANVILLE

Glanville is the first lawyer not in holy orders to leave his initials on the page book of history. Glanville's classic text book (finished 1189) lays down secular law in their courts for the benefit of legal representatives of the holders of actionable rights. The two systems of jurisprudence that had developed thus far, and which had been the subject of such thought at Clarendon, were now on an equal footing, indeed, to the advantage of the king's court, as the following incident related:

— Court of Exchequer case — judgment for poor man against a man of wealth — an itinerant justice congratulates Glanville C.J. on the swift and equitable disposition of the court:

'Yes, we certainly do give judgment quicker than the Bishops in their cathedrals; although if our king was as far from us as the Pope is from them, I imagine we would be as slow.'

The twelfth century is traditionally regarded as the first spread of cloth on the table of the Common Law, although the old oak table was much older, with wood hewn from the sixth century or so by the missionaries from Rome. This original law, made up of folk-lore and scholarship with the retributive concept of an 'eye for an eye' was bound to be superceded by later development.

The reign of Henry III, looming as it did over the major portion of the thirteenth century, may be taken as the starting point for the existence of professional lawyers in the sense of the word as we know it. From this century onward, the Common Law was to be built by a single race of men unconnected to the traditional seats of learning — the great monasteries — which, up to this era had been the enclave of the ecclesiastical and not the secular movement of jurisprudence. It is rational to conclude — and contended by some historians — that the forensic development of the English Common Law may have influenced the Continental systems of jurisprudence more deeply than suspected: a cursory recital of sister developments in medieval Europe is thus necessary before continuing along the path of the glorious Common Law.

NORMANDY

Normandy has for long been a forerunner in the historical development of the French legal system, a superiority attested by 'the number and the fame of the Anglo-Norman lawyers'.

French writers have sadly confused the institutions which arose in Norman times — for example, the customs of the English courts as synthesised by the Norman kings of England — with the Norman institutions themselves. Probably every positive thought collected into contemporary manuscripts had one of its roots in an English writer which the early Norman kings had extended to Normandy and adapted to local usage.

FRANCE

It is known that the precincts of the Palais de la Cité and the Temple, Paris, were seething with lawyers before the same was true of London's sister precincts but their origins, their establishment and the procedure and system they expounded seemed lacking.

It is conjecture to indicate the predominance of one or other school of thought upon an organic state the size of France especially because of the dearth of manuscripts; however, various facts emerge to infer a reliable conclusion. The school of Bologna, and the name of Placentinus, is to be found in contemporary archivists' commentaries on the records, but the system that Philip of Novara implanted when he returned from the Levant and which he had worked out at the Jerusalem Assizes seems to have had a similar direct bearing on Frankish thought. The Summa Aurea, produced at Oxford by William of Drogheda, who had studied at Bologna, greatly influenced French thought.

LES ASSISES DE JERUSALEM

The Letters of the Holy Sepulchre, or the 'Assizes of Jerusalem' has been called the most curious monument to feudal jurisprudence ever erected in the Middle Ages. It will be recalled that Godfrey de Bouillon, in 1099, had convened in Jerusalem — the freshly taken citadel — a meeting of the knights and learned men of Europe . . . 'there charged to draw up a code of laws for the new Kingdom'. The laws were hand-made for the new Kingdom and soon a source of instruction for the jurists in Europe. In this treatise, as later modified, are the feudal procedures studied. The effect of this military feudalism was to co-ordinate the jurisprudence of Europe, which had devolved in an unctuous and spartan manner (since the withdrawal of the Roman eagle's protective wings), in a material way. Whatever the systems individually practised in one or other territorial domain, be it Gallic, Saxon, Teutonic, or Latin, the common machinery, with the single exception of the Norman administration, was an ill-equipped vehicle of the warrior court which periodically lapsed into jealous confrontation with the ecclesiastical body of the state, who were at that time, the traditional 'conscience' of mankind.

An example of this dichotomy, which was only later resolved by the advancement of a legal profession, was that of Thomas à Becket: A man skilled in great and learned thought, custodian of scholastic science under the tutelage of the royal prerogative, and, suddenly appointed the repositor of ecclesiastical doctrine caused Henry to become the scapegoat of the terrible anguish which rippled across Europe. This episode was no more and no less than the conflict between the church and state, as elaborated further in this Chapter.

Sir Matthew Hale in the seventeenth century lost no time in declaring that the origins of the Common Law were as undiscoverable as that of the Nile. Until the accession of Edward I, Britannicus Justinian, the records in English Legal history had been at best few, and worst indistinct. It is now known that the Anglo-Saxon rule whereby every suitor was to a degree his own advocate was altered by the Normans under whom a body skilled in the law administered the laws of the realm, adding from among their own the 'Conteurs of Rouen'.

The Curia Regis was the name given by the Anglo Saxons to the great assembly convened by the King in the Aula Regia of the Palace where from time to time the Court resided. The Aula Regis as it became (and is properly described), supplanted the function of the Saxon Witan Council, or 'witenagemote', and was bidden for the dual purpose of the affairs of state and as the chief tribunal of the kingdom. The convention probably followed the orthodox feasts: Christmas — the court resided at Gloucester; Easter — the court resided at Winchester; and at Whitsuntide, the court was at Westminster, as Shakespeare knew so well: '. . . that they object against your house, shall be wiped out in the next parliament, call'd for the truce of Winchester and Gloucester.'

Apart from the Order of the Coif, and its serjeant counters, the profession of lawyers lay nascent in the chest of the clergy until in the latter part of the twelfth century, a century or so after the Conquest, an attempt was made to exclude the clergy from legal practice as recounted in the previous chapter. This conflict was finally resolved by our great monarch Henry II, who, with one hand struck out the secular power of the church which at that time was ministered by Thomas à Becket, an unscrupulous and ambitious ecclesiastic, most generously treated by batches of later historians. When this contest had been settled, the Order of the Coif undertook the regular tradition of instructing the apprenticii ad legem (as enunciated by the Parliament Roll of 1292, which apprentices became in time the court pleader below that of the rank of Serjeant), and who, some two centuries later formed the nucleus of the Bar.

It is intriguing to note that a legal profession in more than one country, sprang up as a result of the itinerant contact by the Knights' Templars, the Crusaders. The reason for this advent may have been the influence of Eastern culture on those 'Euro-

Cell B and Paulus,
revealed...

54

peans', namely, the practice whereby a pleader relied on the ability of his superior to state his cause, and thus the lord commissioned a 'conseil' to speak in the name of the court and thereby avoided the snares of litigious involvement.

Philip of Novara, was an Italian from the neighbourhood of Bologna, although he is still spoken of as a young Frenchman from Navarre. Philip became a crusader and embarked for the Holy Land in 1218. Doubtless he conversed with Louis IX at some length, and provided for him a draft Direction which the monarch later imposed on his country. The upshot of this is twofold: Firstly, the most prestigious medieval document ever written relied on the impact of Syrian practice. Secondly the derivative of the writings of William of Drogheda, were thus incorporated in this far reaching treatise and it may be said that England had contributed, before that event and not after, to the development of the continental systems of jurisprudence.

It is also instructive to glance at a summary of Jurists' work, in chronological order between 1250 and 1350, from which it will be seen that Bologna is the fulcrum of learning.

Rhetorica Ecclesiastics   by unknown At France? 1160-80.
Summa de Ordine Judiciarius   by Richard Anglicus
                                             at Bologna, 1196.
Summa Libellorum   by Bernard Dorna At Bologna, 1213-17.
Ordo Judiciarius   by Elbert of Bremen, 1191-1204.
Ars Notariae   by Rayner of Perugis, at Bologna, 1224-34.
Summa Aurea   by William of Drogheda, at Oxford, 1239.
Ordo Judiciarius   by unknown At France 1235-40.

Ordo Judiciorum	by Martin of Fano, At Arezzo, 1254-64.
Summa	by Magister Aegidius, Bologna, c.1264.
Summa Minorum	by unknown At Paris 1254.
Curialis	by unknown, France, 1251-70.
Ordo Judiciarius	by Aegidius de Fuscarariis, Bologna, 1262.

Richard Anglicus was the first English-born legal writer who, very systematically, enunciated the rights and duties of the professional representative and who attended and influenced the seat of learning at Bologna.

It was left to a teacher of law at Oxford 'half priest, half lawyer', one William of Drogheda, to complete the study of the art of advocacy, and who confirmed that English procedural practice grew out of ecclesiastical quarter of the pre-Norman conquest system. His analysis included the early distinction between the two functions of the professional lawyer, that of the procurator, or the solicitor, and that of the advocatus, the barrister.

GERMANY

The insignificance of the tribes of Germany on jurisprudence till the reign of Charles IV, is witnessed by the absence of mention by legal writers of the time, whereas —

SPAIN

Spain perhaps is unique among the continental countries to have recognised and developed a mature procedure by the twelfth century. The common view is that its historical mastery of the Moors, which early recognised procedural representatives, left aspects of an eastern culture embodied in its own customs before this system spread northwards into Europe.

THE DOCTRINE OF PRECEDENT

'Tis Precedent he said he meant,
And sediment is precedent'.
(James Harkess).

In theory the Common Law is there all the time, and always has been, just waiting to be discovered or revealed to the judicial mind. But the judicial mind, like Moses on the Mount Nebo, must not be exposed to the strain of too close a view of the Promised Land. The judicial eye must peer murkily through the spectacles of its predecessors. Stare decisis – *let that which has been decided stand.* The Common Law court must pay respect to – but is not bound by, the decisions of courts of superior standing. Even a court of superior standing should be reluctant to overturn a decision as to the Common Law of an inferior court which has stood and been acted upon for a long time. These decisions are set out in the reports of earlier cases, 'Law Reports', in commentaries on such decisions, and on the law by text-book writers. The earliest of these was Glanville, whose 'Law and Custom of England' was written towards the end of the twelfth century. Characteristically it does not pretend to disquiet the law as such to any great extent, but merely sets out a description of legal remedies and the various writs available to the suitor who wishes to claim his rights. Glanville does not contain the many reports or discussions of decided cases, but the next great legal author, Bracton, takes up much of his mid-thirteenth century treatise with descriptions of decided cases. The first real series of Law Reports, the 'Year Books', first appeared, written on parchment for Norman French in 1285, and continued until 1535. These brief notes of cases heard in the Court were used by Counsel as precedents in arguing later cases and by Judges when deciding them. The sixteenth and seventeenth centuries produced a host of distinguished legal writers and reporters, whose text books and reports are still cited in the Courts today. Foremost among these were Sir Edward Coke, Chief Justice, with his Commentary on the earlier work of Lyttelton; Sir Francis Bacon, the essayist and Lord Chancellor disgraced for taking bribes; and Sir Matthew Hale. Coke recommended his readers to study old reports and precedents 'that, out of the old fields must come the new corn' but did not himself baulk at inventing precedents to support his arguments for Parliamentary rights when he could not find any suitable reality. For the most part, succeeding law reports are to be found in the English Reports, an encyclopaedic collection of their work produced in the nineteenth century, but many lawyers still prize intrinsically, the older Reports themselves. Today the law must struggle to keep abreast with an ever increasing flow of reports on everything from everywhere: The English series alone range through the alphabet from Criminal Appeal Reports through Industrial Law and Road Traffic Reports to Tax Cases: but the 'with it' practitioner must seek to keep at least a nodding acquaintance with cases from the United States, the British Commonwealth, the International Court, and the Common Market. Thank goodness for the Americans who are devising a computer system to help us withstand a floodtide worse than that which faced King Canute.

THE ADVERSARY

The English Court is still run like a medieval tournament: The parties do battle through their champions, their Counsel, while the Judge merely presides, holds the lists, sees that the rules are observed, and declares the results. His function is not to seek justice at all costs, nor to find out the truth but merely to decide what facts have been proved by the evidence called before him. Alas, the fair damsel who traditionally encouraged the competent and rewarded the winner is no longer with us.

Written pleadings in a civil case, or a plea of 'Guilty' or 'Not Guilty' in a criminal case, decide who has to prove what. The Advocate for the respective party will lose, unless he proves his version of the case to the satisfaction of the court. Each witness is first examined by the Advocate who has called him, then cross-examined by the Advocate for the opposing party, and finally re-examined by the Advocate who called him. The Advocate who calls a party is not allowed to ask 'leading questions' which suggest the answer which should be given to them, nor is he allowed to introduce matters which are deemed irrelevant or so prejudicial that the law of evidence excludes them. No such restrictions hamper the cross-examiner, so that his right to refer to or bring out previous convictions of an accused is not severely limited in a criminal trial. Finally, the Advocates make their closing speeches, summing up their cases and pleading for the result their client desires, in reverse order to that in which they opened them. After this, the Judge delivers his judgment, often, in England, immediately afterwards.

To the Civil or Roman Law practitioner from continental Europe, this system sometimes seems to be a mockery or justice. For him the Court should be a tribunal of investigation, guided by the Judge in its search for the truth. In France, by way of an example, an examining magistrate, the *Juge d'Instruction,* is in charge of a criminal case from the very beginning. The police must report to him at an early stage, and follow his instructions, and submit themselves and their witnesses to his interrogation, as does Inspector Maigret in the novels of Georges Simenon. At the Court of Trial itself the evidence is therefore largely documentary: the papers prepared by the examining Magistrate merely examine and cross-examine the witnesses and the parties argue the cases under the supervision of the Judge (who can himself insist on witnesses being called). In many Civil Law jurisdictions the Judge himself questions the witnesses, and the advocates merely request him to ask certain questions, or, perhaps 'put questions through him', and then sum up the evidence and address the Judge on it and on the law.

The accused who is brought immediately before an examining Magistrate may have much better protection from tyranny and injustice than the Englishman who 'helps the Police with their enquiries' for lengthy periods before being formally charged. The poor litigant struggling against the might of a government department or a wealthy corporation might, it has been argued by some authors, benefit more from the investigatory powers of a Civil Law Judge than he can from the financially circumscribed efforts of his own lawyers.

THE DISTRUST OF THE PROFESSIONAL

The Englishman still distrusts the career Judge, and relegates him to the Colonies. In England itself the Judges are appointed from the ranks of practising Advocates, mainly from Barristers, and many of them are only part-time Judges, who return at the end of their judicial stint to a practice at the Bar. A remarkable fact is that the vast majority of cases in England are heard by lay Justices of the Peace. These Magistrates are ordinary people who sit in Court once or twice a week, taking the day off from their normal occupations, to do justice to their fellow citizens. All these judges are appointed by the Lord Chancellor, but it is a tradition that he shall not let political considerations guide his appointments. In some American States some Judges are elected, by popular vote, but this does not find favour in England. In most Civil Law systems the aspiring Judge leaves his University, having passed his examinations with the necessary distinction, and goes into the Judicial service, either as Judge or Prosecutor in a minor Court, and slowly works his way up until, if he is

61

fortunate, he achieves a seat in the highest Court in the land. Judicial promotion from lower to Higher Courts exists in England too, and has increased of late, but it is hoped and believed that the traditions of independent advocacy and an independent judiciary — free from political control — will continue to prevent anxious Judges from trimming their judgments to suit whatever they may believe to be the political wind of change in their countries. The fact that Judges are experienced Advocates, with a personal knowledge of most of those who appear as Advocates before them, makes English Court proceedings go with a speed which astonishes those more familiar with the Courts of other lands.

THE RULE OF LAW AND THE COMMON LAW

The Common Law rapidly developed into the sword with which the citizen has sought to rely and to defend himself against 'the insolence of office, and the slights which patient merit of the unworthy takes'. In particular it sought to protect the individual against arbitrary levying of taxes by the monarch. Even the great Elizabeth abandoned all efforts to tax her subjects without Parliamentary consent, but the Stuarts were less wise. The Petition Right, presented to the Stuart Parliament in 1628, included at Coke's suggestion a declaration of the illegality of taxation without Parliamentary consent, and one of the main causes of the Civil War in England was Charles I successful attempt to raise taxes without Parliamentary consent for the building and maintenance of his

Navy. John Hampden, a Buckinghamshire squire and Member of Parliament, refused to pay this tax, but the Court declared he had to. In 1688 the *Glorious Revolution* overthrew James II, and shortly afterwards the Bill of Rights affirmed the supremacy of Parliament and the independence of the Judiciary.

The Common Law seeks to ensure that the citizen shall live under the rule of law, and shall not be subject to arbitrary taxation, imprisonment, confiscation, or other manifestation of tyranny. The Common Law writs provided the means for this protection. *Habeas Corpus* secured the production of the body of any man who was unlawfully imprisoned, even by order of the King, so that the Judge, on being satisfied of this, could order his immediate release. *Certiorari* enabled the Courts to quash any unjust decision of any inferior tribunal or other quasi-legal body. Prohibition was the means by which the Common Law Court forbad the commission of illegal Acts, including illegal or unjust trials, while, by *Mandamus* the officials of the King could be ordered to perform their duties as required by law. The Police, the Magistrates and every arm of the Executive was subject to the control of the Courts of Common Law by means of these remedies. Now, however, the complete triumph is Parliament's, and perhaps the Common Law itself can pose a solid threat to Parliament *supreme and omnipotent,* where it has shown to have failed the electorate and otherwise eroded the civil liberties of its people. The Government, which is to a very great extent under the influence of such outside bodies as Trades Unions and Employers' Associations, and the Parliamentary power so jealously vindicated in the seventeenth century may itself become an instrument of tyranny. Parliament has delegated many of its legislative powers to Ministers (often in a form called after its origins: the 'Henry the Eighth Clause'), which effectively prevents the Court from questioning the legality of ministerial decres. More and more of the rights of the citizen are delegated to tribunals, which the Common Law Courts cannot of right control. The Courts have no power to declare an Act of Parliament unconstitutional merely because it takes away rights given by Magna Carta or the Bill of Rights. The scandal of Watergate was uncovered and remedied in the United States, but in England the Government could have used its powers under the Official Secrets Acts to prevent any such revelations. Now that Parliament is 'supremo', and the Government supreme within it, the Englishman probably needs the protection for his liberties in a written constitution, as have been given the citizens of the United States. The price of liberty is eternal vigilance, and never must our pride in the Common Law, and its own achievements, blind us to the need to modify, adapt and extend it anew to cope with the dangers of our modern age, where previously Kings ruled their Englishmen and Parliament benevolently.

THE GREAT INHERITANCE

The frontiers of the United States are formidable; were forged by the branding iron of the Common Law. When the Founding Fathers — and, perhaps their stalwart predecessors in Virginia — set their hand to the greatest modern state since Greece, they adopted that system of jurisprudence common to their heritage, the English Common Law as it stood in the seventeenth century.

The Common Law has proved an indestructible anvil for the United States and, as in instances discussed, has retained the spirit and strength of the summary power of the bench more accurately, perhaps, than in the mother country. In a federal sense there is no Common Law, notwithstanding its adoption by the rules of the Supreme Court of Justice of procedural matters in determination of its own. The various States however, acting within their own jurisdiction, and empowered under the Constitution to regulate and advance their own jurisprudence have carried forward the Common Law in original jurisdiction with scarce exceptions (e.g. Louisiana, New Mexico, Texas, Missouri, Arizona and the Pacific States): and periodically embodies it, so far as it is not inconsistent with the Constitution or the Public Statutes enacted by Congress. Each state, and particularly the older states, enjoys a settled body of legal precedent beyond which its judges seldom need to travel.

The mantle of the English Common Law was decisively dyed with the colour of the Civil War. That period, an adolescent conflagration, ennobled the country towards maturity, but weakened the distinctive character of the southern states. Reference to the XIV amendment, adopted in 1868, well illustrates the subtle transition made by the Supreme

Court and which guaranteed its throne in the young democracy. This principle was firmly laid down: That citizens of the United States are protected by their common rights, as enshrined in the constitution, against state legislature. The year 1868 marked the watershed of the devolutionary system of American jurisprudence and heralded the beginnings of a Supreme Court which re-enforced its infinite residuary power over the definitive jurisdictions of the various states. From then onwards, to the present day, the Supreme Court became the bastion of personal liberty and sectarian rights in the community. Of historic interest was the cause of the nineteenth century Negro who found refuge within the portico of the Supreme Court in the Capital.

'Other changes of no less importance may be made in the future, and while the cardinal principles of justice are immutable, the methods by which justice is administered are subject to constant fluctuation and . . . the constitution of the United States, which is necessarily and to a large extent inflexible and exceedingly difficult of amendment, should not be so construed as to deprive the states of the power to amend their laws so as to make them conform to the wishes of the citizens as they may deem best for the public welfare without bringing them into conflict with the supreme law of the land,' as was written by the renowned jurist, Mr Justice Brown.

The American Judiciary follows a distinguished path steeped in legal alumni which began with the Puritan thinkers of the seventeenth century, and the finer traditions of legal scholarship. In the old days of course, the leaders in civil life were often the repositories of literary and academic knowledge, as by way of example was one of the first, Sewall, C. J., whose Diary remains a masterful work (1652-1730), or the eminent theologian, Dr Jonathan Edwards, 1703-1758, sometime President of Princetown, where he in fact died. Of those in the law, mention may be made *inter alia* of Judges Marshall, Bushrod, Washington, Story, Kent, Ware, and Bradley to name but a few, though transatlantic admirers of Cardozo and his style of English prose perforce includes his name.

Even below the Supreme Court, the true literature of the State and Federal judges may be found across every volume of the law reports, and although the major distinction with brethren across the Atlantic used to be that holders of judicial office at State and at Federal level were elected politically (unlike their English brethren), the practical consequences have merged in the common integrity, inherited in both systems of jurisprudence. The progress of both have brought the two sides of the Atlantic closer together than at any time in their histories – whether from the point of view of the judgments handed down in the Federal courts and taken cognisance of by the English courts – or from the views of the practitioners' bodies, such as in the field of negotiable instruments as also in the Employer's Liability, for example, where the American Bar Association leaned on British law.

THE DECLARATION OF 1776.

The most wonderful work ever struck off at a given time by the brain and purpose of man.

W. E. Gladstone, The American Constitution.

Five signatories of the Charter were members of the Middle Temple, and gave rise to the saying: 'Blood runs thicker than water: but the law runs thicker than ink'. A sixth gentleman, and scholar, commonly associated with the great work was a member of the Inner Temple. His name was Edmund Burke.

The import of the American Declaration of 1776 has been incalculable. It confirmed and reiterated a faith in the Common Law from the birth of the Nation. Although the American Constitution may be called 'written', it is also an epistle of principles of faith which were handed down by the Anglo-Saxon ideology of the Common Law.

It was a young country squire from Virginia — a lawyer who 'abandoned a talkative and dubious trade', a retiring intellectual whose habits and lips knew no unkind deed, and yet who became the President of the States which he had united, one Thomas Jefferson who inspired the certificate of the Articles of Confederation.

THOMAS JEFFERSON, born 13th April, 1743: deceased 4th July, 1826 (on the fiftieth anniversay of the Declaration). Author of the Declaration of American Independence, of the statute of Virginia for religious freedom, and father of the University of Virginia (written on his tombstone). In 1774, Jefferson was elected to the first Virginia convention, and, prevented from attending by illness, forwarded an elaborate set of resolutions, for the delegates to the Continental Congress at

Philadelphia in September, which met to consider colonial grievances. The resolutions were published in a pamphlet, entitled, A Summary View of the Rights of America. In England, this pamphlet ran into many editions, although probably modified by Edmund Burke (who was in 'opposition') and this procured for Jefferson the seat of honour offered him by his countrymen of drafting the Declaration of Independence, whose historical portions were a revised transcription of the Summary View.

It is intriguing to consider that the 'eternal truths' may have been in part the hand of Burke, as laid down by Jefferson: the evidence tends to support this opinion – repeated and detailed knowledge, for example, of the deficiences of the English administration; as well might be spoken by the champion of English liberty who was firmly entrenched against his own monarch's government, and repeated here:

'We hold these truths to be self-evident, that all men are created equal, That they are endowed by their creator with certain inalienable rights, that among these are Life, Liberty and the pursuit of Happiness; That to secure these rights, Governments are instituted among Men, deriving their just powers from the consent of the governed; That whenever any Form of Government becomes destructive of these ends, it is the Right of the People to alter or to abolish it, and to institute new Government, laying its foundation on such principles and organising its powers in such form, as to them shall seem most likely to effect their Safety and Happiness.

Prudence indeed, will dictate that Governments long established should not be changed for light and transient causes; and ... Such has been the patient sufference of these Colonies; and such is now the necessity which constrains them to alter their former Systems of Government ... To prove this, let Facts be submitted to a candid world. (Here follow eighteen paragraphs of King George III historic blunders — poor old trout.)

... He has combined with others to subject us to a jurisdiction foreign to our constitution, and unacknowldeged by our laws; giving his Assent to their acts of pretended legislation; For ... abolishing the free system of English Laws ... for taking away our Charters ... He has abdicated Government here ... Nor have we been wanting in attention to our British brethren ... We have reminded them of the circumstances of our emigration and settlement here.

God bless America; the Common Law has reason to be grateful.

CHAPTER 3

THE COURTS

THE COURTS

The Courts of the United Kingdom — Parliament: the bi-cameral system — The House of Lords — The Lord Chancellor — The Judicial system — The Supreme Court of Judicature — The High Court — The Chancery Division — The Queen's Bench Division — The Family Division — Crown Courts — The Old Bailey — County Courts — Magistrates' Courts — Justices of the Peace — Bow Street — Judicial Titles — Some Rule of Evidence.

THE UNITED KINGDOM

England is a part of the United Kingdom of Great Britain and Northern Ireland, and the United Kingdom itself is only a part of the British Isles. Other parts are the Channel Isles, ruled by the Queen: not as Queen of England or even as head of the Commonwealth, but as a Duchess of Normandie. They still have their own Norman/French law courts, and feudal rulers, such as the Dame of Sark, who are subordinate to the Duchess. Another British Isle is the Isle of Man, purchased by George III from its feudal but independent lord, the Earl of Derby, wherein the legislature is the House of Keyes, the lone survivor of Norse Parliaments.

The Government of the United Kingdom is conducted, and its justice bounteously administered, in the name of Her Majesty the Queen, the hereditary Monarch and head of the State. Her Majesty acts on the advice of her Ministers, and those same Ministers are responsible to Her Parliament for conducting the affairs of the Kingdom of England, the Principality of Wales, the Kingdom of Scotland and the Province of Northern Ireland.

PARLIAMENT

Parliament consists of two Houses, the House of Lords and the House of Commons. The House of Commons is made up of 630 Members of Parliament elected in secret ballot by all citizens (save Peers and, for example the mentally unfit) over majority (18 years of age). The Member of Parliament who leads his Parliamentary Party which can command a majority of votes in the House of Commons is invited by his and their monarch to be Prime Minister. He becomes Prime Minister and selects persons who are usually his supporters in charge of the one or other various departments of government. Twenty or so of the most senior Ministers form the Cabinet, which decides the policies for governing the country. If the House of Commons votes against a major government policy, the Prime Minister either requests the Queen to dissolve Parliament or resigns with his government. If they resign the monarch then either sends for the Member of Parliament who leads an alternative party which might assemble a majority in the House and who appoints him her Prime Minister; or Her Majesty dissolves Parliament in order that a new House of Commons may be elected.

The State Opening of Parliament by the Queen is a magnificent spectacle, when the Commons and the Judges foregather in the Chamber of the Upper House of Parliament — the House of Lords, to attend upon Her Majesty's presence, who reads her speech from the Throne. This occasion opens Parliament and bestows the programme that her Ministers intend to follow for the coming Session. This splendid occasion is a reminder of the days of the medieval feudal system, when power resided either with the House of Lords or with the Monarch, and the Judges attended there as part of the Court to give their advice when called upon to do so.

THE HOUSE OF LORDS

In those days the peerages were hereditary, and the House was composed of Dukes, Marquises, Earls, Viscounts, and Barons, who and whose heirs male have been ennobled by the Crown. Hereditary Peers are still entitled to sit in the House of Lords, and many of them do so, but no more have been created since 1958 and now an increasing proportion of the House consists of Life Peers — 'Lifers' — as they are affectionately known. Of these ladies and gentlemen (who are created peers of Parliament for life by the Monarch on the recommendation of the Prime Minister), are included an appropriate proportion of persons nominated by the leaders of his and other Political Parties.

The machinations of Parliament first see the light of day as 'Bills' which can be introduced in either House of Parliament. Bills must be passed by both Houses, and receive the formal assent of the Crown, before they become statute law. (Common or Judge made Law is sometimes compared to Statutary Law, its antonym.) The House of Lords has no power over money Bills, that is, Bills imposing taxation, and has the power to delay other Bills for one year only. It frequently amends Bills, but the Commons may and in its usual fashion usually does disagree. When this occurs a compromise is usually reached, the nature of which depends — inter alia — on the strength or weakness of the Government in the Commons, the length of time before there must be a general election, and the power of the Commons to overrule the Lords.

Centuries ago there was no clear distinction between the legislative, executive, and judicial powers of the state. When the King in his court stated what was to be, no one was concerned whether he was legislating, administering or judging. The House of Lords retains to this day a judicial function as the highest appellate tribunal in the United Kingdom. There remains, too, one important servant of the Crown whose office combines the legislative, executive and judicial functions, and he is the Lord Chancellor.

THE LORD HIGH CHANCELLOR

The head of the judiciary is the Lord Chancellor.

He is selected by the Prime Minister of the day and is usually an active member of the Prime Minister's political party. He is a senior member of the Cabinet and the principal legal spokesman for, and adviser to, the Government. He is also the Speaker of the House of Lords and (unlike the Speaker of the House of Commons) partakes in debates and divisions. He is the senior Judge in the country, although he seldom sits in Court himself. On his recommendation all Judges and many other persons concerned in the administrative hierarchy of justice are appointed, and the Lord Chancellor's Department is responsible for the management of the Courts and the whole judicial system. His powers of patronage are great, and are exercised in modern times without regard to political affiliations but solely on grounds of professional ability.

The Lord Chancellorship is not a stepping stone to further political advancement, unlike other ministerial appointments.

The House of Lords exercises its judicial functions through Appellate Committees. The House of Lords is not bound by its previous decisions.

One of its most regular litigants, Mr. Albert Haddock — The fictitious creation of (Sir) A. P. Herbert, sometime M.P. for the University of Oxford — describes a typical day's work of the House of Lords, presided over by the Lord Chancellor:

> '... Your lordships must wearily consider once more the question to which for so many decades, so many judges, juries, and jurists have given so much time, thought and toil: Have we

here libel or a slander? We shall, I fear, be
discussing it for many decades more... My
Lords I need not tell You, but I must — for the
instruction of less learned men and the full
employment of typists and printers — what that
distinction is... Your Lordships have never had
a similar case before you, and so have no
decision of your own to guide you. Parliament
has declined to abolish the distinction between
Libel and Slander: and your Lordships, I
conceive, are bound to abide by it...'

Lord Wool:
'Stuff and nonsense!
... Who made the Common Law? The Judges.
Who are we? The top judges. And who's put the
Common Law right when it's old and silly?
Why, we of course... You're all afraid. I'm not.
I'm 73. But I'll race any of you across West-
minster Bridge...'

Lord Middle:
'I do not agree... It will be a sad day for British
justice if ever we interrupt the orderly march of
precedent and case-law...'

Lord Orff:
'... The distinction of which (Lord Wool)
complains is due to an historical accident.
Slander, in ancient days, was dealt with by the
feudal, and later by the ecclesiastical courts.
Then printing came in, and the apprehensive
Star Chamber made the new invention its
particular care, so that an action for libel has
retained some of its criminal character of that

78

Court's proceedings, and no proof of damage is required . . .'

Lord Laburnum:

'My Lords, I am only 87: but I am not going to race my brother Wool across Westminster Bridge . . . Of course . . . the simplest thing is to stop all this talk about 'special damage'. then we could stop distinguishing between libel and slander. People will be more careful what they say, and litigation, in my opinion, will be less, not more . . .'

The Sky-Writing Case, 1966, HL, reference W at W, *Law Reporter:* Sir Alan Herbert, to whom, many thanks.

THE PRIVY COUNCIL

The judicial Committee of the House of Lords — plus a few distinguished Commonwealth judges, also sit as the Judicial Committee of the Privy Council, the Supreme Court of Appeal from some parts of the Commonwealth and from some domestic tribunals such as the General Medical and the General Dental Council. Their decisions are persuasive but not binding precedents for the English Courts. Their quotations go a long way.

THE SUPREME COURT OF JUDICATURE

The Supreme Court has three parts: the Court of Appeal, the High Court, and the Crown Court.

The senior Judge of the COURT OF APPEAL is the Master of the Rolls and the other Judges are 14 Lords Justices. They sit in benches of three. Decisions may be by majority. The Court hears appeals from the High Court, the Crown Court, County Courts, and from certain other Tribunals. Appeals lie to the House of Lords with leave of the Court (or with leave of the House of Lords itself).

Although the House of Lords is the 'supreme' court of judicature, The Supreme Court of Judicature (as created by Judicature Acts) does not include the House of Lords, but consists of the Court of Appeal, the High Court of Justice, and the Crown Court. The Master of the Rolls, whose medieval predecessor looked after the Rolls on which judgments were then recorded, is now the third ranking Judge in the land, preceded only by the Lord Chancellor and the Lord Chief Justice. His Lordship is the head of the Court of Appeal, and usually presides over the senior of the several — three or sometimes five, — divisions in which this Court sits. These divisions are staffed by the fourteen Lords Justices of Appeal, who are usually supplemented by one or two retired Lords Justices or High Court judges. It seems that old Lords Justices, too, never die but only fade away. They are supplemented when necessary by Lords of Appeal in Ordinary, judicial members of the House of Lords, or by puisne judges of the High Court. The Lord Chief Justice, and the President of the Family Division are also members of the Court of Appeal, but they, like the Master of the Rolls, are usually made Lords of Appeal soon after their appointments, and so sometimes sit as judges in the House of Lords as well. This interchange of personnel helps preserve the unity of the judicial system. Where judges of the Court of

Appeal disagree, the view of the majority of those sitting (in the particular division of the court in question) prevails.

The Court of Appeal hears appeals from the High Court, Crown Courts, County Courts, and from certain other specified decisions of other tribunals and judicial officers. For some appeals leave is necessary, but on some matters there is an absolute right of appeal. The Court appeals on both Civil and Criminal matters, (but a court hearing a criminal appeal usually contains at least one High Court Judge who normally tries criminal cases at first instance). Appeal does itself lie from the Court of Appeal to the House of Lords, but only with the leave of the Court of Appeal or the House of Lords. Provision has recently been made for certain appeals to 'leap-frog' the Court of Appeal and go straight from High Court to the House of Lords, but this rarely occurs.

The HIGH COURT, is the principal civil court of first instance in the land, but it also exercises criminal jurisdiction over inferior courts, on points of law, hears appeals from certain tribunals on certain other matters, and hears the applications for prerogative writs which were discussed in Chapter 2. It is divided into the Chancery, Queens Bench, and Family Divisions. Each of its 72 judges, known as puisne ('puny') judges is assigned to one of these divisions. The rigidity of the medieval system of law provided — inter alia — that any division or judge can exercise the powers of any other division or judge, and any judge can sit in any division. On occasion, too, judges of the

Court of Appeal or even of the House of Lords sit as judges of the High Court.

The CHANCERY Division is, as explained in Chapter 2, the modern descendant of the old Court of Equity where you get justice without delay. Today it deals mainly with cases concerning companies, mortgages, wills — their construction and validity, patents, bankruptcy, trusts, and with other cases in which equitable remedies, such as specific performance or injunctions are the principal relief sought by the litigant.

The QUEEN'S BENCH DIVISION is the largest division of the High Court. The distinguished minds of its 44 judges, headed by the Lord Chief Justice, are normally concerned in the adjudications of contract and tort (the majority of which are in fact actions in personal injuries). Its two specialised Courts, the Admiralty and the Commercial Court deal respectively with shipping and with commercial cases. Most of its judges, however, spend much of their time trying actions in the Crown Court in courts outside London, including criminal cases. Their distinguished minds are sometimes known to be sorely tried also. Its Divisional Court, which is usually presided over by the Lord Chief Justice, is really one of the most important Courts in the land, because, through its hearing of criminal appeals on points of law, and of applications for the old prerogative writs and orders already described, it keeps a firm finger on the pulse of judicial and political administration throughout the land. Judges in Crown Courts and the 'Red'

Judges try the more serious criminal cases, and civil cases such as those heard in the Queen's Bench Division in London.

The FAMILY DIVISION of the High Court consists of a President and 16 puisne Judges, but these are usually supplemented by a large number of circuit judges sitting as deputy judges sit in Crown Courts like their Queen's Bench colleagues, but perhaps not quite so frequently. Often, for a change, they hear Common Law cases, and sometimes crime. Their normal work in the Family Division consists of arguments over family matters, such as defended divorce cases (quarrels over the disposition of matrimonial property and the care of children during and after divorce, alimony and maintenance for divorced wives, and cases concerning the property care, control and education of minors, persons under 18 years of age). They therefore exercise the old jurisdiction of the Lord Chancellor over wards of court, as well as the jurisdiction in adoption and guardianship cases, and their skill, patience and expertise very often saves human beings from ghastly embarrassment of a personal nature.

High Court judges usually sit alone, save when they sit in a Divisional Court, to hear appeals, except in the rare cases when they sit with the jury. A jury is very rare in civil cases nowadays, although it is still usual in defamation cases as Kojak recently discovered to his satisfaction. In the Admiralty Court the High Court judge usually sits with 'assessors', retired Master Mariners whose experience will help on technical points. High Court judges also staff the Restrictive Practices Court, the Industrial Court, the special tribunals which the government sets up from time to time to conduct special enquiries. They also hear disputes concerning validity of elections to Parliament and to local government authorities.

The old Assize Courts, described in Chapter Two, to which the Common Law judges used to go on their assize circuits, have now been abolished and replaced by the new Crown Courts. The circuits themselves still linger on, as societies of Barristers who practice in the areas of the country which comprised the old circuits, and as administrative areas into which the new Crown Courts are grouped. In those Crown Court centres where what used to be High Court business is still transacted, and where High Court judges sit as Crown Court judges, the Barristers still dine in their messes, but not always every night.

THE OLD BAILEY

There are few law-abiding citizens, if there are any indeed, who have not heard of the Old Bailey. The Central Criminal Court, otherwise known as the Old Bailey, is the principal criminal court-house of Greater London.

The old building was built in 1902-7 by the architect E. W. B. Mountford — much restored after heavy bomb damage (1941). The new extensions were completed in 1971 and opened by Her Majesty the Queen. Again, bomb damage of a different character took place recently: fortunately for the criminals, the Death Penalty was abolished some years ago.

The site revealed, when excavations in 1966 were under way for extensions to the precincts, sections of the Roman wall which encircled Londinium, A.D. 200. Newgate Prison, made more intimate to the public in the writings of Charles Dickens, dated from the thirteenth century and was demolished in 1902. It adjoined the Sessions-House. Public Hangings were removed, to the west facade of the Old Bailey in 1783, from Tyburn, and continued with unfortunate repetition perhaps until 1901.

William Penn, the Quaker and pioneer, was confined to this prison in 1670, when he was tried with his friends for unlawful assembly. An Anglican Parliament took a very dim view of his religious leanings, and he very nearly did not get an opportunity to go to America: A plaque in the main hall records the famous incident, as a result of which judgment was established, the right of impartiality of a Jury and freedom from political fear in the expression of their conscionable verdict.

'Near this Site WILLIAM PENN and WILLIAM MEAD

were tried in 1670

for preaching to an unlawful assembly

in Grace Church Street

This tablet Commemorates

The courage and endurance of the Jury Thos Vere, Edward Bushell and ten others who refused to give a verdict against them although locked up without food for two nights and were fined for their final

Verdict of Not Guilty

The case of these Jurymen was reviewed on a writ of Habeas Corpus and Chief Justice Vaughan delivered the opinion of the Court which established 'The Right of Juries' to give their Verdict

according to their Convictions

Other famous prisoners have included:

Titus Oates, perjurer,
Daniel Defoe, novelist,
Jonathan Wild,
Lord George Gordon, the rioter, 1780,
Oscar Wilde, playwright,
Dr. Crippen,

and more recently,

Lord Haw-Haw.

'Poise the Cause in Justice in Equal Scales', as does our lady in bronze astride the dome. This famous statue was designed by F. W. Pomeroy. She is not blind-folded. She may wish she was with the changing face of London's ugly skyline.

Of the many incidents of trials, personalities, and yarns that have been around in this famous court-house, it is impossible to select a particular text: books have been written, volumes will continue to flow into libraries. An often little know procedural habit may divert the reader's attention nevertheless. In the old days, when the literate class was confined to a small section of the people, a valid defence in the Common Law Courts was available to a defendant, who could recite verse one of psalm 57: 'Have mercy upon me O God, according to Thy loving kindness; according unto the multitude of thy tender mercies blot out my transgressions'. This 'neck-verse' as it came to be known, originated with the clergy and persons in Holy Order who were exempted from secular jurisdiction and if tried by an ecclesiastical court, saved their neck at the least since there was no power to hang a convicted person. Gradually this defendant's claim extended to all those who were eligible for ordination. This contention between the King's jurisdiction and that of the clergy was an example of the differences between King Henry and Thomas à Becket.

In 1490 a statute was passed which limited this right of Benefit of Clergy to a defendant once and once only: he was branded on the thumb as a precaution. The Benefit was abolished in England in 1827 but continued in parts of the United States thereafter, and was successfully pleaded in Carolina in the year 1855.

COUNTY COURTS

COUNTY COURTS, which sit in 356 places, divided into 65 County Court Circuits, deal with the less important civil actions; their jurisdiction is limited in general to £1,000. Cases are tried by Circuit Judges or Recorders. These latter judicial appointments are from practising members of the Bar who are usually Queen's Counsel. Appeals lie to the Civil Division of the Court of Appeal.

MAGISTRATES' COURTS

These exercise a criminal jurisdiction, but they deal with some civil matters, mainly in the sphere of family law. Every criminal charge must be brought before Magistrates. A person accused of an offence which it is beyond their competence to try is committed to the Crown Court for trial by Judge and jury if the Magistrates' Court is satisfied that there is a *prima facie* case. Magistrates themselves dispose of over 95 per cent of all criminal charges (two-thirds of which are traffic offences) in England and Wales. For certain offences the accused may elect to be tried in the Crown Court. Appeals from Magistrates' Courts lie to the Crown Court or, on points of law, to the Divisional Court. Nearly all the Magistrates in the country (there are nearly 20,000 of them) are unqualified and unpaid laymen, who are appointed Justices of the Peace by the Lord Chancellor. They sit in Lay Benches of a minimum of three. The clerk of the Court must be a qualified barrister or solicitor. In London there are 39 full-time Magistrates (on a 'stipend') appointed from barristers or solicitors and 10 in certain other cities. Stipendiary Magistrates are fully qualified lawyers and thus may exercise a wider jurisdiction, e.g. the Chief Magistrate, Bow Street, London.

BOW STREET

The most famous Magistrates' Court in the

Kingdom is probably that at Bow Street, the seat of the Chief Metropolitan Magistrate who usually shares extradition cases and those concerning deportation. The first Bow Street Magistrate, for whom the Court was opened in 1748, was the blind Sir John Fielding, brother and predecessor of the novelist Henry Fielding, and founder of the Bow Street runners, the famous force of 'Thief-takers' on whose model the Metropolitan Police force was later based by Sir Robert Peel. Bow Street takes its name from its curling path running southwards 'in the shape of a bow'. It seems strange that Bow Street runners did not choose a straighter street for Headquarters. A morning spent at Bow Street Court-house is a rewarding waste of time which drives the spectator to wonder how the Chief Metropolitan Magistrate who sits in the Number 1 Court contrives to be so perfect a gentleman despite a company he is paid to keep.

OTHER JUDGES

Some judicial functions in the High Court are performed by Masters and Registrars,who adjudicate upon interlocutory or other pre-trial issues, some of which are however of the utmost importance and may in fact decide the disposition of hundreds of thousands of pounds' worth of matrimonial property, and who also play a part in the administration of the Courts. Appeals lie from these Masters and Registrars to a Judge of the High Court, but in some instances appeal is direct to the Court of Appeal. County Court Registrars have similar functions in the County

Courts. Magistrates' Clerks, however, cannot deputise or perform judicial functions for Magistrates.

CORONERS' COURTS

Coroners' Courts are a relic of the medieval enquiries of the Coroner, whose function was to investigate all matters which might entitle the Crown to revenue or to forfeit man's goods or lands. These were once extensive duties but are now limited mainly to investigating deaths where other than natural causes are suspected, although treasure found and royal fish, such as the sturgeon, still fall within their jurisdiction.

STATUTORY TRIBUNALS

Statutory Tribunals grow apace in this modern age, and often supplant or replace Courts, dealing with apparently administrative matters such as compensation under the National Insurance Acts, land valuations, assessment, Income Tax assessment, commercial vehicle licensing, rating valuations, and many similar matters. With the growth of State control of and participation in everyday life, these tribunals play a more and more important part in the life of the ordinary system, and many think that the time has come to organise them into a proper and properly controlled, judicial system. Many of these tribunals have a full or part-time legally qualified Chairman, e.g. The Criminal Injuries Compensation Board, whose chairman is a distinguished and senior silk (Michael Ogden, Q.C.). Barristers and Solicitors have a right of audience to some, but not all, of them. Still other tribunals are outside the State system altogether, though they may be regulated by Statute. Appeal from them lies sometimes to the High Court and sometimes to the Privy Council, which is the judicial committee to the House of Lords sitting under another name. The tribunals are subject to some statutory control. There are also those set up to govern the more important professions such as Solicitors and Doctors and Dentists. Other professional bodies have less formal tribunals, as do Trades Unions, Clubs, and the numerous other bodies which reserve the right to expel persons from membership, or even to punish their members. Alas and alack that the system which protects their liberties is so often abused by the less decent members of their organizations. Any domestic tribunal of this sort, however, is subject to the powers of the Queen's Bench Divisional Court to control injustice by prerogative writs.

The influence of the Common Law and the Judicial system is also to be seen abroad in the South African context: Despite the political trials, the patience and courtesy shown by the South African Courts to the poorer and more ignorant defendants of both races is a reflection of common standards.

THE SMALLER THE BETTER?

The smaller the Better? Thanks largely to the institution of the lay Magistrate, and the use of part-time services of Recorders and Deputy Judges, there are remarkably few full-time Judges in England

and Wales when one considers the size of the population. For nearly forty-nine million people there are fewer than 100 High Court Judges and only about 260 Circuit Judges. There are only 330 Recorders but there are 20,000 Justices of the Peace. Perhaps the very smallness of the salaried judiciary assists in preserving its high standards, integrity, competence, unity and cohesion.

TERMINOLOGY

It is worth including a few words on Judicial titles since they do confuse those unfamiliar with English customs of address.

A LAW LORD

A Law Lord is officially styled The Rt. Hon. Lord Campbell. (All Peers are entitled to the style Right Honourable, as are Members of the Privy Council.) In Court his Lordship is addressed as My Lord, and in informal conversation or correspondence as Lord Campbell. His wife is Lady Campbell.

A LORD JUSTICE

A Lord Justice (Court of Appeal Judge) is not yet a Peer but is made a Privy Councillor on appointment and his style is The Rt. Hon. Lord Justice Jeffries. He is a Knight Bachelor and is therefore The Rt. Hon. Sir George Jeffries, and his wife Lady Jeffries. In Court he is addressed as My Lord, and in law reports will be referred to as Jeffries L.J. In private conversation or correspondence he should be addressed as Lord Justice or Sir George.

A HIGH COURT JUDGE

A High Court or Puisne Judge is a Knight and his prefix and proper style is The Hon. Mr Justice Blackstone. In Court he is addressed as My Lord and he is referred to in law reports as Blackstone J. Informally or socially he is addressed as the Hon. Sir William Blackstone and his wife, Lady Blackstone. He should not be referred to as Judge Blackstone.

JUDGES

A Circuit Judge is His Honour Judge Smith. He is addressed in Court as Your Honour. In private life he is Judge Smith and may be addressed as Judge.

A Magistrate is a Justice of the Peace and places the letters J.P. after his or her name; an envelope to him would be addressed John Wilkinson Esq., JP. In Court he is addressed as Your Worship, or, if by a member of the Bar as 'Sir'.

A visit to the Courts can, undeniably, provide information, entertainment and education (the three admitted aims of the B.B.C. as Baroness Stocks so rightly observed).

Whether it is a point of law, such as the late A. P. H. made so readable:—

SOME RULE OF EVIDENCE

Sir Ethelred:
Have you got varicose veins Mr. Stanley?
Witness:
No.

Sir Ethelred:

I put it to you, Mr. Stanley, that you *have* got varicose veins?

Witness:

Must I answer that your honour?

His Learned Opponent:

Milord, I object. Me learned friend . . .

Sir Ethelred:

Milord, I do submit — I have a reason for asking, milord.

H.L.O. & Sir Ethelred:

Milord!

(The two famous advocates here engaged in a violent altercation in undertones.)

The Judge:

. . . I think it right to say that so far as I understand the law, I shall at a suitable moment be prepared to say that the question is relevant and shall be answered, subject to the consideration that this sentence has now continued so long that it may be arguable that the law has altered in the meantime.

Sir Ethelred:

I am very much obliged, milord'.

. . . Or the drama of human life played out in the courts of law, English Justice maintains to this day the high standards of integrity and fairness which has set an example to the world.

CHAPTER 4

LEGAL LONDON

Dragon

Wyvern

LEGAL LONDON

Temple Bar — Early London — Palace of Westminster — Chancery Lane — Public Record Office — Sergeants' Inns — The Law Society Hall — And President's Chamber — Royal Courts of Justice — St. Clement Danes — The Liberty Bells — The Temple and Legal London.

(Appendix: Historical Associations Of Temple Bar)

TEMPLE BAR

INTRODUCTION

At the confluence of two great thoroughfares, the Strand and Fleet Street, there once stood Temple Bar, Gateway to the City of London. A fearsome dragon guards this site, though, as a matter of heraldic fact, the supporters of the City's armorial bearings are sometimes displayed as wyverns. The memorial *in situ* was erected in 1880, two years after Temple Bar had been demolished and removed to a nobleman's palace outside London where it remains to this day. Many monarchs and national pageants have been associated with this grand portal . . .

99

Because the City administers to its own needs, and has since time immemorial displayed its own talent for jurisdiction – it still is, and it is hoped will ever remain, a law unto itself – the Lord Mayor tenders the symbolic sword of the City, which the sovereign deftly returns, at the entrance Gate to the City.

Temple Bar was designed by Sir Christopher Wren, and erected in 1672 to replace an earlier structure. It is a magnificent pièce de résistance and lent grace and dignity to England's capital for two hundred years. It was when the 'new' Law Courts in the Strand were built that Temple Bar was pulled down, and thus ended an association for which it is hard to forgive our City Fathers.

THE MEMORIAL

The Memorial was designed by Sir Horace Jones and erected in 1880. On its south side, in a niche, is a statue of Queen Victoria; on the north side (facing the Law Courts) is a niche, bearing a statue of Edward, Prince of Wales; both are by Sir E. Boehm. The bas-reliefs which adorn the base of the monument are: on the south side, Queen Victoria going to the Guildhall on the first Lord Mayor's Day in her reign (9 November 1837); on the north side, the Royal Procession to St. Paul's Cathedral on 27 February 1872 to return thanks for the recovery of the Prince of Wales (afterwards Edward VII) from typhoid fever. Eastwards to St. Paul's, a bas-relief depicts Wren's Temple Bar and there follows a description of its removal; westwards, is a commemorative plaque giving the exact position of Temple

Bar gate relative to this monument, and both are by C. H. Mabey Esquire.

The monument is surmounted by a very fierce dragon rampant, designed by C. B. Birch and represents one supporter of the achievement of the City of London. Often incorrectly, the dragon on this monument is cited as a griffin and is a grave insult to this noble beast. Both dragons and griffins are heraldic and mythical beasts — the dragon with scaled body, pointed tail and tongue, wings and sharp claws — perhaps the best known of the Royal beasts, whereas the griffin is a hybrid creature with eagle's head and wings and a lion's body; but by no stretch of the imagination can the creature on this monument be called this, or even — that.

'High over roaring Temple Bar' — with Alfred Lord Tennyson — can be seen the masterpiece of English classical architecture, St. Paul's Cathedral. Sir Christopher Wren, 1632-1723, had decided to build a fitting Gateway to 'his' Cathedral — indeed to the City — and a summary account of its erection will leave no one to doubt, either his authenticity or its great bearing in contemporary secular architecture.

The older gateway as depicted in engravings of this period was a structure almost as high as the buildings on either side of it, constructed of wood and ornamented with carvings, and there was a large central archway with lesser arches on either side, covered by a pitched roof clad in red tiles, and gables. This gateway began to show signs of age when, between 1632 and 1642, Inigo Jones was restoring St. Paul's and rebuilding its West Front. Inigo Jones completed a plan but it was never utilised and the old gate was still standing at the time of the Great Fire in 1666. The fire stopped just short of it on the east side, although various reports were written at the time that the gate was destroyed. These reports were probably circulated by the 'insolent' Dutch and passed to other war-mongers throughout Europe, in one account they even went as far as to say that the gate had been reduced to ashes but the roof still survived!

In 1669 it was decided to remove the old gateway and replace it with the new Temple Bar which had been designed by Dr. Christopher Wren (he was not yet Sir Christopher). Work started in 1670 and was completed in 1672.

The new gate is typical of the English Renaissance style soon to be brought to the degree of perfection by Wren, and renders a fine example of the late Italian Baroque Roman triumphal arch. The gate served as a screen to be approached from either side, through a central arch flanked by two lesser arches. Above the central arch is a room with a window placed central in its wall, on either side of which is a niche of equal dimensions between Corinthian pilasters. The thrust from this upper storey is transmitted through buttreses which are a motif of wing trusses decorated with scrolls. The design is unified by the curve of the segmental pediment which carries in its tympanum a flat sarcophagus supported on either side by a cornucopia (the symbol of plenty), and above, a tablet decorated with oak leaves and acorns in rich relief. The elevations of this gateway are identical except for the statuary and carvings.

There are four effigies each standing on its own niche: on the west side, facing Westminster, Charles I in the north and Charles II in the south; on the east side facing the City were James I on the north side and his wife, Anne of Denmark — the Monarchs are dressed in Roman style and are wearing the Order of the Garter on their left legs. There has been doubt concerning the effigy of the Queen and is believed by some to be of Queen Elizabeth in her young days. This theory has merit in the fact that certain contemporaneous portraits painted of the two Royal Ladies at a comparable age are not unlike each other, and if this theory is correct it would also make the statues read in chronological (anti-clockwise direction) order of succession.

Above the keystone of the central arch on the west side is a cartouche carved with the Royal Arms of Charles II, surmounted by a large Crown, and on the parapets over the posterns were positioned the supporters of the Royal Arms; on the south the unicorn and on the north the lion. The cartouche over the keystone facing the City contained the City Arms and the supporters on the parapets were dragons with shields, and all the heraldic arms and beasts were gilded and coloured.

The four effigies are approximately life size and are by John Bushnell. They are considered to be amongst his best work, sculptured at about the same time as the statues of the Kings and Queens of England which he produced for Edward Jarman (who designed the

103

second Royal Exchange in 1667-71 to replace the Exchange destroyed by the Great Fire. Unfortunately this one was also destined to be burnt to the ground in 1838). All the statues were thus destroyed except those of Charles I, Charles II and Sir Thomas Gresham (founder of the Royal Exchange) and are now at the Old Bailey, on the first floor landing; which royal effigies are identical to those on Temple Bar. From the accounts for Temple Bar it seems likely that Bushnell carried out all the carved work. Although Sir Christopher Wren was in fact the designer of the gateway, no drawings unfortunately, or separate building accounts even, have survived, except the ledger in which is recorded interim payments made to the master craftsmen for work carried out. However, in the light of the Bute Collection of drawings, discovered in 1951, there is hope that other records of Temple Bar may one day be found.

The professional architect as such was entirely unknown in Restoration England. The large contracting companies were still people of the future. In taste and design the educated amateur reigned supreme, and the master craftsmen — stone-masons, joiners, bricklayers — were only beginning to ascend to the position of contractor. Until this time the person who was 'professional' — ranking perhaps the higher in both the practical and theoretical sense — was the Clerk of the Works, who fulfilled his centuries'-old duties.

Wren's life and achievements are too well known to be narrated in these pages. Suffice it to say he became, by his talents, the truly great architect and builder without the benefit of formal training and with scant opportunity of studying at first hand continental architecture of his, or his preceding age. For it is remembered that until the advent of his predecessor, Inigo Jones, some forty years before, architecture in England had stagnated for upwards of a century, and therefore Wren had little enough reference to architectural styles which were well out-dated by continental standards. Far from a detriment, this was turned to advantage as he was given to sheer originality and inventiveness: his hand showed this genius. It may be asked why Wren, a brilliant mathematician, turned to architecture. It is probable that having acquired mathematical equations for construction problems he changed horses.

In 1663 when he was appointed a member of the Commission for the repair of Old St. Paul's (and in the same year designed his first building, Pembroke College Chapel, Cambridge, 1663-5), he undertook the Sheldonian Theatre in Oxford (1664-9) where he resolved some and many problems of structure and design, particularly that of the span, by his prowess as an inventor and mathematician.

His one and only visit to the continent, between July 1665 and 1666, took him to Paris. He did not keep a diary but it is doubtful that his tour took him further afield than Holland and Belgium. This important impression in his career revealed to him 'modern' styles of architecture by architects of talent. The enormous impact this short visit made on him may be found in and judged by his later work. While

Queen Elizabeth I
(Statue at St. Dunstan's)

in Paris he studied Baroque architecture for the first time and saw what at that time were the major domed churches — the Sorbonne by Jacques Lemercier and the church of the Val-de-Grace begun by Francois Mansart and completed by Lemercier. We know the influence these domes played on Wren, and the upper storey of the West Front of the Val-de-Grace has a certain resemblance to Temple Bar, particularly where the thrust of the clerestory is taken by buttresses as wing trusses decorated with scrolls. Good examples of wing trusses in brick and stone also appear on the north elevation of the Royal Observatory at Greenwich built by Sir Christopher Wren in 1675, the same year he commenced building St. Paul's. When Wren was engaged on the chapel at Cambridge he could not fail to have seen the Gate of Honour at Gaius College (1572-3) which up to its pediment gives a familiar outline but without the posterns. He met Bernini during this visit, but his style never developed into the heavy Italian Baroque but was in keeping with the conservative school of the French and Dutch. We know (from the Wren Sale Catalogue of 1749) that he owned and therefore read a large number of books on Italian architecture including 'De architecture libri X' by Vitruvius, 'Architettura' by Sebastiano Serlio, and many more by worthies such a Palladio, Vignola, etc., and from that he was thoroughly versed in the latest continental styles. Wren used to full advantage the pediment motif and its tympanum with or without carving — the former as the focula point of the façade — and the use of the niche, with or without statuary, to relieve a large expanse of plain masonry or its use in giving colour in light and shade to a building. All these points and many more he employed to great advantage. Soon after his return to England in September, 1666, came the auspicious fate of the Great Fire of London to his talents, which were thenceforth plunged into showmanship. He was appointed a member of the Commission for the rebuilding of London, and, in 1669 was appointed Surveyor General of the Royal Works by Charles II.

Wren's son, in 'Parentalia' (1750), tells us that Wren was appointed Surveyor General and Principal Architect 'for the rebuilding of the whole City, the Cathedral Church of St. Paul's, all parochial churches' (in No. 51 enacted by Parliament in lieu of those that were burnt and demolished) 'with other public structures and for the disposition of the streets' and 'he took as his assistant Mr. Robert Hooke to whom he assigned chiefly the business of measuring, adjusting and setting out the ground of the private street houses to the several proprietors, reserving all the public works to his own peculiar care and direction'.

In the rebuilding programme was included the widening of the streets and City gates on the western edge of the City. Beyond the limits of the fire the widening of Temple Bar brought this improvement to fruition, and it was entirely due to Charles II and his promptors. The City fought shy of the cost of rebuilding and did its best to avoid the issue but Charles peremptorily ordered the Commissioners at Scotland Yard to grant £1,500 towards the cost of

Temple Bar and thus forced the City to act. Parliament provided the money, and naturally this was passed to its own Surveyor. It is unlikely in the extreme that Wren would in turn have passed that authority to the City while still retaining overall responsibility, especially as he 'reserved all the public works to his own peculiar care and direction'.

The Temple Bar ledgers which exist define the master masons to have been Joshua Marshall and Thomas Knight: the bricklayer one Anthony Connor, and the (black) smith to have been Thomas Hodgekins. It is interesting that during this period of building Temple Bar, these same craftsmen were also working on another contract of Wren's, the building of the 'Pillar' or The Monument as it is known, commemorating the Great Fire itself. Joshua Marshall was well known to Wren and in the accounts of St. Paul's Cathedral (dated 2 December 1668) he received a payment as master mason for carrying out various works, and again, in the accounts for the building of the new cathedral, he, with Thomas Stong, signed the first contracts for the construction work on 18 June 1675, three days before the foundation stone was laid for that building. The entry in those accounts show him indeed as the Master Mason to the Crown. Joshua Marshall along with his ageing father, had dominated the London scene of artistry in stone and in their stone yard in Fetter Lane many works of art were produced, among their accomplishments was the tall pedestal of the equestrian statue to Charles I in Trafalgar Square. Wren preferred to make his major appointments on a personal knowledge of his men and their attainments, and unfortunately Marshall died in 1678 or he would have figured very prominently in the building of St. Paul's and the rash of City churches.

Joshua Marshall and Thomas Knight received their first payment on 3 May 1670 which was authorised by the Lord Mayor (dated 29 April 1670), since all work other than the ecclesiastical building was a civic responsibility. However it is interesting to note that the payment made to Thomas Hodgekins, the smith, in the sum of £60 was paid for out of the Coal Tax and not from the money granted by Parliament. The total in the ledger amounted to £1,397 10s. but this cannot be the final cost as certain trades were not listed, for example the plumber for leadwork to the roof, the joiner for making and hanging the gates and doors, the glazier (in those days probably carried out by the plumber), the plasterer for work in the upper room, painting, etc.

A STUDY

A study of the gateway itself is revealing: the wing trusses decorated with scrolls and their decorative carved details are identical with the scrolls mounted on the stall screens in the Sheldonian Theatre but at Oxford they are placed and fixed on an axis of horizontal plain, whereas at Temple Bar they are on the vertical (their use as wing trusses with the scrolls also appears on the external walls of the Theatre). The use of these wing trusses for buttresses, which he had seen in Paris, also appears along nearby Fleet Street on the tower of St. Bride's Church which he commenced also in 1670, and they are also to be seen on the towers of St. Martin, Ludgate and Christ Church in Newgate Street. And, this motif is used by Wren as a carved decorative feature on either side of the lunette windows on the triforium level inside St. Paul's Cathedral.

In the flank or end walls of the upper storey of Temple Bar are circular windows, the dimensions of which are different but for obvious reasons, and the detail of the moulding is similar to the circular openings which occur in the bastions of the peri-style around the drum of the Dome of St. Paul's, and appears identical with those on the towers of St. Bride's and St. Vedast in Foster Lane.

The window surrounds on the Temple Bar are in a lighter moulding but nevertheless are similar to those on the lower storey on the exterior of St. Paul's. The use of the heraldic beasts on the parapets as a means of decorating the building is similar with his plans for St. Paul's and his designs of statuary there, and so the use of such beasts on Temple Bar fit in neatly with his characteristic ideas for decorating a building. There are too many instances of details on Temple Bar closely following those we find by Wren on his other buildings, for this to have been a sheer coincidence or for Temple Bar not to have been his handiwork. It is so obviously his design. Wren had very little to copy in this country, but many people copied Wren.

Probably the most eminent in these matters today are the craftsmen and artists who have spent many recent years — some a lifetime — working on and rebuilding Wren's work after the two World Wars. In so doing they have had ample cause to study his styles, his minute and often intricate details, and probed deep into his mind to find the faithful avenues of his thoughts. The craftsman engages in this mental excercise from the sheer necessity of acquiring the maximum knowledge before undertaking the faithful replica of works of art, which, when completed will be scrutinised by all those who doubtless call themselves 'experts'. Such thought to the craftsman becomes second nature. Those who after a few hours of study, will pronounce at random an incorrect opinion that may be far reaching may do well to remember this.

Even Wren's life and work was made difficult by some in high places, but it is only to be expected that one so brilliant should make enemies and Wren certainly had his share, for there were many only too ready and eager to pounce upon him at every opportunity yet it seems strange that when his contemporaries were alive and we presume knew the facts, not one voice seems to have been raised that Wren had not designed Temple Bar, had this not been true. Scholars have studied Wren and his work during the past two hundred and fifty years – and obviously the farther one goes back the nearer one should be to the truth. Be that as it may, it behoves us to remember the inscription on the tablet above the tomb of Sir Christopher Wren, in the Crypt of St. Paul's Cathedral:

> Beneath lies buried the founder of this Church and City, Christopher Wren, who lived for more

than 90 years, not for himself, but for the public good. Reader, if you seek his monument, look around you.

SI MONUMENTUM REQUIRIS, CIRCUMSPICE

It is also true of Temple Bar.

Outside the City walls 'in olden days ere witch-craft did begin; before polygamy was made a sin', there grew up a community of warriors. This husbandry distinguished itself from the militia: they dedicated their activities to God's calling, which they interpreted as being their duty to wrest the Holy Land from the Oriental infidel. The avowed aim was to provide Christian pilgrims a free access to Jerusalem.

The site of the Temple was this home of the Crusaders, the Order of the Holy Sepulchre of Knights Templars (whence its name). These strong men chose the close proximity of the city for the obvious protection that an orderly citizenship bestows on its flanks. In medieval times, it must be noted, only the godly or the brave dared live outside a fortification. The Knights' neighbours then included the Whitefriars, the Carmelites, the Blackfriars, the Carthusians at Smithfield, the knights of the Order of St. John at Clerkenwell, and the occasional bishop safely inside his palace. One bishop, His Right Reverence of Exeter, was unhappily beheaded by a cockney mob on his way home to Sunday luncheon in 1326. Times change.

Within the Temple precincts, long before that year, the knights suffered students to read the law. No doubt in so doing they contravened their own ordinance: 'that the Temple Palace be not put to profane uses.' The Temple is situate in the Ward of Farringdon Without, i.e. outside the city wall. Close by Temple Bar, which marked this division, the 'Middle' Temple grew on the verge beside the 'Inner' Temple, inside the city boundary. There was once an Outer Temple westward of the two, since lost to redevelopers.

Westwards the 1680 apse of St. Clement Danes, a Wren architectural curtain-raiser leading up to St. Paul's, makes a cleft ear for Dr. Johnson reading from his pedestal, which was erected in 1900 to commemorate the great parishioner. Back and beyond is St. Mary-le-Strand, built by James Gibb in 1714, and noted for one of its rectors, Thomas à Becket. Further West, a spiritual appetite is well satisfied by the secular premises of Simpson's Restaurant in the Strand, famed for its traditional English saddle of mutton trolley. The Savoy Hotel adjoins it, built with the profits of the Gilbert & Sullivan operettas, and is situated in the only street of London where you drive on the right. This enabled Mr. D'Oyly Carte's patrons to alight from their carriages at the entrance doors to the Savoy Theatre.

Opposite the Law Courts, note the 'Spy' cartoons in the window of the Wig & Pen Club. Nearby is Messrs. Twining's, the tea merchants who were responsible for the speedy tea-clipper trade to the Far East. At five and twenty past four of an afternoon, a worthy patron, Codrington Edmund Carrington by name, may be encountered (by asking the nice waitress Julia for your introduction to him). His ancestor was the great Chief Justice of Ceylon, the other tea isle, through whom England learned to drink tea. He welcomes visitors from abroad and readers are recommended to make his acquaintance.

Closeby is to be found the Old Cheshire Cheese, a haven well worth the honour of Dr. Johnson's ghost. The delectable port-wine is most conducive to a full enjoyment of old England.

Cast your eyes across the roofs that lean over their street facades. This reveals their age more vividly than the shopfronts. The famous 'street of ink' has been associated with printing since 1500 (Caxton's assistant). The Solicitors' Law Stationery Society is where you buy a real writ for five pence. In close view are Coutts Bank (founded in 1692), bankers to Her Majesty the Queen, and Child's (established 1671), bankers to little Nell Gwynne.

The church of St. Dunstan's in the West gave its name to the Home for the Blind, and was mentioned by Dickens in 'The Chimes' of the lantern tower.

Backstage is Dr. Johnson's House (open to the public) at No. 17 Gough Square, where he compiled the great Dictionary. The learned Doctor died in Bolt Court hardby. Marvel at the newspaper superstructures that do so much to belittle the written word; and at the bottom of Fleet Street a stone marks the spot where young Edgar Wallace remained a street newsvendor, till he achieved world renown as a thriller writer.

Down the hill is St. Bride's (alias Bridget, and not of monogamous union), noted for the Roman

Dr Johnson & his house

excavations discovered there after the war. The Church is well associated with the lines of Richard Lovelace: 'Stone walls do not a prison make, nor iron bars a cage . . .' or the prose: 'I could not love thee dear so much loved I not honour more . . .' Samuel Pepys was baptised here on 3rd March, 1632. Beside the Wren church stands a Public House, built by Wren as a dosshouse for his workmen.

The Chanticleer sign that swings over the Cock Tavern replaces the original carved by Grinling Gibbons (and hung inside). Linger awhile at No. 17, Prince Henry's Room, the ancient Council Chamber of the Prince of Wales: it has been well restored by the Greater London Council. The badge of the three feathers finely carved below the upper windows indicates the ancient plaster and panelling within the Chamber, which ceased to keep its secrets when Prince Henry died in 1612. (A report of the Election Case at West Looe, a town in the Royal Duchy of Cornwall, mentions a 'Commission-House in Fleet Street', 25th November, 1635.)

Chancery Lane is named after the ancient writ office (viz. 'Cursitor Street') of the Lord Chancellor, and more especially after the resident Bishop of Chichester, later Chancellor, whose palace was in Lincoln's Inn. This bustling thoroughfare connects Gray's Inn with the other Inns of Court. Until recently, a future occupant of the Woolsack could be espied astride his bicycle en route for luncheon in Lincoln's Inn Hall.

Wending left up the Lane we pass the Law Society to which body all solicitors belong. The building

(1832) is protected by iron railings with gilded lions' heads. Opposite, the Public Record Office houses all the historic State Papers, including Domesday (1086) and Magna Carta (1215). On its site stood the Rolls Chapel in which a Bishop once preached the text from Psalm 22 vv. 21: 'Save me from the lion's mouth for thou hast heard me from amongst the horns of the unicorns'. The monarch of the day promptly dismissed the minister of God for levelling against the Royal Arms.

Ede & Ravenscroft, wig and robe makers, have their shop at No. 93, at the back of which Mr. Marsh makes the judges' wigs. Recently a young and impecunious barrister threatened the wig makers with the Monopolies Commission (because wigs are expensive and 'Ede & R' are the only surviving wig-makers in London): 'Delighted', their manager replied, 'Let any rival come hither and ease the burden of our orders.' At Star Yard a street lavatory in the Parisian taste often fascinates the passer-by; on the decorative ironwork can be seen the Royal Coat of Arms.

THE PUBLIC RECORD OFFICE

Close to Rolls Buildings is the Public Record Office.

The gaunt splendour of the façade was much lauded at the time of its building, in 1851, and completion in 1902. Sir James Pennethorne and Sir John Taylor, respectively, acquit themselves well of the mock Tudor-Gothic style, though one does deprecate the modern planner who must be blind as well as thoughtless when he suffocates the view of buildings by allowing neighbours to congest *ad nauseam*. Cities of the world need good fresh air as it is, and fast it is coming upon us, when any sight-seer who uses his eyes, will perforce use them to better advantage from an aeroplane, whereas the street level is where architects must be presumed to have intended the admirers of their works to stand.

Be that as it may, the repository for the National archives and legal records struggles on without complaint, and once within, too many fascinating documents soon rid our minds of itinerant grumbles. The Keeper of the Records is the most acquisitive gentleman I know:

– the two pristine vellum volumes of Domesday Book, a statistical survey of 34 counties of England commissioned by order – else, execution – of William the Conqueror in 1086;
– the Magna Carta in its final form as issued by King Henry III in 1225 (the British Museum houses the scroll of the original articles of the barons, as accepted by King John)
– the Plea Rolls dated from 1194, the Exchequer Rolls including the earliest surviving Pipe Roll of 1129
– the confession signed by Mr Guy Fawkes in 1605
– Shakespeare's last will and testament dated 1612
– the 'olive branch' petition from Congress to King George III in 1775, signed by, among others, John Adams and Benjamin Franklin; George Washington's letter of 1795 to his 'great and good friend' George III, and many other treasures.

120

It occupies the site of a house and chapel founded by Henry III in 1232 for converted Jews, the 'domus conversorum'. The chapel came to be used for the custody of the Rolls and Records of Chancery and parts of it have been embodied into a large room of the modern building used as a museum, which may be visited between 1 and 4 p.m. from Monday to Friday.

THE SERJEANTS' INNS

A few steps down the Lane a blue plaque marks the site of one of the old Inns of the Serjeants.

There were two, if not three, sites of Serjeants' Inn where membership was the venerable status of Serjeant-at-law and on which appointment a member of one of the four Inns of Court duly left his Inn and proceeded to the ranks he had joined, as explained in Chapter One.

On the site of the Royal Insurance Group building, at number 5 Chancery Lane stood the Serjeants' Inn and the chapel hall and chambers from which the stained glass now rests in the Hall windows of the Law Society, near opposite in the lane. The Serjeants' Inn existed from 1415 until 1909, when one of their number, one Serjeant Cox, purchased it for £57,100 and removed for safekeeping the heraldic stained glass armorial windows to his residence Mote Mount, Mill Hill, and which in 1926, were given to the Law Society and thereafter displayed in the Hall. Serjeants' Inn was itself demolished in 1909.

The second Serjeants' Inn, whose premises and precincts survive this day, was in Fleet Street, where from 1424, accommodation was known to have been given to the serjeants, and but for a few interruptions, as when in 1442-59 the Inn removed to Chancery Lane, and when in 1666 the Great Fire consumed the premises which were speedily rebuilt, the society continued there on the south side of Fleet Street until in 1733 they failed to obtain a renewal of the lease, and the Norwich Union Insurance Group ultimately purchased the precincts, part of which we see to the day.

This Inn was first called Farringdon's Inn after Robert Faryngdon, a clerk of the Chancery, who acquired the land in 1404; his name has been given to a nearby street and to an Underground 'Tube' railway station. Serjeants used the Inn from 1484, as well as another Inn in Fleet Street, and it was there that the judicial commission sat which settled the boundaries of properties in the City of London after the obliterating Great Fire of 1666.

With the demise of the order of the Serjeants in the second half of the last century, and the eclipse of the societies, the judges found themselves homeless and were offered a home in the Inns of Court, previously unheard of, and the institutions of practitioners, as were the Inns of Chancery, which were hospitable to both attorneys of the Common Law and the solicitors of Equity.

THE LAW SOCIETY'S HALL

The façade is made attractive by the little row of 'legal' lions, designed by Alfred Stevens for the railings of the British Museum, but which the Keeper now keeps out of sight. These delightful copies guard the 'den of equity' and the law.

The Law Society's Hall was designed in Classical style by Lewis Vulliamy and opened in 1831. Extensions were added from time to time, the final addition, the common room, opened by King Edward VII in 1904. It contains the Council Chamber and the offices of The Law Society, the governing body of the solicitors' branch of the legal profession, and the library and other facilities for the use of its members. It stands on the site of one of the Inns of Chancery, known at various times in its history as Harfleet Inn, Kederminster's Inn and Six Clerks' Inn. More detailed reference to the Hall and the Law Society is made in an earlier chapter. Around the corner at 60 Carey Street is a beautiful house which belonged to The Law Society since 1929. It was built in 1731-32 for Richard Foley, M.P., a Bencher of Lincoln's Inn, and second Chief Notary of the Court of Common Pleas. Unfortunately he had not time to enjoy his new creation as he died in 1732 having just paid for it!

AND PRESIDENT'S CHAMBER

'He saw a lawyer killing a viper
On a dunghill hardby his own stable;
And the devil smiled,
For it put him in mind
Of Cain and his brother Abel.'

(The Devil's Thoughts).

The doors leading to the staircase deserve special mention. They are panelled in the same polished wood as is used on the staircase; their brazen, double-action locks and elongated hinges are of unusual design. Beyond the saddler's headquarters nearby, Richard Foley had at an earlier date built a stable and it was on the site of this stable and the land which lay between it and the saddler's property that Foley erected the house now known as 60 Carey Street 'situate in the Parish of St. Dunstan in the West and St. Clement Danes in the County of Middlesex'.

Much of the original building has since been carefully restored and preserved. The ground floor is now used for administrative purposes of the Society while the first floor, with its gracefully proportioned and panelled dining and sitting rooms, is used by the President as a town residence where he can entertain, and we trust, be entertained.

'Over the chimney piece in the dining room hangs a very fine oil-painting of ships at anchor, presented by Sir Douglas Garrett and Col. W. Mackenzie Smith, past Presidents of the Society, the work of Peter Monamy, the marine painter, who worked in London in the early eighteenth century. The work is interesting because, although it is called 'Ships at Anchor', the larger vessel is clearly making sail and has just fired a signal gun to port to warn her Consort. These facts, as well as the boat pulling towards it, seem to show that it is about to weigh anchor imminently, perhaps indicating that the vessels in the background could have hostile intentions – Dutch vessels sailing up the Medway perhaps.'

The Law Society is, and the housekeeper, Mrs

Moore in particular, keenly aware that it owns one of the finest examples of an early Georgian business and dwelling-house still surviving in this part of London and has constantly sought to show that, in carrying out its functions in today's world, the Society can both preserve and make daily use of gracious survival from a bygone age.

The Worshipful Company of Solicitors of the City of London is one of the many venerable companies in the City. The Company held its first meeting in 1909 whose members included, it is interesting to find, one David Lloyd George, who was a solicitor by profession but an advocate at heart, as England's tormentors learnt to their cost, in the first World War. The Company was made a Livery Company in 1944 which, considering that no new Livery Company had been created since 1709 (with one exception), was a singular honour and recognition of the profession's great bearing and status. Over the years, the Corporation of the City has called upon no less than four distinguished members to hold the office of Lord Mayor: they are: Sir William Phene Neal (1930), Sir William Waterlow (1929), Sir Cullum Welch (1956), and Sir Gilbert Inglefield (1971).

At the Annual Banquet in 1951, if this occasion may be thus recited to conclude the few words written of this illustrious body, the chief guest, Lord Goddard, then the Lord Chief Justice, had this to say to the assembly: 'I have stood at the Bar and sat on the Bench: I have got stout on, but never bitter with You!

THE ROYAL COURTS OF JUSTICE

The Royal Courts of Justice are the centre of a judicial system which goes back to Magna Carta and beyond, but the present building is less than a hundred years old. For 700 years the Royal courts were housed in the Palace of Westminster, but in 1866 a competition was held for the design of new Law Courts to be built on a site of some 5½ acres to the north of the Strand and Fleet Street. Eleven architects submitted their plans and these were exhibited in 1868 when those of George Edmund Street, R.A. (1824-81) were accepted. Street was one of the most important and influential of the Victorian ecclesiastical architects and pupil of Sir George Gilbert Scott (1811-78).

– AT THE PALACE OF WESTMINSTER –

An understanding why a thirteenth-century Gothic building was fashioned during the mid-nineteenth century is given in a study of the architectural trends of those days. Every generation of architects have striven to create a new style of architecture with which they can be identified. Those of the nineteenth century were no exception, but – with one difference – instead of searching for original ideas they chose to return to the Middle Ages and to recreate – and further develop – those architectural styles. Throughout the nineteenth century there had been an increasing interest in a secular Gothic Revival as though there were the need of religious orders from the past. On the night of 16 October 1834 the Palace of Westminster was burned to the ground. It was quickly decided that the new and larger Houses of Parliament should be built and to that end a competition was launched in June 1835. One of the conditions in the terms of entry stipulated that the building should be designed in either the Gothic or Elizabethan style. This was remarkable as it firmly established 'Gothic' as a national form of architecture.

The competition was won by (Sir) Charles Barry (1795-1860) who undertook the task of providing the working drawings and supervision necessary to complete the building. In this he was fortunate to have the co-operation of Augustus Wilby Northmore Pugin (1812-52), an architect who was dedicated and devout to the Gothic style; and so came about one of the largest – if not the largest – Gothic-style creation in the world. The seal of approval having been put on this style, it quickly gained momentum and became a great influence in the creative thoughts of many architects, so much so, that soon some of them behaved as though they really believed that the form of a cathedral or abbey was in reality a hotel, a railway station, town hall and so on. The Albert Memorial (1864-72), St. Pancras Station and Hotel (1864-74), both by Sir George Gilbert Scott, are good examples of this inventive line of thought.

THE LAW COURTS

Street's new Law Courts follow this trend and are a splendid 'example' of Early English Gothic of the thirteenth century. Work on the building commenced in 1874 with the foundation stone being laid in that year, and work continued beyond Street's death in 1881 until its completion by his son and Sir Arthur Blomfield in 1882.

The Courts were opened in 1882 by Queen Victoria and a bust of her is displayed under the balcony in the central hall to commemorate the event. There is also a painting showing the scene in the central hall which includes twenty-nine judges. It is interesting to note that the last survivor of that group was Lord Linley who also happened to be the last of the Serjeants-at-law and who died in 1921.

The central hall is a magnificent apartment, 238 feet long, 48 feet wide and 82 feet high, and is entered by a fine Gothic archway over which is a statue of Christ, on the west side of Him is King Solomon and on the east is Alfred the Great. The hall, which is the principal apartment, bears a very strong resemblance to a cathedral: is singularly bare, is rib-vaulted with blank arcading, and richly foliated.

The windows, lancets or grouped lancets with geometrical tracery, are emblazoned with the escutcheons of Lord Keepers of the Seal and Lords Chancellors. Street also designed the tessellated pavement which covers the entire length of the hall.

Of the statuary in the hall, that of Lord Russell of Killowen is by Sir Thomas Brock (whose best-known work is probably the Victoria Memorial (1911) standing at the west end of The Mall outside Buckingham Palace). Lord Russell (1832-1900) was the first Roman Catholic to become Lord Chief Justice of England since the Reformation, and was the leading counsel for Parnell and the Irish members before the Parnell Commission. There is also a statue to the famous Sir William Blackstone (1723-89) who became a judge in 1770 and was author of the classic 'Commentaries on the Law of England'. This statue was presented by the American Bar Association in 1924. The monument to George E. Street is by H. H. Armstead and was carried out in 1886. He is shown seated while studying a drawing and holding a pair of compasses; the plinth of the monument is a bas-relief showing the artists and craftsmen at work on the building during its construction. The hall also contains a number of fine paintings.

In 1918 this great hall was used as a dormitory for 600 sailors of the United States Grand Fleet who visited London.

There are twenty-three courts grouped around three sides of this great hall, four of which date from 1911, and in a room leading off the hall in the south-east corner is housed a permanent exhibition of court dress worn by judges and barristers from 1800 to the present day. There are a number of legal documents on display including the appointment by Queen Elizabeth II of the late Sir Gerald Upjohn as a Lord of Appeal in Ordinary and his summons to Parliament as a Law Lord.

There are cells in the basement for prisoners in attendance at the Court of Criminal Appeal. Altogether there are over 1,000 rooms in the Royal Courts, and in the main building alone are over 3½ miles of corridors.

If the Law Courts have in the past been less

popular in the London public mind than other national buildings since the cleaning of the stonework of the Strand façade in 1973, the intricate carvings and mouldings together with other long hidden details have once more been brought to light, and perhaps now it may find new friends. The 514-foot-long Strand elevation of the building was restored to something like its original freshness when in 1973 a thorough cleaning operation removed the accumulated grime of 90 years. It is now possible to appreciate details of Street's elaborate design and his subtle touches of colour. The façade has been described as 'an object lesson in free composition, with none of the symmetry of the classics, yet not undisciplined where symmetry is abandoned'. Along the outer screen walls the metalwork deserves notice; this was made by James Leaver and Thomas Potter & Sons and designed partly by George Street himself, partly by his son A. E. Street, and partly by Arthur Blomfield.

The cost of the building was in the order of £700,000 which was paid for out of unclaimed funds in Chancery, with Parliament paying over £1 million for the site, a large but never too large a sum of money to spend on dispensing justice.

Street created the Royal Courts of Justice in keeping with the trend of the Gothic Revival, but in doing so he probably contributed more than anyone else to its downfall. Although the Victorians came to accept and even to like the Houses of Parliament, they never took to the Law Courts; possibly they came to realise that as a style, Gothic was not really suited for large, secular buildings, and so the great Revival went into decline and large buildings were never again built in that style.

Since the war new buildings have been added to the Royal Courts, the first of these was the Queen's Building situated at the west end along Carey Street and built 1966-8 and opened by Queen Elizabeth II in 1968. This building provides twelve new courts, and in 1972 cells were built in the basement.

Since then another building has been constructed, the eleven-storey Thomas More Building — named by the then incumbent Lord Chancellor, Viscount Hailsham after an illustrious predecessor — this building houses the Bankruptcy and Companies Courts, and replaces the old offices which gave rise to the synonym that bankruptcy meant to 'finish up in Carey Street'.

During term time the Courts sit from 10.30 a.m. to just after 4 p.m. with an hour's adjournment at 1 p.m. Members of the public can go and watch any trial (except when the Judge is sitting 'in chambers') although it may be difficult to find room if the trial is one that is attracting much public attention. It is, of course, a fundamental principle of English legal procedure that justice should be 'seen to be done.'

The church of St. Clement Danes, which stands almost outside the Law Courts in the Strand, was bombed on several occasions until it was reduced to a ruin in the air raid of Saturday, 10 May 1941 (Temple Church was destroyed in the same raid). It was however, rebuilt (1955-58) by W. A. S. Lloyd and reconsecrated as the church of the Royal Air

131

Force. Its peal of bells were cast in the last decade of the eighteenth century.

THE LIBERTY BELLS

The most famous and least known bell foundry in the world is in the sound of Bow bells (East London), which were cast in the seventeenth century. The Whitechapel Bell Foundry was founded in the reign of Elizabeth I, in 1570, by one Robert Mot, and apart from removing across the thoroughfare, in 1738, stands in its original situation.

It was here in 1752 that the original Liberty Bell was produced at a cost of £54 10s. 6d. by 'Order of the Assembly of the Province of Pennsylvania for the State House in Philadelphia'. In those days a member of the firm, Thomas Lester, made the mould although the method has remained unchanged over two hundred years.

The famous tone of the Liberty Bell, heard throughout America by the convenience of the electric transmitter, which rang out the triumphant independence of the nation in 1776, carries an apt quotation from the book of Leviticus: 'Proclaim liberty throughout all the land unto all the inhabitants thereof'.

Other churches to which the foundry has sent its peals across the centuries have been:
Christchurch, Philadelphia (cast in 1754),
St. Michael's, Charleston.S.C. (cast in 1764),
Trinity Church, New York (cast in 1796),
the Bow Bells,
St. Clement Danes (Oranges and Lemons),

132

Great Tom of St. Paul's,
Great Peter of York,
the eight peals of Westminster Abbey (cast variously
from 1583-1919).

Of all professions, perhaps, Dr. Johnson would
have said that of bell-casting was the most worthy.
Most travellers in most cities, most persons in most
places share a spirit of thanksgiving when peals ripple
across the busy air of the day, and hearts uplift with
the infectious laughter of these great and wonderful
legacies.

Returning to London, a short pause may be made
in the City:

DOCTORS' COMMONS

The medical profession is far too sensible to mix
itself in with the law, and even the Doctors'
Commons cannot be pinned on their back door. The
mystery of the place hard by St. Paul's Cathedral, is
even greater, when, not a little research reveals that
the Archbishop of Canterbury runs this outfit — or
did so down the centuries.

Recalling the period of the law as it stood before
the Reformation, it will be remembered that a
gradual removal of those in holy orders from the
practice of the law took place as the Common Law
took root, and, the common lawyers stealthily
enlarged their field, compass, and of course pockets,
to the exclusion of the former except in Chancery
matters. Thomas à Becket died in the cause that his
brethren duly lost against the King and the King's

courts. However, one grey area of the law continued to be dispensed exclusively by the ecclesiastical body, that of probate, and some aspects of admiralty. As to the former, the old rule that the Bank of England refused to acknowledge a probate of wills except from this source, and, as to the latter, the Common Law refused to take cognisance of such matters 'since the Law was unclear' (until Lord Mansfield came forth and declared 'the law of nations in its full extent is part of the Common Law of England').

It was Henry VIII who in 1538 forbad the further study of Canon Law, but founded instead professorships of Civil Law at the universities of Oxford and Cambridge — there have ever been only two. Twenty-seven years prior to the Royal prohibition, the civilian lawyers had established their own Association of Doctors of Law, and were incorporated in 1565 in Doctors' Commons, a variation of an Inn of Court. The chief courts of Doctors' Commons were the Court of Arches, the Prerogative Court, the Consistory Court, and the Court of Admiralty, of which venue was in the Hall of the Doctors' Commons. With the decline of domestic ecclesiastical influence, and the transfer of international matters to the arena of the law officers of the Crown, the Doctors' Commons was dissolved painlessly in 1837, and so ended what was to Charles Dickens, and no doubt many others 'a very pleasant, profitable little affair of private theatricals, presented to an uncommonly select audience'. What is their greatest legacy is perhaps the appellation of academic degrees being termed 'doctor in this — or that'.

THE TEMPLE AND LEGAL LONDON

Outside the city walls, 'ere witchcraft did begin in olden days before polygamy was made a sin' the warriors of the church militant pitched their camp,
There when they came, whereas those
   bricky towers,
The which on Thames broad aged bank
   do ride,
Where now the studious Lawyers have
   their bowers
There whilom wont the Templar Knights
   to bide,
   Till they decay'd through
    pride.
    from The Prothalamion:
     Edmund Spenser.

The Temple became the hospitium of the Crusading Order of the Holy Sepulchre of Knights Templars in 1116, when they removed from Holborn. The Temple Church (b. 1185) remains a devout yet magnificent memorial to the ill-fated denizens of that part of London which assumed their name. When the property was seized by Edward II in 1313 as a result of the machinations against the order throughout Europe's capitals, the Temple became the subject of Court favour. Passing briefly through the occupancy of one Aimes de la Valence, and Hugh Despencer, it was arranged at a Parliament held at Westminster in 1324 that: '... it pleases the King, magnates and others, for the health of their souls, that their lands shall be assigned to other men of religion, it is therefore agreed, proclaimed, and enacted, by the

King, Prelates, Earls, Barons et alios Proceres, that all
the lands shall be assigned and delivered to the order
of the Hospital of St. John of Jerusalem, etc' (Parl.
Writs, 11;17 Edward II, st.1) . . . One can only say:
tempora mutantur nor et mutamur in illis. Since these
knights of St. John were amply provided for in
Clerkenwell (where vestiges of their fine dwelling still
survive and warrant at least an excursion) they had no
intention of removing to the lair of their unfortunate
comrades. The property was thus let at a rent of £10
to 'divers apprentices of the law' who, according to
Dugdale, 'came from Thavie's Inn in Holborn', which
had no doubt, accommodation fit for a king. One of
such famous apprentices was indeed Geoffrey
Chaucer himself whose recollections of keeping terms
fills part of the Prologue to the Canterbury Tales:
A manciple there was of Temple,
Of which all catours might taken ensemple,
For to been wise in buying of vitail;
For whether he payed or took by taile,
Algate he wayted so in his ashate
That he was aye before in good estate.
Now is not that of God a full faire grace,
That such a leude man's wit shall pace,
The wisdom of an heape of learned men.

Of masters had he mo than thrice ten,
That were of law expert and curious.
. . . The profitable office of Purveyor or Manciple did
not escape the humour of one of his customers.—Man
profiteth by example.

Reverting to the dry scheme of things, which is to
define the historical divisions of the area in London

known as the Temple — and for convenience, that of its environs — the Inns of Court have certainly been there for donkey's years, although that answer will not do. The societies of the Inns of Court, and those of the sister Inns of Chancery, came into possession of their great arenas in the period between Chaucer and the advent of the Elizabethan age. There is one remarkable circumstance which is common to each Inn of Court: they all evolved out of ecclesiastical property.

The Temple, as has been mentioned, was the legacy of the grand old military order before the 'students of the law' acquired possession, and in due course title divided between the two societies of the Inner and Middle Temple.

The society of Lincoln's Inn first acquired a northern portion of their property from the See of Chichester, referred to earlier, and mention is made by Dugdale of the lawyers' leases, until, in the time of Henry VII, the Dean and Chapter sold the property to the Benchers of the Inn.

The fourth of the Inns of Court, Gray's Inn, was the old manor of the Grays, or De Greys of Wilton, forming part of the ancient manor of Purtpool or Portpole. The society received title from the prior and monks of Shene to whom it was conveyed by the de Grey family for the use of the students.

When Henry VIII suppressed the monasteries in England the property of the Hospitallers became, in 1540, vested in the Crown. The Societies, however, as sitting tenants, were undisturbed and each paid to the Crown the same annual rent of £10 as they had to their previous landlords. They continued as tenants at will for the rest of the Tudor period but in 1608 a charter of James I gave them security in the form of tenure known as socage. Each Inn paid a fee-farm rent of £10 a year to the Crown which was not finally extinguished until 1705. The grant was originally to trustees appointed by each of the two Inns in 1732 the property was divided by mutual agreement and the boundary was established which may be seen on the maps displayed in various parts of the Temple today. The Church remained the common responsibility of each Inn and the Master's House, garden and Churchyard are Common Property.

The Inns are thus owners of their property by virtue of the Royal Charter or Letters Patent, of 1608. In gratitude for the grant the Inns presented the King at his Palace in Whitehall a valuable 'stately cup of pure gold'. Charles I later pawned it in the Netherlands and it has not been seen since. The Charter, a long document in Latin, is kept beneath the altar in the Temple Church. Extracts are worth quoting, for they describe the status and functions of the Inns of Court in terms which have not lost their validity to this day.

. . . The King states that he 'is sensible that great part of the welfare of our Realm of England is justly owing to the ancient and proper laws of that Realm'. Then he goes on to describe the Inns as:

> Those four colleges, the most famous of all Europe, as always abounding with persons devoted to the study of the aforesaid laws and experienced therein . . . to which, as to the best

seminaries of learning and education many young men have resorted from all parts of this Realm ... and from which many men have by reason of their very great merits been advanced to discharge the public and arduous functions as well as the store of justice, in which they have exhibited great examples of prudence and integrity, to the no small honour of the said profession and adornment of this Realm and good of the whole Commonwealth.

It proudly continues to the present day.

THE INNS

THE HONOURABLE SOCIETIES

of the

INNS OF COURT

FOREWORD TO THE FIRST EDITION

— The Inns of Court was dedicated —

To the memory of

LORD GODDARD

in gratitude

Starting at the Bar now is very different to what it was. Called to the Bar in 1899, I accepted my first brief in the reign of our Sovereign Queen Victoria. In those days there was no scheme of Legal Aid to which everybody can now turn. Half a century later, in 1948, the Legal Aid Act was introduced. How far that has been an advantage to the Bar may be doubted.

I have read this book. Mr. Daniell is to be congratulated in showing the uninformed layman what the Inns of Court represent in history and in the present day.

[signature]

Easter 1971

The Rt. Hon. Lord Goddard, G.C.B.,
Lord Chief Justice of England 1946-1958.
Bencher of the Inner Temple.

CHAPTER 5

THE INNS

Our Glorious Legacy – Origins – The Inns of Chancery – New Inn, Strand Inn – Thavies Inn – Lyon's Inn – Clement's Inn – Staple Inn – Barnard's Inn – Clifford's Inn – Furnival's Inn – The four Inns of Court – Honourable Societies – A word about them all.

THE INNS – OUR GLORIOUS LEGACY –

'The most notable example of the "professional enclave" are of course the Inns of Court. They were built as such and still serve their purposes remarkably well. Where they have been damaged by bombing, I cannot see that much would be gained either by replacing them or rebuilding them on substantially different architectural lines. I say this in spite of the fact that . . . the architecture in these places is . . . with certain exceptions, routine carpenters' work of the 17th and 18th centuries' . . .'

(Sir) John Summerson,
'Heavenly Mansions'.

The Inns of Court, which have survived those of Chancery, are ancient institutions shrouded in as

much history and mystery as the layman suspects. The words 'Inn' of 'Court' at once sound far-fetched and may be mistaken for a 'grey area of London where the lawyers revive themselves in an unknown ritual, nightlife, or more bizarrely, associate with a curious Inn or public house which even has a Temple Bar'. There is thus enough difficulty in presenting a rational and substantiated record of the Inns' existence without facetious ignorance to confound us all!

The four Inns of Court that we know today: Lincoln's Inn, Inner Temple, Middle Temple, and Gray's Inn (which will be described in detail in later chapters), are ancient unincorporated 'Honourable Societies'. They grew up about the time of the Ordinance of 1292 (see Chapter Three), which accelerated the growth of 'apprentices and attorneys' in the place of clerical practitioners in the Courts.

(It is indeed romantic to think of an era, albeit so long ago, when once upon a time, society could exist without lawyers.) When the professional lawyers were put on this firmer footing, by being placed under the control of judges, the demise of the clergy – hitherto the educated body in matters of law or state – was begun in earnest at the end of the thirteenth century.

'The four Inns', writes Mr Justice Megarry, 'seem to have been voluntary associations of these lawyers, congregating in some convenient place. "Inn" (as we translate "hospitium") was the name given in those days to a town house, or mansion, and in particular a mansion used as a hostel for students.'

The Inns of Court, and Chancery, were the meeting

house of these lawyers who found it convenient to congregate together, and organise their extra-curricular activities under one roof.

In the course of history there have been a number of Inns in the area of Legal London. Altogether the some thirty are recorded, though some are merely alternatives for other names. Apart from the Inns of Court, few have left any physical presence and none survive as an institution. There were three Serjeants' Inns — one north of Holborn, one in Fleet Street and one in Chancery Lane — which at various times were the abodes of the Order of the Coif, the Serjeants-at-Law, of whom no more were appointed after 1875. The remainder were Inns of Chancery, and in 1468 there were said to be ten of them.

THE INNS OF CHANCERY

The Inns of Chancery perished in the main in the course of the nineteenth century. Some vestiges of their rich and colourful tenure in the law remains by association of their names in streets, buildings, passages and pathways.

It was from the Chancellor's office that all writs emanated for half a millenium (that is, from the latter end of the twelfth century up to the beginning of the seventeenth century). The clerks in Chancery foregathered variously near the Chancellor's court, Chancery Lane, and Cursitor Street, and apprentices congregated about them. Thus clerks in Chancery soon evolved a viable professional existence much on the lines of the later Inns of Court. An Inn of Chancery became a suitable starting-point for a law student and in time the principal source of recruitment to the Inns of Court from the reign of Elizabeth I onwards. The Inns of Chancery were within walking distance of the respective Inn of Court to which it became affiliated, and, in common its members enjoyed a Hall, Library and workplace, although not a chapel. No doubt several of the Inns of Chancery did as Clement's Inn, which enjoyed reserved pews at St. Clement Dane's.

The constitutions of the Inns of Chancery were similar in many respects to their parent bodies, and had, Principal(s) (for Treasurer(s)), Ancients (for Benchers — both still abound!) and Juniors (for Members). The Inn of Court provided Readers for the Juniors who were appointed for the respective law term.

The Inns of Court cannot be particularly proud of their feeble actions in the last century when they allowed various Inns of Chancery to be abandoned, sold and disembodied. It is a tribute to a commercial institution who bought up and refurbished two Inns of Chancery that posterity is enabled to enjoy one particular Inn of Chancery — Staple Inn — that has survived the traditional shortsightedness of its own professional estates.

The best account of the Inns of Chancery — apart from the ubiquitous pen of Charles Dickens is in a separate ramble over the history of each Inn of Chancery: By the time of Edward Coke, C.J., 1613, there were but eight Inns of Chancery, the Strand Inn having been demolished in 1549 to make way for the new Somerset House 'of' Sir William Chambers.

NEW INN

New Inn was built in lieu of the Strand Inn. In 1608 the Middle Temple bought the freehold. The Inn was affiliated to the Middle Temple, whose other Inn of Chancery had, as previously said, extinguished itself. In 1899 the London County Council in high-handed fashion compulsorily acquired the site for its grandiose Kingsway improvement scheme, and shades of New Inn may now be contemplated beneath Australia House, hard by New Inn Passage. The decision cost our metropolitan masters a penny or two: there was a dispute at the time as to who was entitled to the proceeds, beyond public indignation at their philistine act. *In The New Inn* (1902, Chancery Reports), Farwell J. awarded less than a half of the sale proceeds to the owners, the Middle Temple, a nominal portion to the leaseholders themselves, and the sum of £55,000 to the office of the Attorney-General for the benefit of legal education. This established rather late in the day that trustees of these ancient establishments were *custodians* of their possessions and not absolute owners, for the real beneficiary was to be the student of the law.

A list of the Inns of Chancery and affiliations is given:
FURNIVAL'S INN . . . (Lincoln's Inn),
THAVIES INN . . . (Lincoln's Inn),
STRAND INN,
NEW INN . . . (Middle Temple),
CLEMENT'S INN . . . (Inner Temple),
CLIFFORD'S INN . . . (Inner Temple)

LYON'S INN . . . (Inner Temple)
STAPLE INN . . . (Gray's Inn),
BARNARD'S INN . . . (Gray's Inn)

And of others that there were, SYMOND'S INN, EXETER INN, et cetera, the first to go, was as stated, Strand Inn.

There followed a lull of two hundred years, until 1769, when the Honourable Society of Lincoln's Inn allowed Thavies Inn to be trodden underfoot.

THAVIES INN

Lincoln's Inn had bought the freehold in 1549, and when the lease came up for renewal, refused to renew it on terms that Thaviesites could meet. The Inn was sold for £47,000 and the proceeds were used to erect the Stone Buildings in 1775-80.

Another hundred years elapsed when the fate of Lyon's Inn was decided:

LYON'S INN

On the site of the Globe Theatre, Aldwych, stood Lyon's Inn for a very long time. Its origins were traced to 1413 after which the Inner Temple purchased it in 1583. It perished in the eighteenth century.

Now it was the turn of Clement's Inn, a century on.

CLEMENT'S INN

Clement's Inn, again the property of the Inner Temple — and in the gardens of which may still be

149

seen their statue — was sold in 1884 for £60,000. The worthy Law Society took counsel's opinion on the sale — unfortunately the law did not regard it as a breach of trust — so the legacy is left in the form of a signpost: Clement's Inn Passage, a stroll from the Law Courts, and an office block.

STAPLE INN

Old Holborn's Elizabethan row saunters along the pavement at the northernmost part of Staple Inn. The timber-framed façade is a rare example of Elizabethan domestic architecture which survived the Great Fire of 1666, and is attributed to the year 1586 (although it was restored substantially in 1950). Staple Inn was reported to have been a hostel for wool merchants before it ever acquired legal status as an Inn of Chancery in the fifteenth century . . . when wool became the Tudor bullion of England and lawyers the indispensable fleecers.

Staple Inn lingered on into the nineteenth century when it was fortunately bought by 'the Pru' (the Prudential Assurance Company, that ever benevolent institution), who later leased it to the Institute of Actuaries, the present residents. Much damaged in the Second World War, the Inn was courageously restored to its former style and its treasures both in the whole and in the particular are a treat for the traveller.

BARNARD'S INN

On the south side of Holborn is the precinct of Barnard's Inn, of which the Hall alone survives the

500 years since its inception in 1454. Pip and Herbert Pocket shared rooms in the nineteenth century described by Dickens — in a visit — 'the dingiest collection of shabby buildings ever squeezed together in a rank corner as a club for Tom-cats' (Great Expectations). Shortly afterwards (in 1877) the members bought the reversion of the lease from the Ecclesiastical Commissioners (who held it of Gray's Inn) for the sum of £23,000. 15 years later, the senior Livery Company of the City of London purchased the entire collection of 'dingy' buildings for £43,000 and gave the Inn a new lease of life as the home of the scholars of the Mercers' School. Another £30,000 was spent on the general refurbishment of Barnard's Inn, but unfortunately, the school ceased to reside there in 1959, and worse still, after 512 years of academic distinction (founded 1447), the school was closed down.

The restored Hall (1931) houses fine examples of sixteenth century glasswork and panelling, and, with a few tenements of nearby structures, are the lone survivors today, presently occupied by the Prudential Assurance Company.

CLIFFORD'S INN

Hard by St. Dunstan's in the West, was Clifford's Inn which went that way in 1903, and a block of flats makes do for what was one of the earliest Inns of Chancery. The Inn comprised three small courtyards over which the grand Hall presided, where Hale C.J. sat to determine the 'boundaries' following their erasure by the Great Fire.

In 1903 William Willett bought the Inn for £100,000 of which some £77,000 was bequeathed to legal education as a charitable trust. Seven years later the Society of Knights Bachelor were in residence (until the 'Four-tenn'ay'een' War) and 40 years ago saw the virtual disappearance of the Inn in a collegiate sense.

FURNIVAL'S INN

On the site of the Gothic encampment of Victorian red brick, in which the army of the Prudential men assure us of *our* lives on paper, was Furnival's Inn. The Pru are forgiven for demolishing this Inn to build their own arsenal — (1879 by Alfred Waterhouse) — because they have preserved some other Inns of Chancery across the way. This Inn was one of the larger of Chancery, beginning circa 1383. In 1547 Lincoln's Inn purchased the freehold to which the Inn became affiliated as previously explained. It was here that Justice Shallow spent his mad days (viz Henry IV pt.ii, Act 3, scene 2), and in 1817, Lincoln's Inn refused to renew the lease of £6.00 per annum to the unfortunate Inn of Chancery, and greedily sold the property to Henry Peto, who later demolished most of it. In 1888 the Pru bought the freehold. The name survives in Furnival Street on the south side of Holborn. Charles Dickens lived there, 1834-7, where he began the Pickwick Papers, which is commemorated in a plaque and bust, by Percy Fitzgerald, resting in the arch to the inner court.

Although these Inns of Chancery were in some degree the precursor of the solicitors' branch of the legal profession, The Law Society has rightly pointed out that, unlike the Bar who keep their company in the four Inns of Court, the solicitors, of necessity have their offices near and for their clients. Thus no surviving Inn is relevant to the needs of the members of The Law Society beyond the fine premises in Chancery Lane.

Thus the only Inns that survive today as going concerns are the four Inns of Court, and they have never been more active.

THE FOUR INNS OF COURT

Gray's Inn for Walks,
Lincoln's for your call,
The Inner for a garden,
And the Middle for its Hall.

The Inns of Court are institutions which for centuries have had a special place in the English legal structure, the proper title of each Inn is 'The Honourable Society of . . .' whether it be Lincoln's Inn, the Inner Temple, the Middle Temple or Gray's Inn. They are voluntary societies bound by the same rules and founded upon similar constitutions. Although the four Inns are equal in rank and status, nevertheless they retain their own traditions and customs. The governing body of an Inn is composed of Masters of the Bench (known as Benchers) in whom is vested the sole power to fill vacancies. Annually each Bench elects a Treasurer from among its Benchers: this is normally the most senior Bencher who has not already held the high office which

153

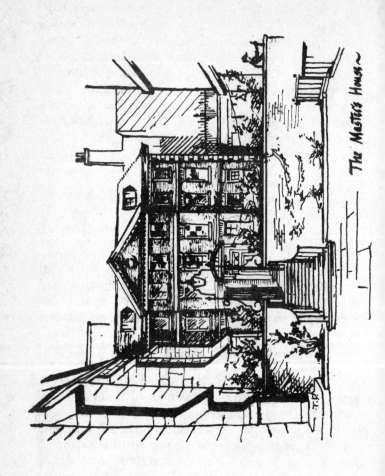

The Masters House

commences on the 1st January. During the ensuing year he is the head of the Inn: primus inter pares.

The Benchers, all of whom hold office for life, include practising members of the Bar, Judges, and a few Honorary Benchers. A member of the Royal Family is on the Bench of each Inn, for Lincoln's Inn, HRH Princess Margaret; Inner Temple, HRH Prince Philip; Middle Temple, HM Queen Elizabeth, the Queen Mother; and for Gray's Inn, HRH The Prince of Wales. Eminent people from other walks of life are occasionally made an Honorary Bencher.

The day-to-day administration of each Inn is carried out by a permanent staff of people from many trades and professions; other aspects of the work of an Inn is supervised by Committees whose tasks are varied, for example the administration, welfare and training facilities for students, to which we should probably add the most important function, for which the Inns are justly proud, of providing the splendid and large libraries to the benefit of students and barristers alike. The Library buildings in Inner Temple, Middle Temple and ·Gray's Inn were unfortunately destroyed in the last war but have since been rebuilt to great advantage; the library of Lincoln's Inn remains housed in the buildings which were completed in 1845.

Because the Inns own sizable areas of land and property they may be considered as land-owners or land-lords on a grand scale. However this property is largely to be found in buildings of architectural and historic value, its plate, paintings and so on, all assets which cannot be realized. They are therefore large but not necessarily rich landlords. To be the owner of such valuable and very often old property is a great responsibility and a very costly one if planned maintenance is properly carried out to ensure the buildings are fit for their present use and preserved for posterity.

Tenants in the Inn properties fall into three categories, the practising barristers, professional people mainly solicitors and the occupiers of the residential flats. The former mainly occupy the ground floors of the buildings which they form into Chambers — except Gray's Inn who have few sets of Chambers at the present time, and the latter group who occupy most of the upper floors. It can be seen that each Inn performs the function of an Estate Agent in the administration of its properties. In all there are approximately 190 sets of barrister's Chambers catering for the business accommodation of some 2,800 practising members of the Bar, it should then be remembered that this is not the largest of the three groups already mentioned.

Amongst the facilities afforded the Benchers and their guests is that of dining in the Halls of the Inns during the legal terms and part of the periods of vacations. Each Inn can be likened to a medieval village or large manor house of that period with the Hall forming the central or focal point of the community, in which social events of every kind take place and on occasion the Halls may be hired for the private functions, of the Benchers, for the Members.

Each Inn maintains its own chapel except the Inner and Middle Temples who are jointly responsible for

Temple Church. The gardens and or Walks are to be likened to an oasis in a City which has become a brick and concrete jungle. The Law's pastures are free.

THE INNS OF COURT MISSION

At the Bar, there are two important charities. Unlike the Barristers Benevolent Association — which is the vehicle whereby practitioners provide for retired colleagues — the Inns of Court Mission is an 'outward giving' charity formed for the purpose of providing the unprivileged youth of an area of London with recreational and other facilities. The Honorary secretary has drawn attention to the appalling state of the Mission's finances. Any reader who customarily enjoys ready access to an outdoor life, may like to remember less fortunate Londoners. To enclose a gesture to the Mission in a tangible form, the address is: 44 Drury Lane, London WC2.

CHAPTER 6

THE HONOURABLE SOCIETY

of

LINCOLN'S INN

LINCOLN'S INN

THE HONOURABLE SOCIETY OF LINCOLN'S INN

Before the lawyers, who settled on the banks of the River Thames had put their house in order, a Fellowship of lawyers had taken possession of an equally endearing quarter: Lovely Lincoln's Inn.

The records of this Inn, the 'Black Books', present a remarkably complete portrait of the Society over a period of five and a half centuries. They began in 1422, which is considerably earlier than those of any of the other Inns. It is not clear whether this is the reason that Lincoln's Inn is always placed first when the four Inns are listed. But it is certain that then Barristers of Lincoln's Inn were already possessed of the site as tenants of the Bishop of Chichester and the Hospital of Burton Lazars of Jerusalem in England.

According to Stow, a Judge, Henry de Lacy, 'Earl of Lincoln Constable of Cheshires and Custos of England' (1286-1311), had a house near Holborn Bar at the upper end of what is now Shoe Lane. It is probably that this was a similar hostel or 'Inn' for law students as was the Manor of Portpoole belonging to the de Grey family on the other side of Holborn (see chapter on Gray's Inn), which were founded after the Order in Council of 1292. This story cannot be confirmed as de Lacy's residence was in Shoe Lane. In 1350 there is a reference to 'Lincolnesynne', which premises were those of Thomas de Lincoln, King's Serjeant. By 1422, the Society was known in its present site which was, partly owned, on the southern part, by the Bishops of Chichester, who, as explained in Chapter 1 had a Palace in Chancery Lane, and when the gatehouse was built in 1517-21, the arms of the Earl were carved upon it. Up to 1535 there was a rent of ten marks a year payable to the Bishop, who ceased to reside there in 1536. In 1580 the Society bought the episcopal land, freehold.

The Inn has always been more closely associated with Equity than have the other Inns, and the professional chambers are for the most part occupied by members of the respected Chancery Bar. This congregation of conveyancers and 'paper-work' lawyers lies in the historical proximity of the Chancery offices down the lane.

THE GATE HOUSE

The Gate House opening on to Chancery Lane was the main entrance to the Inn until the Lincoln's Inn

Fields entrance was made at the time New Hall was built in 1845. The present building dates from 1521 and the grand oak doors from 1564. The bricks were baked within the Inn from clay dug in the coney-garth. This good work was the responsibility of Sir Thomas Lovell, K.G., a member of the Inn who had been attainted by Richard III, and fought for Henry VII at the Battle of Bosworth. Gratefully His Majesty appointed Sir Thomas to the post of Chancellor of the Exchequer for life. He contributed one-third of the cost, £345, of the gate house.

All the nuns of Holywell
Pray ye both day and night
Pray for the soul of Sir Thomas Lovell
Whom Harry Seven made Knight:

This benefactor also contributed to the cost of Gaius College, Cambridge, and the Benedictine Nunnery at Holywell, which explains the inmates' felicitations. But rarely are women grateful.

Part of the rest of the money was lent by one of the Inn's more famous sons, Sir Thomas More, who was later Lord Chancellor and then beheaded by Henry VIII in 1535. The Gate House has been renovated many times, most recently in 1969 under the Treasuryship of Lord Upjohn, and the arms on the lane side now glow with fresh colour. They are from left to right those of the de Lacy family, Henry VIII, and Sir Thomas Lovell. There are only three other such gatehouses left in London; St. James's Palace, Lambeth Palace, and St. John's' Clerkenwell.

MEMBERS OF THE SOCIETY

The list of great lawyers cut deep through history, with alumnae: Sir Thomas More; Lord Keeper Egerton (later Lord Ellesmere); Richard Cromwell; Sir Matthew Hale, who entered as a student in 1626; Earl of Mansfield, called to the Bar in 1730; Lord Chancellor Bathurst; Lords Campbell, St. Leonards, Brougham, Eldon, Erskine, Lyndhurst, and Fortescue: and in Queen Victoria's reign, the society gave the British Empire no less than twelve of the fourteen Lords Chancellors. And to date, Denning, M. R.; Lord Parker, Lord Hailsham, Lord Widgery L.C.J. have endowed England.

Of famous men: John Donne; Tillotson; Warburton; Hurd; Heber; Horace Walpole (who entered as a student in 1731); William Penn; William Pitt; Macaulay; Rider Haggard; George Canning; Cardinal Newman; Disraeli; Gladstone and more recently President Eisenhower, the well loved honorary member; and Dean Acheson, a contemporary.

THE ARMS OF LINCOLN'S INN

The blazon is: 'Azure, semé des fers de moline or, on a dexter canton or a lion rampant purpure.' The purple rampant lion on a golden ground was the emblem of the family of de Lacy, Earls of Lincoln. Up to 1702 the Inn used these arms only. The golden millrinds, on a blue field, were added in memory of Henry Kingsmill, the Bencher who negotiated the purchase of 1580. Millrinds are the iron supports of millstones and they formed the punning device of the Kingsmills' necks! The original de Lacy arms may be seen on the south archway from New Square, above the premises of a well-known firm of law booksellers.

OLD BUILDINGS

Once inside the lordly protection of the Gate House, a small square, well fortified by the Old Hall immediately opposite and the Chapel to the north, is occupied by the mellow red brickwork of Old Buildings. These date from the sixteenth century and formed part of an extensive rebuilding which started in 1524 with the making of 'a bevy of new chambers at the back side of the Hall by the Kitchen'. Nos. 20-24 were modernised in 1967-69, while the old façades were carefully retained. At the same time a new building, Hale Court, named after Chief Justice Hale, was built behind those houses.

John Thurloe, a member of the Council of State under the Lord Protector, Oliver Cromwell, occupied the ground floor of No. 24 from 1647-1659 and then No. 13 (now disappeared) until 1661. In the latter house his State Papers were discovered in a false ceiling and published in 1742. Other occupants of Old Buildings have been John Donne and Benjamin Disraeli. About the latter, little need be said, such is his fame; of John Donne, long associated with the Inn, the story is told:

His inspiration was his 'cherry-love' Anne, with whom he eloped. She was the niece of the

165

Chancellor to whom he was secretary. No sooner did 'uncle' (later Lord Ellesmere) discover his young secretary's commitment than nephew-in-law was dismissed. This resulted in the famous line: 'John Donne, Anne Donne, Undone.'

Old Buildings runs north of the chapel into Old Square, again of red brick but quite as pleasing.

OLD HALL

Old Hall is undeniably the oldest, the stateliest and the finest building in Lincoln's Inn. Occupying the site of the hall of the Bishops of Chichester, it was built, as recorded in a tablet on the north wall, 'in the fifth year of King Henry VII', that is in 1489 or 1490. It was originally smaller than it is now, until it was lengthened by 12 feet in 1642 and two oriel windows added.

Dining has not taken place here since its function was replaced by the much larger new Hall, built in 1845, but it is still used for meetings, social gatherings, and as an additional lecture room for the students of the Inns of Court School of Law.

One of the most famous dinners to have taken place in Old Hall was on 29 February 1672 when the Benchers entertained Charles II, his brother (later James II), the Duke of Monmouth, and other members of the Royal Family. When the time came to drink King Charles' health the company was incapable of rising to its feet, whereupon he allowed them to drink to him sitting down. And to this day in Lincoln's Inn the Loyal Toast is drunk sitting down.

166

Over the dais hangs the huge painting of St. Paul before the Roman Governor Felix, depicting the trial recorded in Chapter 24 of the Acts of the Apostles. In 1745 the Inn received a legacy of £200 under the will of a Bencher, Lord Wyndham, and Lord Chancellor of Ireland 'for adorning the Chapel or Hall or both'. Another Bencher of the Inn at the time was Lord Mansfield (a famous Lord Chancellor). He was a friend of the painter William Hogarth. Hogarth chose this subject, which was both religious and forensic. The correspondence with him and his receipt for the £200 are extant in the Inn archives. He also suggested a frame for the painting, sketching the design in one of his letters, but the Benchers must have considered the price too much for it was not pursued. Nevertheless the frame is to Hogarth's design for it was made a hundred years later, from his original sketch. The picture was much tampered with in the early nineteenth century and altered in accordance with contemporary tastes. Some parts were painted out and others painted in. In the course of years the picture had become very dirty: In 1970 it was thoroughly cleaned and the overpainting removed so that the visitor may again enjoy the delicate harmony of the colours of the various robes and the assured feeling of the composition. This is a magnificent painting, revealing an aspect of Hogarth's genius that may not be known to those acquainted only with his popular studies of the life of his time.

At the other end of the Hall is a wooden screen of intricate design, dating from this time of the building of the extension in 1624, believed to be the work of

167

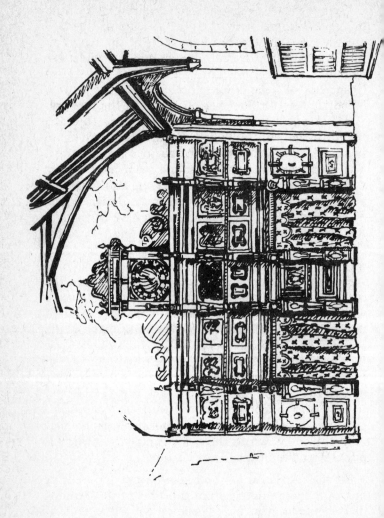

Inigo Jones. It was executed by Robert Lynton, joiner, at a cost of £40.

Dickens's readers will remember the opening chapter of *Bleak House:*

> London. Michalmas Term lately over and the Lord Chancellor sitting in Lincoln's Inn Hall. Implacable November weather ... fog everywhere. Fog up the river, where it flows among green aits and meadows; fog down the river, where it rolls defiled among the tiers of shipping, and the waterside pollution of a great (and dirty) city ... And hard by Temple Bar, in Lincoln's Inn Hall, at the very heart of the fog, sits the Lord High Chancellor in his High Court of Chancery.

Grammatili certant et adhuc sub indice lis est. (Scholars dispute, and the case is still before the court, as we may agree with Horace.)

Fortunately, since the Clean Air Act, London no longer has the same pea soupers, and fortunately, too, Chancery procedure is no longer the impenetrable muddle that it was in *Jarndyce* v. *Jarndyce,* although opinions differ!

THE CHAPEL

'Ordered by the christian bench' in the year 1609 and completed fourteen years later, the chapel replaced an earlier 'insufficient and ruinous' place of worship. Ben Jonson, who later became famous as a playwright (and whose father was a master bricklayer), was one of the masons who may have worked on the building. The Dean of St. Paul's, the great John Donne, who had previously been Preacher to Lincoln's Inn, preached the sermon at the dedication service on Ascension Day 1623. So great a reputation had he that it was reported that there was 'a great concourse of noblemen and gentlemen, whereof two or three were endangered and taken up for dead at the time, with the extreme press and thronging.' The architect of the chapel was once thought to be Inigo Jones, but it is now known to have been designed and built by the mason, John Clarke. The Chapel was much altered by Wyatt in 1797 and Salter in 1882. There is exquisite stained glass in the windows, including figures of the Apostles, ascribed to Bernard van Linge and his brother and said to be commissioned by 'friends of Shakespeare'.

Below the chapel is an undercroft, open on its four sides. This was early described as a place for students and barristers 'to walk and talk and confer for their learnings'. It was also a rendezvous where barristers met their clients. At one time the undercroft was a place where foundling babies were sometimes left: the Inn gave them a start in life by bestowing on them the surname 'Lincoln'. 'Indeed, there were plenty of "Abrahams" in their rockers, but none so illustrious as our American cousin.'

The chapel bell tolls a curfew every night at 9 p.m. It is also tolled on the death of a Bencher of the Inn and it is possible that it inspired John Donne, who was Preacher to the Society from 1616 to 1622, to write the famous lines:

No man is an island entire of itself. Every man is a piece of the continent, a part of the main. If a clod be washed away by the sea, Europe is the less, as well as if a promontory were, as well as if a manor of thy friend's or thine own were. Any man's death diminishes me, because I am involved in mankind. And therefore never send to know for whom the bell tolls; it tolls for thee.

The Sunday services in the chapel are open to the public.

NEW HALL

The trees of yore are seen no more,
unshaded now the garden lies
May the red bricks which here we fix,
Be lasting as our equities.
The olden dome with musty tone,
of Law and Litigation suits:
In this we look for a better 'cook'
than he who wrote the Institutes.

> . . .Translated from the Latin Inscription near the Butteries.

Lincoln's Inn was flourishing in the first half of the nineteenth century: its membership was increasing and the Old Hall had become too small. The Inn commissioned the architect Philip Hardwick to design a new galaxy of buildings on the west side, to comprise Hall, Benchers' rooms, Treasury offices and library. He did just that in what was described as 'the collegiate style towards the end of the sixteenth century before the admixture of Italian architecture.'

171

The buildings were started in 1843, the date in the brickwork of the south wall. The 26-year-old Queen Victoria accompanied by the Prince Consort, opened the New Hall on 30 October 1845.

The New Hall, or the Great Hall as it is often known, is the largest in the Inns of Court, 120 feet long, 45 feet wide and 62 feet high. Inside it is dominated by the enormous fresco by G. F. Watts, R.A., 40 feet high and 45 feet wide, completed in 1859, which he called 'one of my very best efforts.' The picture is called *Justice, a Hemicycle of Lawgivers* and it depicts, under allegorical figures of Truth, Mercy and Justice twenty-three 'lawgivers' and a number of attendant figures. Several of the personages were modelled by friends of the artist. Lord Tennyson appears as Minos, King of Crete, Holman Hunt as Ina, King of Wessex, Sir William Harcourt as Justinian, so on and so forth.

... Unfortunately the fresco soon suffered the malady of the English climate that inflicts itself upon us all, but in 1890 it was successfully restored. This must have pleased the artist for he had earlier written:

> the faith I have in the justice of the time would console me, for the few who care to see my very best effort ... I hear it is beginning to decay. I suppose it will go the way of all frescoes in England and speedily crumble away ... Time is the only judge whose dictum is a serious matter to serious workers, but the destruction of one's work before it can receive judgment is a regret — even to the least vain.

Skilful treatment in 1955 has further saved it from the elements.

The Interior is extremely gorgeous (in the choice words of Col. Blackham), to members and strangers alike: the rise of the gallery to the ornamental roof and the two semi-octagonal oriels at east and west, lend dignity to this great chamber.

Behind the high table is a bust of William Pitt, M.P., called to the Bar by Lincoln's Inn in 1780, Prime Minister at the age of 25, and Treasurer of the Inn in 1794. It is a replica of an original by Nollekens. Pitt may be remembered for his prophesy: 'You cannot conquer a map', when he looked at the battle lines drawn up, which depicted the revolting colonies.

THE LIBRARY

The first and oldest library in London dating back to 1497 was begun with a legacy of forty marks. Many of the orignial volumes were tethered to the shelves by iron rings; the reason suggests Dugdale: 'The Temple has no library so they cannot attain to the divers learning there, by buying of such books as they lust to study.' The ugly exterior encroaches upon every aspect of the Inn. Hardwick's original design was squeezed into a disproportioned corridor by Sir George Gilbert Scott, but it bears the discomfort well. The mouldings are a fine example, nevertheless, of the Victorian depth for detail, in an Age that rendered a stone mason as economical as today's re-inforced concrete.

STONE BUILDINGS

Sir Robert Taylor designed this classical building in 1775, a precursor to the complete redevelopment of the Inn. Fortunately the scheme proved too expensive and was abandoned. On the garden façade is a sundial placed there by William Pitt when he was Treasurer; see 'T.Rt.Honble W.P. 1794–'Qua Redit Nescitis Horam'. Hardwick finished the building in 1845 while his quill was still awash the drawing board for the New Hall. Notice the Inns of Court Volunteers' Regimental Drill Hall opposite; they are nicknamed the 'devils own' — (You will realise 'why' when you meet one off the battle-field) — attributed to King George III's descriptive answer to Lord Erskine.

NEW SQUARE

The original southern boundary of the Inn ran along an open space known as Ficket's Field where at one time the Knights Templars performed their military and jousting exercises. It lay between the Inn and the Strand, part of the area now heavily occupied by the Royal Courts of Justice.

At the end of the seventeenth century a dispute, and considerable litigation, arose between the Society and one Henry Serle (whose name lingers in the neighbouring Serle Street), as to the ownership of the land: a compromise was reached and the dignified houses were built in the period between 1682-93. New Square is a charming quadrangle typical of the late seventeenth century. The Square was originally known as Serle's Court. His arms, and those of the de Lacy family (Earls of Lincoln), with the date 1697 may be seen over the archway in the south-east corner where resides Wildy's bookshop. There was originally a bleak area of gravel and a Corinthian column in the middle of the square but this was replaced by grass, trees and flowers in 1843, surrounded by iron railings. The railings were stolen in 1940 to be melted down for armaments but the tall gates at the northern end were preserved because of their artistic merit and they stand there now rather forlorn.

This action by a pillar of the establishment may be compared to the Barberini family: 'Quod non fecerunt barbari fecerunt, Barberini'. A little passageway in the south-west corner is known as More's Passage after Sir Thomas More (an indifferent statue of him stands on the corner of a building just outside) and is much used by members of the Chancery Bar, whose Chambers are in Lincoln's Inn, in 'going to the fray and fro' between the Inn and the Law Courts, on the other side of Carey Street.

THE GARDENS

There once was a garden to the eastern border by Chancery Lane boundary and also a coney-garth (rabbit warren) to its west. Throughout the early history of the Inn rabbit formed a staple item of food in Hall. From 1506 onwards clay was dug here for making bricks to the Inn's requirements, which included the Gate House. Elms from the site were also used. (The rabbits disappeared. The elms have disappeared.) At some stage, avenues were laid out in a pleasing manner, fresh trees planted and the present

175

terrace walk, near the Under-Treasurer's house north of the Library, was completed in 1584.

The impressive Stone Buildings commands the fine gardens. As a counterbalance to the loss of the coney-garth's wider area, in 1843, the lawn and gardens of New Square were laid out in the same year. Today the Inn has a pleasing aspect from the North Lawns with their stately plane trees, past the gardens between New Hall and Old Square (with its tiny Gothic tool shed, the 'head-gardener's castle' built by Gilbert Scott in 1852) and to the expanse of New Square with its grass and ornamental trees.

The old gardens rivalled the Temple's in the days of Addison and Steele: The Tatler's own Isaac Bikerstaffe, delighted to walk here 'being privileged to do so by his friends amongst the benchers'.

LINCOLN'S INN FIELDS

Lincoln's Inn Fields, Lincoln's Inn Fields . . . the name sings with associations of every type, and is fixed in the Londoner's memory. The majesty of the great sweeping boughs of plane trees freshen the heart of Legal London and provide a welcome resting place from the bustle of the town. Much of the Square still stands as it did in the colourful days of the seventeenth century. Long before, as the name of great turnstile shows, the pathway through the Fields was a short cut between the Strand and Holborn.

For long the Fields were the popular resort of duellists, mobs, and 'mumpers', although today it is more noted for the minor speakers' corner (North

East), to which aspiring advocates are occasionally known to acquire the common touch. A 'Lincoln's Inn Mumper' was a proverbial expression in the eighteenth century for a vagabond who used to plague the vicinity ... (a mumper to this day means a beggar, in gipsy cant).

The Fields were planned – possibly – by Inigo Jones and cover twelve acres (the largest square in London). It became the most fashionable address in the eyes of society. One such resident was Nell Gwynne whose son, the Duke of St. Albans, was born under the royal blanket (– lent by King Charles's keeper of the Wardrobe, to the housekeeper of number 57), but Nell lived everywhere.

The Great houses still ponder their hidden secrets on the north and sides of the square, although the south side has made way for the huge brick piles of the Land Registry and stone, The Royal College of Surgeons. Within the latter building, – designed by Sir Charles Barry in 1835, is housed the Museum, to which the curious may be admitted by order. Endless treasures of anatomy may be inspected behind glass jars of preservative wine. On its site stood The Lincoln's Inn Fields Theatre where Pepys was continually entertained ... but not his wife who was often 'mad as the devil' with his capers outside her home.

Numbers 51 to 67 Lincoln's Inn Fields, have still fine examples of the nobleman's town residence: Number 66 was acquired by Mr James Farrer in 1791, whose descendants have occupied it ever since. Newcastle House, as it was formerly known (having

The Elizabethan Staircase
Old and New

178

been completed by, and the residence of the Duke), was converted along with number 67 into the present dwelling. In 1930, Sir Edwin Lutyens faithfully designed the present façade to the instructions of Mr H. L. Farrer (then the head of the eminent firm of Messrs. Farrer & Co), who had wisely decided to rebuild the mansion on original lines after many years of drastic alterations of other occupancies which had been allowed to take place during the intervening period.

Perhaps the most prominent landmark on this side of the square (after Newcastle House) is Lindsey House, at numbers 59 and 60. Both historically and architecturally it is one of the most important structures in the Fields. Spencer Perceval (the Prime Minister who, in his butler's words was 'murdered by the House of Commons'); the head and the body of Lord Russell after his execution in the Fields; and many generations of more fortunate dignitaries have been associated with the mansion, one way or another.

Numbers 53, 54 and 55 were for long the site of the Sardinian Embassy and its goings on fill many a bloody page in continental works of reference. Portugal Street hardby, lives on by name in these associations. Number 56 was once occupied by Lord Mansfield, as he later became, and while the legend of the next door has already been alluded to, more interestingly, Mr Tulkington, well known to readers of Bleak House, had his chambers at number 58. It was here also that the novelist Charles Dickens read the manuscript of The Chimes to a party of friends on 2nd December 1844 ... 'roomy staircases, passages and ante-chambers ... and even in its painted ceilings, where Allegory, in Roman helmet and celestial linen, sprawls among balustrades': under which ceiling was found the dead body of the impenetrable lawyer.

On the north side of the Fields is the SOANE MUSEUM, the interior of which premises – at numbers 12 and 13 – is as it was at Sir John Soane's death in 1837. The rare collection of antiquities, priceless ornaments and other treasures is unique, and will devour many hours of a visitor's intense curiosity. Those persons who choose to 'skip a visit' will be a foolish loser: An infinite variety of good works are displayed although perhaps Hagarth's election series of the 'Rake's Progress' is most often recalled.

Sir John Soane purchased number 12 and occupied it until 1812. In the meantime his collection increased, and he moved into number 13 which he bought, pulled down and rebuilt. He later acquired number 14 which he apparently let, but constructed over its stables (site) an extension of his museum gallery. Unlike any other collection in London, that at number 13 was the effort of one man. What pleasure must have passed through Sir John's thoughts as he acquired like a royal squirrel, a feast of treasures. Soane is too well known to recount his achievements in depth: Architect of the Bank of England, Professor of Architecture at the Royal Academy, Fellow of the Royal Society, etc. By Act of Parliament in 1883,

this valuable collection was preserved for posterity
. . . 'so that free access shall be given at least on two
days in every week throughout the months of April,
May and June, to Amateurs and Students and to such
other persons . . .' according to his wishes, which had
taken into account his realisation that these months
contained sufficient light for a rewarding view of the
contents. The Trustees have generously extended
these hours (in their bountiful discretion) for all and
sundry's convenience.

CHAPTER 7

ORIGINS OF THE TEMPLE

ORIGINS OF THE TEMPLE

Early History — The Order of the Knights Templars
— The 'Lower' orders — The Church of St. Mary —
Exterior — Interior.

ORIGINS OF THE TEMPLE — EARLY HISTORY

The Order of the Knights Templars was founded in
1118 in Jerusalem. They were a military
religious order dedicated to protecting pilgrims to the
Holy Land. Their English branch, founded in 1128,
was first established in the parish of St. Andrew,
Holborn, but sold it about thirty years later to move
to a larger site, 'a fine open meadow sloping down to
the Thames'. The area was called the 'New Temple'
and in due course just 'The Temple', as it is today.

The Round Church, built on the model of the
church of the Holy Sepulchre which stood within the
precinct of the Temple of Solomon in Jerusalem, was
consecrated by Heraclius, Patriarch of Jerusalem, in
1185. The choir was added in 1240.

The Templars, who owed allegiance to no
ecclesiastical authority save the Pope himself, became
a powerful institution throughout Christendom, as is

Knights Effigy~

186

recounted elsewhere. Their Master in England sat as a Baron in Parliament. They were advisers and bankers to the Crown. Documents and treasure were entrusted to their safe keeping. Affairs of state were conducted in the Temple. In 1214 King John received a deputation of barons there and listened to the demands which were shortly afterwards agreed to at Runnymede in Magna Carta and in 1265 Simon de Montfort assembled his Parliament there which presented demands for constitutional government to King Henry III, who had taken refuge in the Tower of London.

The independence and wealth of the Knights Templars later aroused envy and malice. Pope Clement V, living in Avignon under the thumb of the ruthless Philip IV of France, suppressed the Order in 1308 on grounds of alleged immorality and blasphemy, for which the most absurd evidence was extracted by torture from the Knights, to the benefit of the French royal coffers. Edward II was persuaded to abolish the Order in England, though without the same cruelty and loot. Their land and property were given, by a statute of 1324, to another religious order, the Hospital of St. John of Jerusalem. The Hospitallers had their own premises in Clerkenwell (parts of them are still to be seen) and never in fact occupied the Temple.

THE ORDER OF THE KNIGHTS TEMPLARS

The Knights Templars were one of three principal Christian orders founded to wrest Jerusalem from the unfair hand of the infidel, who had captured the Holy

City in A.D. 1076 and thus precipitated the Fall of Jerusalem in 1187 and the Siege of Acre in 1189. The 'poor knights of Christ' 'of the Temple of Solomon', whence their name derived, were a military organisation from the beginning, whereas the Knights Hospitallers, and the Teutonic Knights were not. The Order was founded in A.D. 1118 by Hugo de Payns (or de Paganis), a Burgundian knight, and one Godfrey de St. Omer. Their efforts were duly rewarded when King Baldwin I, King of Jerusalem, granted over part of the royal palace adjoining the so-called Temple of Solomon to the Order, 'pauperes commilitones christi templique salomonici'.

The Order became one of the most powerful institutions in the western world, and with an iron glove decisively influenced European politics. The reasons were obvious: the military power of the Order ensured the safe custody and delivery of deposited bullion (which itself was able to be stored in strongholds stretching from Ireland to Armenia), in contrast to the unstable kingdoms of monarchs; and the saintly reputation of the officers of the Order was a guarantee to more worldly profiteers of the integrity of this mighty brotherhood. The Order became the great international financier of the age, and rivalled the Italian banking houses until their peremptory disbandment in the fourteenth century whilst in their zenith. It is truly said that the Paris Temple was the centre of the World Bourse, and that the Templars held the key to the eastern Exchange. . . . Would that these noble men were survived unto this day of Opec.

The heyday of the Templars was of course shortlived for reasons as follow, mainly of princely avarice, recited in due course; but from the middle of the twelfth century for some 150 years, the Templars strode mightily across the territories of Christendom, propelled by its own momentum, and was very ably protected on its flanks by the illustrious chivalry of its cause. At the great Councils of the church, namely the Lateran in 1215, and Troyes in 1274, the Templars vied with the authority of the Pope himself.

It may be wondered how a Christian body, devoted (as a matter of course) to unworldly reward, were able to turn a few buck in the 'immoral pursuit of usury', for, detested though the Saracens were, their saintly adversaries were soon smitten by their aptitude and soon espoused it quite as well as any infidel. The solution was dream-like in simplicity (and probably came to one of their number in like mode): 'mortgagees' or clients paid to the Templars, as 'mortgagors', a nominal rent which was used towards the reduction of the debt undertaken. For example, Edward I borrowed some 25,000 'livres tournois' at one fell swoop, and the citizens of England undoubtedly paid taxes — high even then — for the benefits of 'loans from abroad'. The difference between this 'nominal' and the real rent represented the interest levied, and was not Biblical usury. By this means, the Order flourished as a mercantile institution, and may be regarded as the precursor of the modern corporate giants who owe no fealty to territorial states or kingdoms, to the chagrin of modern exchequers.

189

It was the Kharizmian Invasion, circa 1240, which finally ousted Christianity from Jerusalem, and, of 200 Knights Templars, some 16 survived the battlefield. ('Charisma' was thus given to the English language, in a dramatic way, although its pedigree is Greek.)

The Order was threefold in itself: the 'Fratres milites' were the knights proper, out of whom were appointed the officers such as the Grand Master in Jerusalem, the Seneschal, and the Marshals of the provinces, secondly, were the 'fratres capellini', or the chaplains, who gradually assumed so it is said more power than 'the archbishops', and thirdly, the 'servientes armigeri', or the serjeants and esquires. Their habit was a white mantle – the purity of Christ in absolution – and emblazoned with a red cross – the ensign which had been granted by Pope Eugenius III (1145-53). It is interesting, although inconclusive, to note that some of the names used by the Templars were later inherited by the lawyers who came to dwell on their possessions: the serjeant-at-law, and The Master of the Temple. (A royal peculiar to this day).

Before turning to the precincts of the Temple, London, which is one of the richest cultural legacies entailed to our generation, the cruel and frightful story must be recounted of the Knights Templars demise. It has been recalled that their influence had grown steadily and surely in the twelfth century and how at the Council of Troyes in 1128 the rule of Templar immunity from ecclesiastical jurisdiction had been endorsed by the Church itself, how for 150 years the order blew its trumpets across the plains of

Europe, the lesser Islands, and the Levant, and because of this the King of France in 1305 ran their gauntlet, to save his mortal soul from debt but in so doing, avarice swallowed his soul.

King Philip IV certainly knew his strengths and his weaknesses: he expelled the Jews from France, and then turned his head to another industrious section of his subjects, the Templars. He had borrowed large sums from the Temple strongholds in Paris, and watched with envy the procession of the last Grand Master enter Paris brimming with 150,000 gold florins and ten horse-loads of silver bullion. He could stand it no longer when one of his fawning courtiers made the suggestion that the title 'king of Jerusalem' might suit him rather well in this world since he was unlikely to better it in the world hereafter. On the election of Pope Clement V (whose interests were devoted to France), King Philip denounced the Order of the Templars to the Inquisition under whose jurisdiction his kingdom sat. Thirty talents of silver were no doubt paid to the venal informer, esquire de Floyran of Beziers, who proffered evidence of heresy, out of which countless medieval legends grew in the nursery. ('Beware of a Templars' kiss' as the saying goes, and worse: 'the old knights kept women devils' − succubi − with whom carnal intercourse was had, and that they roasted and feasted off their illegitimate fruits.) In fact the Knights Templars swore to 'shun the kiss of a woman' as part of their vows, so, the phrase given to the English language, 'to take it (a kiss) on the chin' has some meaning for them.

On 13 October 1307, a blanket arrest of all knights was made in France, although Edward II of England refused to act until the issue of the Papal Bull enforced him on the 8 January 1308 to follow suit. The injustices perpetrated in the name of law and morality have seldom been exceeded and the knights and their brethren were subjected to abominable inquisitions of torture and abuse which culminated, some three years later, in their deaths, impoverishment and banishment by the Order of the Council of Vienne, that was on the 26 May 1312. It is unnecessary to pass any opinion on the sordid affair save so to say that the sermonal edict delivered was in consistory and not in general council, and that the Order of the Temple of Solomon was never formally pronounced guilty of a single crime or charge. After the 'Examinations' of the year 1309-10, fifty-four Templars were burnt alive in Paris, and their Grand Master Jaques de Molay, host so often to the treacherous king in preceding years, was burnt at the stake on the banks of the Seine still protesting to his and his brethren's innocence. He charged the assembled multitudes who had gathered to witness this ignoble atrocity with 'the judgement seat of God', before whom they would one day stand. It is to be noted that no contemporary writer of repute did dare endorse the verdict of guilt levelled at the Order, and Dante himself maintained the innocence of the Templars, in the following verse: 'Veggio il nuovo Pilate, si crudele che cio nol sazia, ma, senza decreto vele, Porta nel tempio le cupide.'

In England, the episode left an indelible imprint on

the course of the Common Law: confessions obtained under duress gained little probative value in criminal cases.

The possessions of the Order, including the Temple Church of St. Mary's were passed to the rival order of St. John, while, in 1540, all these orders were abolished in England by Henry VIII, and thus the mantle of ownership of the Temple was passed to the lawyers for good.

'THE LOWER ORDERS'

The Order of St. John, it is recalled, inherited the precincts of the Temple and all other possessions owned and occupied by the Knights Templars when they were dissolved by the Council of Vienne in 1312. This Order, of ambulance fame, was founded in 1099 and provided a hospice in the holy city of Jerusalem for the 'sick and the slain'. Unlike the Templars, it was not a military order by right, but a Christian dynasty declared to follow that of its patron, St. John of Jerusalem, in charitable conduct. The order in England was founded by Baron Jordan Briset and his ladywife, Muriel.

The Priory of St. John, at Clerkenwell, is but a stone's throw from the Temple, and remains squat, solitary and splendid beside the filth of poorer dwellings of the Borough. The Patriarch of Jerusalem, when he visited England in 1185, came from the Temple Church to consecrate the priory of the rival order and it was there he fell into such a rage with King Henry II (whom he had failed to persuade to undertake a crusade), that he died.

In 1381 the precincts of the priory were burnt down by Wat Tyler, whose men then beheaded the prior himself, Sir Robert Hales. (The Priory, however, was soon rebuilt and unto this day may be seen to advantage by prior appointment with the Porter.) As for the fortunes of the Order of St. John, far from being rebuilt, it suffered suppression by Henry VIII and finally took to the Mediterranean isle of Malta, where it was able to survive free of further interference from outside. Having been evicted from the Holy Land in 1291, and later from Cyprus and Rhodes, their expatriate existence flourished in Valetta until the year 1798 when Napoleon overthrew the island. Since 1800, the Order of St. John has devoted itself to humanitarian needs, a commendable alternative.

It is unfortunate that the crypt of St. John in Clerkenwell should contain the tombs of the parents and other relatives of the assassin Wilkes Booth, the murderer of President Lincoln.

Brief words summarise the third order, the Teutonic Knights, who remained around in Europe to carve their own history, but, one order which must not be confused with any of the above is the present Order of Good Templars, which was founded in 1851, in Utica, New York State. This society was formed of abstaining members of the public who have done so much to set an example to their erring fellow men and women. The order came to England in 1868, by way of a small crusade, and had a great success at the World Prohibition Conference held in London in 1909. Their annals of the habits of nations make very poor reading for those in search of 'home-truths', but the free world retains a clear lead over the soviet bloc who, on their statistics, are an alcoholic disgrace to the patron saint of Marx.

THE CHURCH OF ST. MARY, TEMPLE

So far as the scholar concerns himself, he has reached the apex of the Temple: permutation of a millenium. Indeed, he would have to traverse many frontiers as did the knights of old, to encounter an equal legacy from past civilisation. The Temple Church is quite the finest example of the Round to survive in Europe. The style is that in which the Knights Templars had built their castles of worship wherever their ranks swelled in number to a 'Commandery': in England there were five — those commanderies were formed at Little Maplestead, Essex, at Northampton, at Cambridge, Ludlow Castle and a chapel at Rothley Manor, Leicestershire (now an hotel) was also given over to the Order circa A.D. 1140.

It is an enticing thought to the observer, standing beside the magnificent façade of the ancient Round, to recite the famous lines of Julia Ward Howe, of which the Knights themselves would have heaved proudly their heavy chests in a unison of the fifth verse, the Battle Hymn of the Republic:
'In the beauty of the lilies, Christ was born across the
    sea
With a glory in his bosom that transfigures you and
    me

THE TEMPLE CHURCH

T.P. 1971

The Round

The Quire

1. PORCH 2. WEST PORCH Y NORMAN DOOR
3. FONT. 4. KNIGHTS. EFFIGIES 5. ORGAN
6. STAIRS PENITENTIAL CELL. 7. WREN REREDOS
8. BISHOPS EFFIGY. 9. SELDENS TOMBSTONE
10. PLOWDEN MONUMENT. 11. GOLDSMITHS TOMB.

As he died to make men holy, Let us die to make
  men free
While God is marching on.'

When the knights moved to the Temple from the
south side of Holborn in 1161, they had rightly
desired to erect a memorial to Christ in the reflection
of St. Sepulchre's, Jerusalem: the apple of their
visered eye. The circular nave — the Round — was
completed in 1185 and was consecrated by Patriarch
Heraclius in the same year . . . in the course of his
visit to England from Jerusalem he had also, it will be
recalled, consecrated the Church of the Order of St.
John at Clerkenwell. The spacious chancel — the
Oblong — was added in 1240 and remains a glorious
example of the Early English style. St. Mary's serves
both Inns of Court and is, as repeated elsewhere,
exempt from episcopal jurisdiction. There is a good
rule of common sense to justify this: Lawyers, as we
all know, can do no wrong.

EXTERIOR

This Romanesque jewel has survived the madness
and the follies of the twentieth century wars with
miraculous good fortune. The choir, which was added
in 1240, is entirely Gothic and a good example of its
Early English phase. The whole church was gravely
damaged by fire during an air raid on 10 May 1941
but the main fabric survived and it has been
excellently restored. The symmetry of the Round,
and the subsequent grace of the Quire are of imposing
beauty, and illustrate the transition from Norman (or
Romanique) to Gothic architecture.

The solid drum of handsome stonework linked to the elegant tapestry of the chancel walls still resemble an appearance when first erected. The West Porch is to be admired: it was probably copied from that masterpiece at Loges, the Loire, which returning Templars had noted in the course of their travels through France. This Romanesque west doorway is intricately carved and is protected by a porch of later date. The heavy oak door is of 1842. The actual site is thought to have born witness to the Treasury of the Templars. This may be well imagined by peering beneath the steps by the West Porch, with its chunky mouldings and squat splendour, and peering down the maze of steps below the railings. The deep recess is striking.

INTERIOR

The Interior of the second oldest church in London is an enchantment. In the suggestive words of the late Mary (Baroness) Stocks ... 'and acquire gramophone records of the superb choir which you may hear if your ramble allows you time on a Sunday morning in the Crusaders Church of the Temple. This will enable you to go on hearing it for many a long month, uninterrupted by the roar of London traffic, and the unquiet thought: that time spent in the Temple Church is time filched from something else, that you have come to London to do and probably won't get done'. (Extract from the Prologue, to *the first edition.*)

The cylindrical Round sweeps heavenwards as clasped hands of a saint. Six thin clerestory windows embroider the effect of a cavity between slender fingers, those Purbeck marble pillars.

The old quarry at Purbeck was specially re-opened for the benchers in the nineteenth century when the Church was being refurbished. Consider then the earlier achievement in transporting the marble from the Dorset quarries! On closer inspection, the columns are seen to lean four inches outwards from the centre — akin to the Victorian umbrella frame principle, and the columns disguise their true purpose: to bolster the weight of the dome.

The slumbering crusaders snore peacefully in full armour who from their labours rest, of all, the most comfortable looking is William Marshall, 4th Earl of Pembroke (died 1219), adviser to King John and Regent when Henry III came to the throne as a boy of nine. The crossing of the legs is not the artistry of an imaginative sculptor, it is rather the symbol that imparts a knight in vows who had campaigned in the Crusades and reached Jerusalem, a back-breaking feat in itself. Of the other eight, five are identified as: the Protector Pembroke, son of the aforesaid, and who overthrew the cantankerous prince, Llewellyn of Wales and in recognition of which, King Henry III attended his funeral; William Marshall, his son, who died bizarrely, on a runaway horse at which tournament he had instituted; old De Roos is still with us, and was a signatory to the Magna Carta; Geoffrey de Mandeville, that burdensome knight, who in the course of supposed good works, robbed Romsey Abbey, and was killed by an arrow which pierced his eye while besieging Burwell Castle. He ended up in the Temple because he had been forbidden consecrated ground by his church overlords, and his spiritual advisers remembered in the nick of time that the Templars suffered bodies thus afflicted to be lain in their sanctuary.

Around the circular aisle may one tread, with plenteous place to rest a weary limb on the handsome circle of bench that stands in freestone beneath the wall-arcade. The vaulting, alternate square and triangle, was the method by which the outer wall's divisions could be united to the main hexagonal piers, and thus the west door could occupy a bay to itself.

Eastwards the Quire is shown and may be seen to advantage. It was finished in 1240, and is undoubtedly an example of great accomplishment for the time. On its site was probably an unaisled chancel (which it replaced), and an adjoining terranean level warehouse known as the Treasury. The proximity is necessary since a knight who was on guard-duty would have been expected to attend services simultaneously, and, rather than miss the ritual cleansing of his soul, he could be there in spirit. The lower part of the Treasury may be visited by virtue of a stumbling stair in the south porch. This Plantagenet Bank of England was about the safest place in the world to deposit 'the valuables' and the Kings of England wasted no time in their discovery: rather than be a borrower – as Edward I started, with 25,000 'livres tournois' – it was much better for the royal soul to 'share and share alike' which is what Edward then did, but in a nice sort of way 'seeing', as he put it, 'to his mother's jewellry.'

200

. . . Some mothers have them: both of them.

The stair leading to the penitential cell in the Triforium is close by, and in the undercroft was once St. Anne's Chapel. However, a disobedient Templar was confined to the dress-circle and there sat while his virtuous brethren incantated beneath him until he passed away, among the pinioned arches, the freestone effigies, and the sepulchre of his life's vows, perhaps contemplating:

'And on his bust a bloudie cross he bore;
In dear remembrance of his dying Lord'.

(Spencer)

The flooring of the Round bears scrutiny, and a story is told how, when in the last century, the pavement was being repaired, the Benchers sought and obtained permission from the Deanery at Westminster Abbey to inspect and have taken up the contemporary encaustic tiles of the Chapel House, which enabled them to forward exact instructions of the nature of decorative work to be copied by the artists in the Staffordshire potteries who provided replicas. Upon a dark red ground are set the prevailing colour of amber and combine the symbols of the Lamb (founded on the device of the Order) and the Pegasus (the symbolic circumstance of the Founder of the Order), as mentioned elsewhere.

Indeed, the period of the twelfth century was notable for the rich and exotic decoration which pervaded European architecture: especially did the Templars incorporate the lavishness of the Orient. Magnificence has dwindled with the wear and tear of age, plunder or agression; a glance at the arabesques

201

which chase all over the compartments of the roof of the Nave bear the hand perhaps of imported craftsmen.

The eye is drawn to the reredos, which was designed by Wren in 1682 and carved by William Emmett. The screen was removed to the Bowes Museum, County Durham, by Victorian restorers, but was thankfully replaced unscathed after the second world war. A little to the fore are set the sanctuary chairs, or thrones, and the banners of the two societies illumine as also denote the technical division of the Church since the Deed of Partition in 1732. The paschal lamb and the spiritual rights of the Middle Temple bear northwards of the centre aisle, while the tail of the pegasus and the Inner Temple point southwards.

The organ is one of the finest instruments in England and was built for the chamber by Father Schmidt or Smith in the reign of Charles II. The choice of organ was the subject of a curious episode: when the benchers of the two societies determined to have built a musical instrument fit for their discerning ear, both Schmidt and Father Harris volunteered to undertake the work. The benchers, lest they made a wrong choice, agreed for the two organs to be erected in the Temple on the understanding – or the condition subsequent – that they would keep the better one. The day duly arrived when work was completed and no bencher dared to express an exact opinion as to the finer model. For one whole year Purcell, the composer, fugued for Father Schmidt, and, with a precise division of the benchers' time the

Organist of Queen Caroline made melody with the Harris alternative. Still were the benchers unable to decide one way or tother (the fact being that there was no precedent to follow). Finally, in order to put at ease the entire musical world, who by this time had joined with the excitement of the lawyers and judges, Chief Justice Jeffries was entrusted to make an unreserved judgment, which duty he was known to execute with a decisive style. The judicial ear was caught by Father Schmidt's organ, and the other was dismantled and in part erected at nearby Holborn's St. Andrew's, (and the remainder at Christ Church Cathedral in Dublin). The present fine Harrison organ, built in 1927, was a gift from Lord Glentaner in 1953. Under the long incumbency as Organist of Dr. George Thalben-Ball the choir of the Temple Church has become one of the most famous in the country, and has made many recordings of sacred music. As Dr. George Thalben-Ball pronounces, the Temple organ has, where Westminster Abbey's has but two, 'three 32-foot-stops,' which is praise indeed. The Temple choir comprises fourteen choristers' voices, six of men and eight of boys, with which a full cathedral service is performed.

Beneath the organ-chamber is a low vestry-room wherein is buried the bust of Lord Thurlow, a tablet to dear Goldsmith, and many other memorials of Temple associates. In the triforium are further monuments of Elizabethan and Carolingian period, chief of which is one of Edward Plowden (died 1584), the eminent lawyer and instigator of the building of the magnificent Middle Temple Hall, who

Father Schmidt warming up on another organ.

was buried in the vaults. Selden, the antiquary, was also buried here, and the glass slab set in the floor of the aisle permits a peep at his tomb, 1684. Also in the south aisle are to be noted:

—that of Richard Martin, Recorder of London in 1618.

— The grand effigy of a Bishop, in Pembroke marble, his feet on a dragon, in pristine condition, and possibly the identity of the Patriarch Heraclius or it may be Silvester de Everdon, Bishop of Carlisle, killed by a fall from his horse in 1213;

— Ann Littleton's tombstone, 'for while this jewel here is set, this grave is but a cabinet';

— And a picnic of stone sandwiches set into the church fabric, of which the following are digestible:

— Ye Lady Morton, a ladywife 'orthodox and exemplary for chastity, constancy, and patient suffering with her husband!'

After a shortish prayer, it behoves us to pay homage to both great and simple tombs on the north side of the Temple Church, erected kindly in loving memory of the friends of mankind. The ornate monument to Johannes Hiccocks without, is a rare example of baroque in the austere surroundings of the law.

The church is owned and maintained by Inner Temple and Middle Temple under the provisions of King James I charter of 1608, which is kept under the altar. Since the final partition of the Temple in 1732 between the two Inns the southern half of the church has been allocated to Inner Temple and the northern to Middle Temple. When members of the Inns attend services in the church they sit on the south or north side accordingly, the pews to the east of the choir stalls being reserved for Benchers.

In ecclesiastical organisation the church is a 'Royal Peculiar', not under the jurisdiction of any bishop. The Master of the Temple, the clergyman who officiates in the church, is appointed by the two Inns jointly. The Master's House is next to the church. The present building is a conscientious replica of the house designed by Wren, which perished in the air raid, and it is enhanced by the embracing foliage of wisteria, magnolia and passion flower.

Regular services are held in the church on Sundays during the law sittings and they are open to the public. It is also much used for special services, such as weddings for members of, or sons and daughters of members of, the two Inns, and memorial services for members.

North of the church, contrasting with the ornate monument to one Johannes Hiccocks alongside, the simple gravestone (inscribed 'Here lies Oliver Goldsmith 1728-1774') reflects fate: in his writings, 'but passing illusions, few in number, were of the Temple, and the Temple, in return, neglected him and his grave'.

CHAPTER 8

THE HONOURABLE SOCIETY

of the

INNER TEMPLE

THE HONOURABLE SOCIETY OF THE INNER TEMPLE

INTRODUCTION

The reader will recall why the Inner Temple assumed its name, but not the reason for a second society. The community grew and grew, larger and larger, until it overflowed into its own back garden, behind the Templars' original house. The Inner represents the colony of 'students of the law' who first settled themselves in the premises of the old Orders of Chivalry.

One wag has compared the Middle Temple to a beautiful bride and the Inner to her dull husband. It is a trite comparison. It is more likely that the

700-year-old couple have imbued each other with more grace than the misogamist wag.

The Paston Papers refer to the Inner Temple as a separate society in 1440 (1 October).

In 1505 the archives of the society began their good work which continues in the present day. In 1608 King James I granted the society the limited title, and in gratitude, a delegation of benchers hustled to Whitehall and presented the Sovereign with a stately cup of pure gold; they would have done better to refrain from such overt flattery; the king's son pawned it on the last of his continental tours.

In 1675 the Society purchased full title, and some half-century later, in 1732 to be exact, the Deed of Partition vested the estates of the Inner Temple in the Benchers of the Inn.

ALUMNAE

The Society has contributed an illustrious assembly of great and legal men, in the development of the Common Law:

Sir John Pakington;

Geoffrey Chaucer;

Sir Edward Coke, C.J.
    'father' of the Common Law;

Littleton,
    famed for his Treatise;

Sir Julius Caesar,
    Master of the Rolls, 1614;

Sir Heneage Finch,
    later Lord Nottingham (one of the black

finches of Kensington, due to his dark
countenance);
John Selden,
    antiquarian;
John Hampden,
    statesman;
Judge Jeffries,
    unfortunately tarnished by the 'bloody
    assizes';
Lord Chancellor Thurlow;
James Boswell,
    biographer and friend of Dr. Johnson;
William Cowper,
    poet;
Lords Erskine, and Ellenborough;
George Grenville,
    Prime Minister, 1763;
Lord Goddard,
    L.C.J.

Charles Lamb made illustrious, by his Essay;
'Eleven Masters of the Bench of the Inner Temple':
They were in seniority:

Masters:
    Thomas Coventry, 1766
    Richard Jackson,
    Francis Maseres,
    Thomas Barton,
    The Hon. Daines Barrington,
    Samuel Salt (to whom John Lamb was Clerk),
    James Mingay,
    John Reade,
    Peter Pierson,

The Lord Chief Justice of England 1946-1958

John Wharry,
and Master Joseph Jekyll, 1805.

ARMS

The arms of the Honourable Society of the Inner Temple are: Azure Pegasus with the wings expanded argent. In other words a silver flying horse on a blue ground. The device is to be seen on innumerable occasions throughout the Inn's properties.

The history of the arms is altogether unclear. Certainly one of the emblems of the Knights Templars showed two figures on one horse. Sometimes it is two knights in armour with the red-crossed white surcoat — a modern version of this may be seen in the stained glass of the east windows of the Temple Church. Sometimes it is a knight carrying a wounded comrade, or perhaps a sick pilgrim, across his saddle bow. The Pegasus is apparently derived from this emblem. Or it will be recalled that the knights took their vows of poverty, chastity, and obedience very seriously — that is, before the spoils of victory taught them safer principles. The 'Beausant' banner they chose embodied these virtues three in one: the vow of poverty was explained by two knights riding one horse; the vow of chastity was met by the filly taking flight if compromised; the vow of obedience was dutifully observed by one knight on horseback rescuing another from the field of battle.

Thus the Inner Temple developed its emblem in heraldry: 'azure, a horse bearing two men, argent'. One tradition is that during a Christmas revel in the

213

sixteenth century, a high-spirited student painted out the figures and turned them into spreading wings — and the horse has been flying ever since.

INNER TEMPLE HALL

The buildings of Inner Temple suffered most grievously from air attack in 1941. The very heart of the Inn — Hall, Library, Benchers' rooms, Treasury office — were gutted.

It has been said earlier that the Knights' Templars had a hall on a site south of the Crusaders' Church, which is roughly occupied by the present Hall. There still remain parts of a fourteenth-century building which has been incorporated into the modern building, consisting of the old buttery and the crypt beneath it and the old flint wall to the west.

There is a fine fifteenth-century fireplace in the crypt.

This, the third successor to the ancient halls which have stood on this site, replaced that of Sydney Smirke's (erected 1868: bombed WWII).

The architect of the present Hall was Sir Hubert Worthington, R.A. The foundation stone was laid by Queen Elizabeth II and the building was opened in 1954. A somewhat uninteresting exterior nevertheless provides a commodious and dignified vestibule. From the point of view of the caterer the Hall enjoys the modern kitchen and pantry arrangements that are difficult to achieve in the other, older, Halls. A member of the Inn is no doubt willing to overlook aesthetic shortcomings. The large and graceful windows admit ample light but no air: only a modern architect would design a window not to open. In them is stained glass by Hugh Easton showing the arms of members of the Inn who have held office as Lord Chancellor or Lord Keeper of the Great Seal. In the centre window on the south side are the arms of two Royal Benchers who were variously Duke of York – one becoming King James II and the other King George VI (Treasurer of the Inn in 1949 when his wife and Queen, Elizabeth was Treasurer of Middle Temple).

After dinner the habit of smoking is permitted only when the junior Bencher has asked the Treasurer the ritual question: 'Have twenty minutes elapsed?' This is meant to refer to the time when the port has been passed but if the Treasurer answers 'Yes', irrespective of the actual lapse of time no member challenges his lapse into forty winks.

The first woman admitted to the Bar, Ivy Williams, was called by Inner Temple on 10 May 1922. Since that time the number of women at the Bar has increased slowly but steadily and now about 280 practising barristers are women. Due allowance for their sex is made by their male brethren.

The rooms to the east of the Hall include the Parliament Chamber where the Masters of the Bench (when in formal session are known as a Bench Table) administer the affairs of the Inn. On the lower floor is the office of the Sub-Treasurer, the permanent head of the administrative Offices of the Inn.

THE LIBRARY

The Library adjoins the Treasury Offices and Hall.

As with them, it is a replacement of the previous nineteenth-century building, which was destroyed by bombs in 1941. It was reopened in 1958. The first record of an Inner library was in 1505, and it has grown over the years to become a most valuable collection of law books. Although 45,000 volumes were lost to the air raid, the more valuable manuscripts and books had been removed to places of safety before the war. These include the collection of early printed books which had belonged to Chief Justice Coke and the manuscripts which were bequeathed to the Inn by William Petyt, Keeper of the Records at the Tower of London and a former Treasurer of the Inn, who died in 1707.

On the staircase in the Library is a bas-relief portrait of Mahatma Gandhi, father of Indian independence, who was a barrister of the Inn.

CROWN OFFICE ROW

By the arch, metal rings used to be visible, a legacy predating the Thames embankment when barges tethered here.

Another post-war reconstruction, Crown Office Row, lies south-west of the Hall, looking down to the Embankment across the extensive Inner Temple gardens. It was also designed by Sir Edward Maufe, R.A. The pegasus carving over the doorway of No. 2 is by Sir Charles Wheeler, P.R.A. The building takes its name from the Crown Office, which was here until 1621 and, since 1882, has been housed along with other administrative departments of the Courts in the Royal Courts of Justice in the Strand.

Charles Lamb, whose father was a barrister's clerk, was born in a house in Crown Office Row, which he called 'the place of my kindly engender', where he spent his first seven years, and a plaque on the wall marks its site. He wrote lovingly of the Temple and its way of life.

INNER TEMPLE GARDENS

The spacious lawns run down from Crown Office Row to the Thames. In the days before the erection of the Victoria Embankment in 1865, the River Thames came much closer to the Temple and the fairly small garden front ran continuously from Inner Temple to Middle. Where the quarrel between York and Lancaster started, when the white and red roses were plucked as described in Chapter Nine, is not exactly known, but Inner Temple, for one, still shows a well-tended rosary.

The proud wrought-iron gates invite the eye's inspection of the motifs: the pegasus accompanied by the Gray's Inn griffin, which betokens the accord between the two Inns. Gray's Inn presented the gates to the Honourable Society in 1730.

The sundial near the gates dates from 1707. There is another, more attractive one near the southern end of Paper Buildings, which was originally presented to Clement's Inn by Lord Clare. It is in the form of a kneeling black boy holding a platter and is described in the following doggerel verses:

In vain, poor sable son of woe,
Thou see'st the tender tear;
From cannibals thou fledst in vain,

Lawyers less quarter give;
The first won't eat you till you're slain,
The last will do it alive.

This dates also from about 1700; it may have come from Italy or it may have been cast by a Piccadilly statuary. Nearby is a pond and the statue of a boy by Margaret Wrightson, which bears the words: 'Lawyers were children once', oft quoted in the Family Division.

PAPER BUILDINGS

The oblong block at the north-east of the gardens is called Paper Buildings after the first building on the site erected in 1610 and officially known as Heyward's Building. The method of construction was timber, lath and plaster, colloquially known as 'paperwork', which gave a lasting name to the buildings, although there are those who prefer to think it is derived from the great quantity of paper attached to the lawyer's trade. Nos 1 to 4 were burned down in 1838 and were rebuilt by Smirke, No. 5 being added in 1848. John Selden, the great legal historian, whose tomb can be seen in Temple Church, had chambers at No. 1 of the old buildings. It is said that when the rebuilding was in progress a mason asked the Treasurer if there were any words he wished to be enshrined on the wall, to which the testy answer was: 'Be gone about your business', and these words are to be seen on the building now by those who know where to look.

218

HARCOURT BUILDINGS AND TEMPLE GARDENS BUILDINGS

The symmetrical chunk that punctuates the west verge of the gardens is named after Lord Chancellor Harcourt; the canopied white stone of Temple Gardens Buildings stands near the water of the Thames and was designed by Sir Charles Barry, architect of the Houses of Parliament, that may be seen in the distance.

KING'S BENCH WALK AND NIBLETT HALL

The splendid long terrace running down the eastern boundary of the Inn to the King's Reach of the Thames, past a sea of parked cars and cobblestones, is named after the King's Bench Office which stood hereabouts until it was burned down in 1677. The present buildings, are of various dates between 1678 at the north end to early nineteenth century at the south. They form a happy unity. Those who saw the film 'Love among the Ruins' may recognise the façades and pavement as the settings of some of the episodes. Nos 4 and 5, with elegant doorways, are attributed to Christopher Wren. No. 5 was the home of Lord Mansfield, eminent Lord Chancellor who did so much to adapt Chancery jurisdiction to the needs of commerce, and international well-being.

> 'Graced as thou art with all the power of words,
> So known, so honoured in the House of Lords'

and parodied by Colley Cibber:

The King's Bench Walk

'Persuasion tips his tongue whene'er he talks:
And has his chambers in the King's Bench Walks'
(1720).

(Horace Imitated.)

No. 1 was destroyed in the war, except for the doorway, but was faithfully reconstructed afterwards. It stands on the site of the Alienation Office, an institution responsible for collecting fines when land held of the Crown was 'alienated' to others. In the back garden of this house there was built in 1927 the Niblett Hall out of funds bequeathed to the Inn by one of its members, William Charles Niblett, who had made a few lacs in Singapore. This hall survived the air raids and was used for luncheons and as the centre of the Inn's life until 1955 when Hall was reopened. It is used for lectures, meetings, and as an examination room, and it contains a precinct which provides amenities for student members of the Inn.

INNER TEMPLE LANE, HARE COURT, FARRAR'S BUILDING, DR. JOHNSON'S BUILDING

Hare Court takes its name from Nicholas Hare, who dwelt here in 1567, though his work was replaced in the eighteenth century. The adjoining Farrar's Building was erected in 1876. In a previous house on the site James Boswell, Johnson's friend, had chambers. In the Middle Ages the town house of the Bishops of Ely stood here. Dr Samuel Johnson himself used to live at No. 1 Inner Temple Lane and his name is commemorated in the somewhat sombre block which has stood on the site since 1857.

His literary accomplice records, in vivid broadside, one of Johnson's recurring dilemmas of life in the Temple:

'On Madame de Boufflers leaving, a sound like thunder descended and J. overtook her. On a little recollection he had taken it into his head to do her the honour of his literary residence.'

We may wonder at the lady's departure for Murphy described Dr. J. as living 'mostly in poverty, total idleness and the pride of literature'. Or we may read of Ozia Humphrey's account:

'As J. sat raving over his breakfast like a lunatic, I could hardly help thinking him a madman. Dress'd in w'stco't, breeches also brown, although they had been crimson, and an old black wig; everything he says is as correct as a second edition; 'tis almost impossible to argue with him as he is so sententious and knowing.'

MITRE COURT BUILDINGS AND FRANCIS TAYLOR BUILDING

These adjoining blocks are at the north-east corner of Inner Temple, near the entrance gates to Serjeants' Inn. Here there used to be Fuller's Rents, where Sir Edward Coke had chambers nearly four centuries ago. Mitre Court neo-classical buildings were erected in 1830 but No. 2 is a replica of the house destroyed in the war. Sir Francis Taylor, Q.C., who became Lord Maenan, had been a much loved Bencher of the Inn for 46 years when he died in 1951. The building named in his memory was opened in 1957.

AN AFTERTHOUGHT

El Vino's Wine Bar has played host to the legal

profession for many years, and although it is not true to say that cases are won and lost over its counter, it makes a useful refuge to the weary or heavy-laden traveller who needs to refresh himself.

CHAPTER 9

THE HONOURABLE SOCIETY
of the
MIDDLE TEMPLE

MIDDLE TEMPLE

The Honourable Society — Introduction — Middle Temple Gate — Middle Temple Lane — Brick Court and Essex Court — Fountain Court — New Court — Garden Court — The Temple Gardens — Middle Temple Hall — The Library — Pump Court — Cloisters.

THE HONOURABLE SOCIETY OF THE MIDDLE TEMPLE

The Middle Temple has a spectacular reputation among the four Inns of Court, though for what reason, it is not for a member of another Inn to move or even fathom. The acquisition of the Temple, as later divided into the two societies of the Inner and Middle Temple, was made as previously recounted in Chapter Seven, by the apprentices of the law, not long after the Crown had granted the property to the Knights Hospitallers by Charter. Chaucer speaks only of 'the Temple' (1381), and Dugdale recites a distinct list of Readers and Treasurers of the two societies starting in 1503. During the course of the fifteenth century, the two societies evolved out of a single body, and assumed the present identities of collegiate existence. The oldest records of the society 'that are' stem from the year of 1501.

The Society commands an illustrious pedigree in the Roll Call of English history, as a cursory mention of its distinguished members confirms:

ALUMNAE — some notable Middle Templars —

Of the Arts: John Evelyn, William Cowper, Henry Fielding, Thomas de Quincey, Richard Sheridan, William Makepeace Thackeray, Thomas More, Charles Dickens and Lord Tweedsmuir (John Buchan);

Of Patriots and others: Sir Francis Drake, Sir Walter Raleigh, Sir Martin Frobisher, Sir John Hawkins, John Pym, planatarian, William Congreve, William Penn, Earl of Clarendon, Edmund Burke — it is not what a lawyer tells me I may do, but what humanity, reason and justice, tell me I ought to do — Sir Humphrey Gilbert, Sir Edwin Sandys, who amongst other things, set sail for Virginia in 1618 and was followed two years later by the Mayflower;

Of the American Declaration of Independence: John Dickinson Esquire (1732-1808), member of the Committee of the 13 colonies which submitted the Draft Declaration to the Pennsylvania Convention which ratified the Charter; and the five signatories (of a total of 56) who adopted it, Edward Rutledge, Thomas Hayward, Jnr., Thomas Lynch, Jnr., Arthur Middleton, and Thomas M. Kean;

Of V.I.Ps: American Ambassadors to the Court

of St. James — honoris causa; C. J. Taft, former President of the U.S.A., Gen. C. J. Dawes, Vice-President, and C. J. Jackson;

Of Lawyers: Sir William Blackstone, author of the 'Commentaries', Lord Chancellors Clarendon, Somers, Hardwicke, Eldon, Finlay, Sankey, Jowitt, also Lords Brampton, Carson, Bowen, Harmen, Lindley, du Parcq, Meisey, Moulton, Scrutton, Stowell, Tenterden, Thurlow, Phillimore, and Lords Chief Justices Cockburn, Coleridge, and Reading (Rufus Isaacs);

And of interest, Mr. Justice William Say, one of the bench who was appointed to try Charles I.

MIDDLE TEMPLE GATE

The imposing Gatehouse may be seen to its advantage from the far side of Fleet Street. The regal façade was designed by Sir Christopher Wren in 1684 with a rash of other buildings to replace those destroyed in the Temple Fire of 1677. The Gate House contains ancient scars within the main old gateway where an old iron bar used to lodge to protect the precincts from, *inter alia,* malcontents such as Wat Tyler who threatened the Temple with his presence in 1381.

>As by the Templars' holds you go the Horse and
>   Lamb displayed,
>In emblematic figures show the merits of their
>   trade.
>That clients may infer from thence, how just is
>   their profession,

> The Lamb sets forth their innocence, the Horse
> their expedition
> Oh Happy Britons! Happy Isle! Let foreign
> nations say —
> Where you get justice without guile, and Law
> without delay.

This rhyme was pinned on the gates in 1774.

Had the author his tongue in his cheek? Another
view of lawyers was expressed by Jack Cade's Kentish
rebels in 1450: Shakespeare put in the mouth of Dick
the Butcher the words: 'The first thing we do, let's
kill all the lawyers.' In the end it was Cade's head
which decorated Temple Bar. But his predecessor,
Wat Tyler, also from Kent, who led the Peasant's
Revolt in 1381, had in fact killed many lawyers,
burned the Court records and Temple Bar itself. The
Temple had been barricaded against the revolution-
aries and inside the pre-1684 gatehouse there was to
be seen the marks left by the iron bar, part of the
defences.

An earlier archway was well known and its story
amusing: When Wolsey, Henry VIII fearsome
Cardinal was but a parish priest in Lymington, one Sir
Amyas Pawlett, a local dignitary, had the truculent
padre popped in the stocks for one misdemeanour or
other. This was a misguided thing to do. Wolsey
became the powerful tyrant and avenged the earlier
indignity by confining poor Pawlet to the precincts of
the Temple and forcing him to incarcerate himself in
the Temple Gatehouse for six full years. Pawlett
could think of nothing better to do than rebuild his
home, which he did *with his own pocket*. Mindful of the

Cardinal's levelled finger, Sir Amyas decorated the entrance with the Cardinal's hat, cognisances and other devices, to pacify the tyrant . . . This in part did the trick, but was chiefly done by King Harry who added the Cardinal's head — and no doubt hat — to his fine collection of human mascots.

MIDDLE TEMPLE LANE

Through the gateway the very narrow Middle Temple Lane runs down to the Victoria Embankment, now one of London's main east-west traffic arteries. Before its construction in 1865, the wide and sluggish Thames came almost up to the Halls of Inner and Middle Temples. The Lane roughly divides the two Inns, but the actual boundary, settled between them in 1732, is very involved; it may be studied on the maps displayed at various places in the precincts. The buildings belonging to each Inn may be identified by the arms displayed on them — the Pegasus of Inner Temple and the Lamb of Middle.

Passing within the arch, which acts as the conduit to the Temple proper, the Old Post House may be admired on the immediate left, and is now a shell of a typing office. This site preceded the postal service which England pioneered and which has since been run down as is the wont of national interests. The black supports which continue to do their job miraculously, were the same posts that Dr. Johnson touched on his way to the chambers.

At once we are in the tranquillity of the law and would agree with Charles Lamb: 'A man would give something to be born in such places.'

BRICK COURT AND ESSEX COURT

Brick Court is the sort of name that a lawyer would give to a courtyard; Essex Court has the historical association of the Essex family as earlier recounted. Both names have muddled the courtyard and taximeter cab-drivers who remark regularly on the blessed confusion. It used in fact to be two courts, divided by a transverse building which was destroyed in World War II and not replaced.

The Court whatever-its-name opens on Middle Temple Lane and is a typical example of barristers' quarters and Temple residential accommodation.

The subordinate attendant does what he may to remove the ugly crop of stationery motor vehicles that like some weed keep springing up even when rooted. Indeed, the story goes from the lips of an anonymous author, that if one must park in the Temple, do not park in a Lady resident's lot, or you have had yours. One lady is both an intrepid motorist and distinguished candidate for high civic office, who, when she succeeds — as doubtless she will — can use her best endeavours to alleviate the fate of the hard-run motorist.

Returning to the scene of the law, it is interesting to recall that Spencer alluded to Brick Court (or that part of the Court which is) as 'those bricky towers' although the present building dates from a pile erected in 1882.

At No. 2 resided the warm-hearted Oliver Goldsmith who died therein in 1774 and whose tomb lies gloriously in the shadow of Temple Church. Thackeray writes of weeping women filling the stair, within the black oak door, when the 'greatest and most generous of all men' passed away. Another Denizen, Edmund Burke, the Statesman, followed the women's example and burst into tears at the death of Goldsmith, and Sir Joshua Reynolds laid aside his brushes for the day.

The only person who might have shown less emotion was Sir William Blackstone, hard at work on his monumental 'Commentaries on the Laws of England' (published in four volumes 1765-69, and one of the greatest expositions of the Common Law), who complained of 'the constant racket above'. Perhaps the racket which interrupted the Commentaries was caused by Goldsmith's landlady, as Dr. Johnson explains:

'I received one morning an urgent message from poor Goldsmith and went accordingly as soon as I was dressed. His landlady had arrested him for his rent at which he was in a violent passion. I put the cork into the madeira bottle, desired he would be calm, and seeing he had a book ready for the publisher, looked into it and saw its merits. Telling the lady I should soon return I sold it to the bookseller for sixty pounds. Goldsmith duly discharged his rent but not without rating his landlady in a high voice for having used him so ill . . .'

The tiny building in the north-west corner was until 1912 Albion's shop where barristers bought wigs and took them in to be re-curled . . . Perfidy is Albion.

FOUNTAIN COURT

A few steps down from New Court is Fountain Court, a delightful promontory in the Inns of Court from which there is a pleasing prospect in every direction. The fountain jet splashes in a circular pool, inhabited still by lazy golden carp. It is surrounded by crutched and chained mulberry trees of great age; Dickens, in *Martin Chuzzlewit* described the scene of his young hero's philanderings by the pond:

'. . . such is this arid wasteland. Which renders the Temple Fountain a welcome fixture in the "dry and dusty channels" of the law. There was a little plot between them, that Tom should always come out of the Temple by one way; and that was past the fountain . . . and if Ruth had come to meet him, there he would see her — not sauntering, you understand (on account of the clerks), but coming briskly up, with the best little laugh upon her face that ever played in opposition to the fountain . . . For, fifty to one, Tom had been looking for her in the wrong direction, and had quite given her up . . . The Temple Fountain might have leaped up twenty feet to greet the spring of hopeful maidenhood that in her person stole . . . through the dry and dusty channels of the Law; the dingy boughs, unused to droop otherwise than in their puny growth, might have bent down in a kindred gracefulness to shed their benedictions on her graceful head; old love-letters, shut up in iron boxes in the neighbouring offices, and made of no account among the heaps of family papers into which they had strayed and of which, in their degeneracy they formed a part, might have stirred and fluttered with a moment's recollection of their tenderness as she went lightly by.'

Regrettably, the scene conveys an aridity to this day . . . and one is reminded of Lord Montgomery (of Alamein, no less), meeting an arch-angel, and saying: 'Wot; no barbers in heaven?' 'You celestial devil,' says the angel, 'nothing grows up here'.

Just by the fountain is a building the doorway of which is superscribed 'Fountain Court'. This leads into three houses, the property of Middle Temple, with frontages on Essex Street. One of the houses has an exquisite staircase. This house, it is believed, was inhabited by ladies of the town in the eighteenth century, when the Covent Garden area was the centre of London's night life. Their departure is not regretted.

NEW COURT

The Court was 'renewed' in 1677 (and the pleasing town house on the west side is attributed to Wren), after the Honourable Society acquired a part of the Essex House garden, once belonging to the Devereux family, from Dr. Nicholas Barbon. Indeed, the Earls of Essex and the name of the family, Devereux are recalled in the nearby public houses (much patronised by Temple folk) — hence also Essex Court and Essex Street — whose London house were here-abouts.

The adjoining Little Gate with its iron scrollwork is also attributed to the pencil of Wren. The building on the north side, Devereux Chambers, was acquired by

Middle Temple in 1975 for use as barristers' chambers.

In New Court, as in many other parts of the Temple, may be seen metal emblems on the walls signifying in Georgian times the insurance company with which the building was insured. Each company had its own fire brigade which, allegedly, would deal with a fire in a building insured with it but not with one insured with a rival. '51906' is a policy number and the 'portcullis' or 'three feathers' the badge of a company. The oldest of these 'fire marks' were of lead and date from 1667, but later they were of tin or copper and brightly painted as advertisements. Thus a rhyme of 1816 says:

> For not even the Regent himself has endured,
> Though I've seen him with badges and orders all shine
> Till he looks like a house that was over-insured. . .

Oddly enough it was the same Dr. Barbon who established the Cohortes Vigilum in 1667 or fire-watchers, which continued until the comprehensive Fire Acts of the nineteenth century.

The passage from Essex Court contains a forty-five rung ladder which is so curiously chained to the wall that in the event of 'Fire!' the unhappy helper would commit malicious damage despite his good intentions.

GARDEN COURT

Before the extension of the buildings down Middle Temple Lane these gardens were continuous with those of Inner Temple to the east. The buildings replaced those of earlier date and style both in 1830 and in 1883. This site housed the lodgings of Oliver Goldsmith before his 'Vicar of Wakefield' enabled him to buy rooms in the adjoining Court. At No. 2 were the chambers of Rufus Isaacs, later the first Marquis of Reading and Viceroy of India.

THE TEMPLE GARDENS

Before the Victorian embankment was bedded in 1865, the gardens of the two honourable societies merged into one another and ran to the water's edge where the Temple Pier contributed its business to Father Thames. Thanks to the motor car, all and sundry are back at square one and two.

Nevertheless, the lawns of the fair Temple will not see again the quick steps of England's fighting men — Sir Francis Drake, fresh returned from naval daring, hurrying to the Middle Temple Hall. All things come about for a reason, and because England has lost her navy, and instead builds motor cars, the Temple does without its Pier, and by preference without the other.

Beside the sundial perhaps, or where the lawns sweep lazily off its bank, here haunts the memory of Shakespeare:

Scene IV. The Temple Garden.
Enter the Earls of Somerset, Suffolk and Warwick; Richard Plantagenet, Vernon, and a lawyer.

Plantagenet:
    Great Lords and gentlemen, what means this silence? Dare no man answer in a case of truth?

Suffolk:
Within the Temple Hall we were too loud; the garden here is more convenient.

Plantagenet:
Then say at once if I maintain'd the truth; or else was wrangling Somerset in th'error?

And Somerset enjoins the Earl of Warwick to intervene . . .

Warwick ends his soliloquy thus:
Between two girls, which hath the merriest eye;
I have, perhaps, some shallow spirit of judgment:
But in these nice sharp quillets of the law,
Good faith, I am no wiser than a daw.

And after further argument, Richard Plantagenet concludes:
Let him that is a true-born gentleman,
And stands upon the honour of his birth,
If he suppose that I have pleaded truth,
From off this brier pluck a white rose with me.

After Somerset, who plucks a red rose, Warwick remarks:
I love no colours; and, without all colour
Of base-insinuating flattery,
I pluck this white rose with Plantagenet.

Suffolk sides with Somerset, and Vernon entreats the company then and there to count their blooms, having taken white himself.

Somerset to Vernon:
Prick not your finger as you pluck it off,

Lest, bleeding, you do paint the white rose red,
And fall on my side so, against your will.

And Somerset, testily:
Well, well, come on: who else?
— Lawyers are so slow —

A lawyer, takes courage and a rose in both hands
and says:
Unless my study and my books be false,
The argument you held was wrong in you;
In sign whereof I pluck a white rose too.

When asked his argument, Somerset replies:
Here in my scabbard; meditating that
Shall dye your white rose in a bloody red.

And Plantagenet, a while later:
Hath not thy rose a canker, Somerset?

And rejoined:
Hath not thy rose a thorn, Plantagenet?

And Warwick concludes:
'. . . And here I prophesy — this brawl to-day,
Grown to this faction, in the Temple Garden,
Shall send, between the red rose and the white,
A thousand souls to death and deadly night.

Thus the fatal civil war of the Roses was conceived
upon the casual choice of two Temple roses.

MIDDLE TEMPLE HALL

Dominating the gardens is Middle Temple Hall the
crowned glory of Tudor domestic architecture. Its exterior suffered Victorian *improvement* but the interior

reveals one of the finest Elizabethan halls in the country.

The Gothic windows lend a masterful if incongruous touch to the superb structure. In 1572 glass was still as expensive as salt, a commodity zealously guarded by the glaziers, reliant wholly on the monopoly of the glass-blower. For this reason alone, among structural others, a window was a means of showing off precious coloured mineral, and not an aperture which it is today because the old problem of heating has been solved.

The east window is dated 1570 although the Hall was not completed until three years later. Dividing the entrance lobby from the Benchers' room beyond is an ancient carved oak door set in a low stone arch known as the 'Watergate'. The name recalls the fact that the site was at one time at the very edge of the River Thames, and possibly the doors are the only relic to survive from the Hall of the Knights' Templars.

The great man responsible for this splendid building was Edmund Plowden, a Salopian, Treasurer of the Inn from 1561 to 1567, and afterwards retained as 'procurator and promotor for building the new Hall and making collections'. A rather pallid Victorian bust of him is to be seen inside the Hall under the screen. More dignified is the ornate funerary memorial to him in the Temple Church. Plowden was remarkable in remaining, unscathed, a staunch Roman Catholic during the full tide of Protestant militancy in Elizabeth's reign.

The names of all the Treasurers of the Inn from

1500 to the present day are displayed on panels in the entrance corridor. The earlier records have been lost.

An outstanding feature of the Hall is its double hammer-beam roof. This is an unusual, and very beautiful, construction. It was made by the same craftsman who made the single hammer-beam roof at Longleat, the seat of the Thynne family (Marquis of Bath). Plowden wrote to Sir John Thynne in 1562 asking to borrow him.

The Hall is 100 feet long, including the entrance corridor, 40 feet wide, and 59 feet high in the apex of the roof.

Another wonderful feature of the Hall is the enormous elaborately carved screen, 23 feet in height, surmounted by the minstrels' gallery, and described by Sir John Summerson as 'the queen of all Elizabethan and Jacobean screens'. The carved gates with iron spikes on top were a later addition following an incident of misbehaviour by students when, over one Christmas, they barricaded themselves in the Hall and held a riotous party. . . . The Benchers ordered the gates to be made so that the wretches were locked out on future occasions.

Middle Temple students frequently caused discomfort to their governing body, as students do everywhere from time to time. The records contain many decisions about their discipline. Among other things the Benchers legislated several times against gambling in Hall. Nevertheless, when the floorboards were replaced by Danzig oak in 1730 a hundred pair of dice were found which had slipped through the

241

cracks between the boards. The floorboards were again renewed in 1971, though there is no record of any dice on that occasion. James I encouraged the game 'between members but not between strangers'.

At the other end of the Hall, on the dais, is the high table, at which the Benchers dine. This is twenty-nine feet long and is made from four planks cut from a single oak tree, felled in Windsor Park and floated down the Thames to the Temple. It was a present from Queen Elizabeth I, a discerning friend of Middle Temple, who enjoyed dining here and joining in the dancing and revels. Her portrait hangs in the southern alcove. Queen Elizabeth II and the Duke of Edinburgh dined at this table on 18 February 1976 as when the heads of other professions, the principal Judges, other lawyers, and leading persons from the nation's life, were entertained.

The other monarchs whose portraits hang on the West Wall behind the high table are, from left to right:—

a — Anne
b — Charles II
c — Charles I
d — James II
e — William III.

The most historic piece of furniture in the Hall, which normally stands in front of the high table, is a plain square table known as the Cupboard. This is made from a hatch cover of the Golden Hynd, the little ship in which Sir Francis Drake circumnavigated the globe in 1578-80. Sir Francis was a member of the Inn and a party was given to him here to celebrate his safe return. He presented the hatch cover as a souvenir and also, it is said, the lantern from the poop of the ship, which was hung in the vestibule outside the screen. This was destroyed in the air raids and the present lantern is a fine replica. Although Drake, and indeed Raleigh, Frobisher and Hawkins, were members of the Inn, they were never practising lawyers, for in those days it was common for young men of good family to join one of the Inns of Court, and the social and club-like amenities of the Inns vied with their legal functions in importance.

... Up the wainscot to the sills of the 14 great windows may the arms of the Readers and Members be perused: and canting heraldry be enjoyed: James Whalley — 3 spouting whales, or, Peter Ball — 3 balls. The third on the right, of Sir Walter Raleigh reads: 'Courtier, Soldier, Scholar, and Founder of Britain's Colonial Empire.'

The glass in the windows displays the arms of members of the Inn who have achieved distinction as Lords Chancellor, Judges, or in other ways. The arms painted on the 461 panels around the walls of the Hall are those of the Readers. The Hall used to be not only a refectory but also a lecture room, and Readers were appointed by the Bench to lecture the students. Two were appointed in each year, the principal period of education being in the Lent and Summer vacations. Appointment as Reader (or 'Lector') was an honour for a member of Hall, but an expensive one.

Middle Temple Hall had a narrow escape from destruction during World War II. Restoration of the Hall was completed in 1949 (with generosity in part from the American and Canadian Bar Associations, as plaques in the corridor gratefully acknowledge). The Hall was reopened by the Treasurer, who in that year was H.M. Queen Elizabeth, consort of H.M. King George VI.

The vaults of Middle Temple house a rare and beautiful collection of silver, brought out — before graces — to grace the dining tables on special occasions. A notable benefactor was the first Viscount Rothermere, an honorary Bencher, who presented in all some twenty-five choice items of Tudor, Jacobean and Commonwealth silver, dated within the years 1558-1658.

Octogenarian Benchers recall that this guest would arrive for luncheon with — 'brown paper packages tied up with string: these were a few of his favourite things!' — and not, as some fondly recount, wrapped in the latest edition of the *Daily Mail*.

These, and the valuable Harmsworth Law Scholarships, for which members of the Inn are eligible to compete and many eternally grateful, were given by Rothermere in memory of his father, Alfred Harmsworth, a barrister of the Society.

Underneath are the Under-Treasurer's room, the administrative offices and common rooms for members of the Inn.

THE LIBRARY

Down Middle Temple Lane is the American law

an item of **Middle Temple Silver.**
silver gilt standing salt, of 1565.

library, the finest and most extensive collection of American law books outside the United States, containing over 20,000 volumes. Rokuichiko Masujima (1857-1948), founder of the American library, was called to the Bar by this Society in 1883 and 'honoured by the American Bar'.

On the landing outside the American library hangs a reproduction of the American Declaration of Independence on which the five members of Middle Temple who were among its signatories are identified with a red star. They were Arthur Middleton, Edward Rutledge, Thomas Hayward, Thomas Lynch, and Thomas McKean. The first four were from South Carolina and McKean from Delaware, of which he became President, and Pennsylvania, of which he was later Chief Justice and then Governor. One member of Inner Temple was also a signatory.

At the foot of the Lane, by the Embankment entrance, is the florid set of buildings known as Temple Gardens, designed by Sir Charles Barry, architect of the Houses of Parliament.

PUMP COURT

This little Court, which lies between Middle Temple Lane and the Cloisters, leading to Temple Church, is one of the oldest in the Temple. The previous Templars' Hall stood on its south side. There is a well 27 feet deep in the centre of the court but, alas, the pump is no more. A quick reference to the map will reveal the strategic position of this courtyard in the Temple. This well did not save the court from destruction by fire in 1678. Such was the severity of the frost at the time that the water supply was frozen, as was the Thames itself. The beer in the Hall cellars was used by the pumps but this soon gave out and, after Pump Court, the Cloisters and Elm Court had been destroyed, the spread of the fire was stopped just before it reached the Temple Church by blowing up intervening buildings. The south side and the Cloisters were destroyed again by enemy bombs in May 1941.

Here lived Henry Fielding; the impecunious Alfred Harmsworth — whose four great sons revolutionised British journalism.

The sundial on the north side of Pump Court should be noted with its caption: 'Shadows we are and like shadows depart' — an untimely reminder for us all.

CLOISTERS

The Cloisters, on the east side of Pump Court, were rebuilt by Wren in 1681 after the disastrous fire, and very charming they were. Their destruction in World War II and their replacement by an uninteresting design is a sad loss to the architecture of the Temple. Wren's original sketch plans, which are preserved in the Middle Temple Surveyor's office, show a single row of elegant columns boldly set apart. It seems that the Benchers were doubtful whether these could support the weight of the building above. Wren knew better, but to appease his learned clients he inserted a second row of columns; little did anyone realise that they carried no weight at all, stopping an inch short of the ceiling! — a fact authenticated by Ken and

Willie Sinkins, proprietors of the family firm of Wildy's, whose pre-war premises were adjoining, at 1a The Cloisters.

Sir Edward Maufe is the post-war architect. His drawings for the Middle Temple were inadvertently 'lost' to the University of Pennsylvania in 1970. It occurred when the distinguished architect was moving house; dustmen were paid to remove a stack of papers. Included in these were the Temple drawings. Delight that these historical manuscripts were saved depends upon which side of the Atlantic you were born.

CHAPTER 10

THE HONOURABLE SOCIETY
of
GRAY'S INN

The Serjeants' Inn of
Sir Christopher Yelverton.

THE HONOURABLE SOCIETY OF GRAY'S INN

Introduction — Alumnae — The Badge — South Square — The Hall — The Eating of Dinners — The Treasury Offices — The Holker Library — The Chapel — Gray's Inn Square — Verulam Buildings — Field Court and Gray's Inn Place — The School of Law — Raymond Buildings — The Walks

> 'For two hundred years at the least my ancestors have been members of this House' — *Sir Christopher Yelverton, speaking in Hall at a feast to honour his appointment to the Order of the Coif in 1589.*

G ray's Inn lies to the north of the street known as High Holborn. Holborn, corrupted in London speech to 'Ho'b'n', means the Hole Bourne, the stream flowing into the Fleet River which ran down the valley now occupied by Farringdon Street and out into the Thames at Blackfriars.

The origins of the Inn are woven as deeply into the cloth of history as those of the other Inns although its own records do not survive before the year 1569.

'This certain Inn at Portpole', as the records call it

in the following year, can trace its beginnings to the manor house of the de Grey family which lay just outside the City of London where the Oxford road left its boundary at Holborn Bar. It was known as the Manor of Portpool, a name which survives in Portpool Lane, a turning off Gray's Inn Road. Many members of the de Grey family were associated with the law. A Walter de Grey was Lord Chancellor in 1206-14. His great-nephew, Sir Reginald de Grey, also held judicial office as Juticiar of Chester and became the first Lord de Grey of Wilton. It seems that he was involved in the preparation of Edward I ordinance of 1292, 'De Attornatis et Apprenticiis' (see Chapter Three), and that it was to his house among others in the district that young men came to study law. He died in 1308 and was succeeded by his son John (died 1323), grandson Henry (died 1343), and great-grandson, Reginald. On the latter's death in 1370 the Manor House is described for the first time as 'hospitium' or hostel, and 25 years later, in 1395, the word 'Greysin' is to be found in the records of the family.

The date of the foundation of the Honourable Society of Gray's Inn is not known. In 1505 Edmund, Lord Grey of Wilton, sold his manor and eight years later it was known to be in the ownership of the monks of Sheen, from whom apparently the Society rented it.

The Society's earlier records were burnt and thus detailed accounts of its activities are lost to us, although much may be gleaned from the accounts of others. For example, the Paston Papers refer to a letter written in 1484 by the Chief Justice, who was 'a felaw' of Gray's Inn, and there is a ledger of 1553 which records the sum of 40 pence spent on the removal of a member's coat of arms; he was the Duke of Northumberland, who had led an unsuccessful conspiracy against the accession of Queen Mary and was executed (recounted in the following chapter).

The first heyday of the Inn was in the reign of Elizabeth I (1558-1603), or 'Good Queen Bess' as the Society still calls her in affection. The records are illuminated with the names of great Elizabethans: Cecil (Lord Burleigh), Walsingham, the Bacons (father and son), Gerard, Howard of Effingham, Sir Philip Sidney. During this period the Society became renowed for its revelries and feasting, which may indicate why the Queen was so enthusiastic a visitor.

Before she came to the throne there had been established a tradition of staging plays using wit as a moral art which mocked both human nature and the highest in the land unmercifully. Even the formidable Cardinal Wolsey at his zenith was not spared. It was recorded in the year 1526 by:

> This Christmas was a goodly disguising played at Gray's Inn which was compiled for the most part by Master John Roo, Serjeant-at-law, twenty years past and long before the Cardinal had any authority. The effect of the play was that the Lord Governance was ruled by Dissipation and Negligence which caused Rumor Populi, Inward Grudge, and Disdain of Wanton Sovereignty to rise with a great multitude to expel ... (them) ... and to restore Public Wealth again to her estate... This play was

highly praised of all men saving of the Cardinal, which imagined that the play was devised of him and in a great fury sent for the said Master Roo and took from him his coif and sent him to the Fleet (prison) . . . but by the means of friends . . . Master Roo was delivered at last . . .

The Prince of Purpoole, for such was the title of the dignitary who traditionally organised these events, was not dismayed by official criticism and, with the Master of the Revels, held his court long after the Cardinal had died in disgrace. Queen Elizabeth enjoyed her visits particularly and commended 'their gallant shows'. One of them was Shakespeare's *The Comedy of Errors*, first performed in the Hall in 1594. To this day members of the Inn and their guests on Grand Nights drink a toast from the loving cup 'to the pious, glorious and immortal memory of Good Queen Bess'.

ALUMNAE

The Honourable Society has hosted a distinguished assembly of great and noble men who have been members or honorary members of this, perhaps, the most intimate of the Inns of Court: 'Gray's' men have included:

Sir William Gascoigne, LCJ in reign of King Henry V;
The Elizabethans:
Sir William Cecil (who later became Lord Burleigh);
Sir Francis Walsingham;

Sir Nicholas Bacon, Lord Keeper of the Great
Seal and father of,
Sir Francis Bacon, later Lord Verulam, Lord
Chancellor;
Sir Gilbert Gerard, Attorney-General and Master
of the Rolls;
Sir Philip Sidney, soldier and poet;
Lord Howard of Effingham, Admiral of the
Fleet and Disposer of the Spanish Armada;
Thereafter:
Thomas Cromwell, Earl of Essex;
Earl of Southampton;
Sir Thomas Gresham, Founder of the Royal
Exchange;
Sir Samuel Romilly;
Sir Robert Lush;
Bishops Gardiner and Hall;
Archbishops Whitgift and Laud;
Lord Macaulay, poet;
Mr Hilaire Belloc, poet;
Mr Sidney Webb;
Lord Birkenhead, Lord Chancellor; alias 'F. E.'
Sir Leonard Stone, Master of the Walks;
Lord Atkin, Law Lord and innovator;
Sir Winston Churchill, Prime Minister;
Franklin D. Roosevelt, President of the U.S.A.
(1932-45);
Sir Robert Menzies, Prime Minister of Australia,
(1949-66);
Mr Edward Heath, Prime Minister (1970-74);
Lord Selwyn Lloyd, Speaker of the House;
Chief Justice Windham (ret.) who lives in Capetown;

Lord Elwyn-Jones, Lord Chancellor incumbent;
Sir Dingle Foot, Solicitor-General;
and the recent call to the Bar, H.R.H. Charles,
Prince of Wales.

THE GRIFFIN

The arms of the Society are — Sable a Griffin
segreant or, that is a golden griffin standing on a
black field. It is thought to be borrowed from
Richard Aungier, thrice Treasurer of the Inn, at the
turn of the sixteenth century, and it is a more spectacular heraldic device than the plain bars of the de
Grey arms which were previously used — they may be
seen above the main entrance to the Treasury Office
in South Square. A griffin is the offspring of a lion
and eagle with the body of the former and the head
and shoulders of the latter, but also with animal ears.
It is sacred to the sun, being seen, for example, on the
Temple of Apollo at Miletus and was used by the
ancients to guard treasure. The curator of the London
Zoo has repeatedly made known his regret that there
is no known specimen in captivity but points out that
since the fabulous creature is alleged to grow to eight
times the size of a lion there might be difficulty in
housing and feeding it.

THE SEAL

The Seal of the Society consists of the shield of
arms encircled by the motto 'Integra lex aequi custos
rectique magistra non habet affectus sed causas
gubernat', which means to some of us — 'Impartial

justice, guardian of equity and mistress of the law, without fear or favour, rules men's causes aright'.

SOUTH SQUARE

Most visitors cannot find Gray's Inn through the narrow white archway on the north side of High Holborn (a few metres west of Chancery Lane Underground station). Immediately on the right are Gray's Inn Chambers, a new block erected by the Inn and principally in use by barristers. Through another narrow archway, surmounted by the griffin, one enters the quiet precinct of South Square, with its lawn, flower beds and statue of Francis Bacon. All the buildings are of red brick and, apart from the Hall, are built in the Georgian style. Practically every building in the Square was destroyed during World War II. The only house to survive was No. 1 immediately on the right of the entrance, which bears the date 1759 over the door. A comparison of that house with its neighbours, which bear dates in the 1950s, shows that the original architecture of the Square has been re-created, albeit mostly on a duller scale.

In the south-east corner there stood the office of the attorney Edward Blackmore, for whom Charles Dickens, in 1827, at the age of fifteen, worked unhappily as a clerk for 13s. 6d. a week (rising to 15s.) until he was able to use his pen for better and more lucrative purposes. (In those days the Square was known as Holborn Court.) Dickens lovers, when they have finished their visit to Gray's Inn, should walk a little distance north of it to No. 49 Doughty

STUDENT 2° 1576
BARROS

260

Street, a house occupied by Dickens as a young married man, now a museum, where they may see the actual desk he worked at in Blackmore's office and much else of interest besides.

Dickens described Gray's Inn in *The Uncommercial Traveller* and his contemporary, the American Nathaniel Hawthorne, wrote of it in *An English Book* in words that may still seem apt to the modern visitor:

> Gray's Inn is a great, quiet domain, quadrangle beyond quadrangle . . . It is very strange to find so much of ancient quietude right in the monster city's very jaws, which yet the monster shall not eat up . . . Nothing else in London is so like the effect of a spell as to pass under one of these archways and find yourself transported from the jumble, rush, tumult, uproar, as of an age of week-days condensed into the present hour, into what seems an eternal Sabbath.

At the far end of the neat lawn stands the bronze statue (by F. W. Pomeroy, 1912) of Francis Bacon, essayist, historian, philosopher, statesman, and lawyer, and perhaps the most famous son of Gray's Inn. He occupied chambers in the Inn from 1576 until his death in 1626 and his career in the Society is recorded on the plinth of the statue: Student 1576, Barrister 1582, Reader 1588, Dean of Chapel 1589, Treasurer 1598-1617. Another list records his public service: Member of Parliament for Middlesex 1593, Solicitor-General 1607, Attorney-General 1613, Lord Keeper 1617, Lord Chancellor 1618. He was the son of Sir Nicholas Bacon, and became Lord Verulam in 1618 and Viscount St. Alban's in 1621. As Lord Chancellor he probably had more influence than any other person in establishing Equity (see Chapter Two) as a vital part of the English legal system.

The north side of the Square is dominated by the Hall, with the Treasury office adjoining, in front of which stand four ornamented lead water tanks bearing dates 1702, 1748, 1752 and 1764 now used as jardinières. The Holker Library occupies the whole of the east side. At No. 11, on the west side are the offices of the Senate of the Inns of Court and the Bar. No. 10, rebuilt in 1973, contains the students' common room. Beneath it is the abode of the Head Porter, who is often to be seen about the Inn dressed in black suit and bowler hat. At formal dinners in Hall he carries out his duties wearing a purple gown and carrying a staff bearing a silver griffin.

THE HALL

As long as it has existed the Inn has had a Hall, the centre of the communal life of its members. Little is known about its origins, but it is known that it was 're-edified' in 1556-58 and then assumed its present appearance. Brutally mutilated by bombs in 1941, it was faithfully restored in 1951 to its previous style, largely through the generosity of the American Bar Association, who also presented the additional south oriel window bearing the inscription *Verus amicus est tanquam alter idem.*

The mellow brickwork, which partly survived the

bombing, gives the Inn a warm and intimate feeling, unmatched by the larger Halls of the other Inns.

It is in fact the smallest of the Inn Halls, being 75 feet long. The handsome cupola was copied in 1722 by a member of the Inn for an identical replica at the State House of Philadelphia. Within, the carved woodwork and timber roof, although the chief victim of the incendiaries, were carefully renewed after the war. (It is pleasant to imagine a delegation of 'hand-picked' Benchers making their way to Kent to hand-pick the 106 oaks of antiquity to be felled for this purpose.)

INTERIOR

The magnificent screen that runs the width of the west end of the Hall is of Spanish chestnut and according to tradition it comes from one of the galleons of the Armada, 1588. A jury of amateur historians may like to consider the facts: that the Lord High Admiral of the English fleet was Howard of Effingham, a member of the Society, that the Queen was a great friend of the Society, that of the Armada ships wrecked on the English coast, one, Nuestra Señora del Rosario, was towed to Chatham and that it was large enough to have contained a screen of this size. The screen was saved in the nick of time from the incendiary bombs in 1941. Although the pictures and other valuables had been moved to safety out of London at the beginning of the war, the screen at first remained. Plans were made, however, to saw it in sections and remove it piecemeal. Only some of the sections had been taken out of the Hall when the attack came but through the gallant efforts of fire wardens the remaining sections were towed on to the lawn before the fire spread.

The screen is in three parts divided by six Corinthian columns. The middle section rests on a raised block and is topped by a capital, giving slight extra height. On the block may be seen a charred hole made by a drop of molten lead when the roof was burning during the air raid. In front of it is the cash desk where members of the Inn, having satisfied their hunger and written out their own bills, satisfy the cashier.

Behind the screen are the passages to the kitchens and an old stone archway which is thought to be the original entrance to the de Grey's banqueting chamber.

The plaques in the panelling around the Hall display the arms of each Treasurer of the Inn since 1775. The wooden lozenges are original, having been removed to safety during the war.

Much fine heraldic glass was also preserved and replaced. The north oriel window contains the arms of Sir William Gascoigne, Lord Chief Justice of the King's Bench, who figures in Shakespeare's *Henry IV*.

The Hall is overlooked by the great Parliament Clock. Not many of this type survive in working order. They derive their name from a tax levied on clocks in the eighteenth century which caused many owners to discard their own timepieces and rely on such large clocks specially made and erected in taverns and public places.

By the south oriel window is a bust of Winston

Churchill by Epstein. It was in this Hall that Churchill first met Franklin D. Roosevelt, both of whom became honorary Benchers of the Society.

The portraits on the wall behind the high table, where the Benchers lunch and dine, are of Queen Elizabeth I, painted in her twenty-eighth year by an unknown artist, Sir Francis Bacon and Sir Christopher Yelverton, and on her right William Cecil, Lord Burleigh, greatest of her ministers, Sir Nicholas Bacon, her Lord Chancellor, and Sir Francis Walsingham, Secretary of State and brilliant head of her secret service.

Around the Hall are other portraits of famous members of the Inn.

In the reign of Elizabeth I and for long after the Hall was famous for revelries, plays and masques. John Evelyn, the seventeenth-century diarist, gives a long account, and they were last recorded in the year 1773. On occasions, too, the four Inns staged 'command performances' at Whitehall Palace, which was the residence of the sovereign until 1688. There is an old tradition that in order to settle a squabble as to the order of precedence of their carriages the names were put into a hat and Gray's Inn was drawn out first, and Gray's Inn members like to think that the priority thus accorded is a binding 'precedent'. The tradition, however, was evidently unknown to the publishers of the Law List for 1817 which printed Lincoln's Inn, Inner Temple, Middle Temple, and Gray's Inn in that order, and has done ever since. That is the accepted convention although it must be stressed that all the Inns are of equal status.

F. E. Smith, Lord Birkenhead, Treasurer in 1917, who did as much as any member to build up the Inn to its present stature and prosperity, expressed his own typically outspoken view that a Gray's Inn man was better than any other 'and no damned nonsense about "other things being equal" '.

One other of the tens of thousands of Gray's men who have eaten dinners in this Hall deserves special mention. He was a Bencher named Joseph Ball and he had a fifteen-year-old nephew residing in the colony of Virginia, whom he dissuaded from his youthful intention of joining the British navy. The young man was called George Washington.

eating DINNERS, CALL NIGHTS, GRAND NIGHTS and all that

'Man wants but little drink below,
But wants that little strong'

once spake Oliver Wendell Holmes (in a parody of Goldsmith, entitled A Song of Other Days), and this leads us to the custom of Eating Dinners.

The Hall is the centre of the collegiate life of the Inn. Luncheon is served during the law sittings and is attended by members of the Inn within ambit. Those who have been in Court in the morning may be seen still wearing their bands and will hurry back to their case after a quick meal. The Hall is used for business and social meetings of various sections of the Bar and for receptions and entertainments of sundry kinds such as concerts and theatrical performances.

But it is dining in Hall that constitutes the most significant feature of the Inn's social life. During each of the four law sittings in the year there is a period of three weeks known as dining term, when there are dinners every night. Any member of the Inn may attend, including students. All Bar students, indeed, have to 'keep terms' by dining in the Hall of their Inn twenty-four times before they are called to the Bar. The requirements are the same for all Inns but dining customs differ somewhat from Inn to Inn.

A very pleasant dinner was recently held in honour of Capt. Oswald Terry, retiring Under Treasurer, and much loved by us all. The butler knocks for silence and all stand while the Benchers, in order of seniority, walk in from the door at the back of the dais and take their places at the high table, Master Treasurer in the middle. He then says grace: 'Benedic, Domine, nos et haec tua dona quae de bonitate tua sumpturi sumus. Amen'. ('Bless us, O Lord, and these thy gifts which we are about to receive from thy bounty'.)

Members dine in messes of four, two on each side of the table, and each mess may choose its wine. Barristers are entitled to sherry or port as well as wine, whereas students must make do with just wine. Ancient courtesies attend its drinking. The members of the mess drink to the health of each other and then collectively to the mess below them, saying 'Gentlemen' (or 'Members' if there is a lady among them) 'of the lower mess' adding their names. The lower mess then returns the compliment. Breach of the custom may involve a charge being brought by one mess or a member of it against the miscreant. The charge is heard after dinner by the senior barrister in Hall, 'Mr Senior', who convenes a court for the trial.

If the charge is proved the traditional fine is a bottle of port, although with the present rate of excise duty it may be commuted to a lesser penalty. The trials of these and other alleged breaches of ritual are often hilarious. Mr Senior may also be called upon to exercise his authority during the meal. A young member may rise in his place and when all eyes are silently fixed on him he will solemnly enquire whether the Benchers at the high table are being served with the same bill of fare as his own, whereupon Mr Senior will sternly admonish him with the words: 'Young fellow, your nostrils may lead you to the pinnacle of your profession but your tongue will not'.

The proceedings often continue late into the evening, with debates (Gray's Inn has a renowned debating society) — and with eminent guest speakers, readings, and mock trials or moots. These are an echo of the days when the Bar student's entire education took place in the Hall of his Inn.

An important occasion in each dining term, normally the twenty-first day, is Call Night. The students to be called to the Bar don a barrister's gown over evening dress. Each in turn comes before the Treasurer who formally admits him as a barrister member of the Society and shakes his hand. After dinner the Benchers drink the health of the new barristers and retire to their own quarters. After their departure Mr Senior again proposes their health and each is supposed to make a speech in reply, but by tradition each is shouted down, by 'expert witnesses'.

Once a term, also, there is Grand Night, when the

Inn entertains distinguished guests. They are announced by name and conducted into the Hall by the Head Porter who keeps his eye on them and their refreshment. The Benchers and their guests mingle with members of Hall on their benches while the loving cup is circulated. After dinner, at which the guests sit with the Benchers at the high table, the loving cup is again circulated and, starting with Master Treasurer, every one in turn drinks from it 'to the pious, glorious and immortal memory of Good Queen Bess'. Afterwards the toast to Her Majesty is roundly proposed by Mr Senior and healths are drunk to other members of the Royal Family and to the students. A student then proposes the health of the barristers, and finally all drink to 'Domus' — 'The House', but are not drunk on the house.

THE HOLKER LIBRARY

In 1555 one Robert Chaloner in his will left his law books to the Inn and directed that they were all to be fastened by chains. Since then either librarians have acquired more faith in human honesty or fewer bookworms are kleptomaniacs for the volumes in the Inn's fine modern library are no longer manacled. The Inn appointed its first library Keeper in 1645 at an annual salary of £3 6s. 8d. The first catalogue was compiled in 1669. The collection grew over the years and the library acquired its present name from Sir John Holker, a Master of the Bench, who bequeathed large funds for what came to be known as the 'most comfortable library in London', which was built in 1929. But twelve years later Nazi bombs destroyed books and fabric without trace except the most valuable volumes, which had been removed for safe keeping. After the war temporary premises were erected in the Walks and were opened by Sir Winston Churchill; he called them the 'architecture of the aftermath'. In 1958 Mr Harold Macmillan, the Prime Minister, opened the present Holker Library, which had been designed by Sir Edward Maufe R.A., in recognition of which work he was made an honorary Bencher. There is a comprehensive collection of British jurisprudence and also representative collections of the laws of other countries, particularly the U.S.A. It is contemplated that the Holker Library will become the main permanent home of the international section of the Inns of Court libraries in due course.

THE CHAPEL

A place of worship has stood on the site of the present chapel since 1315. In 1539 the Court of Augmentations, which was set up under Henry VIII to 'augment' the revenues of the Crown by the suppression of the monasteries, investigated the duties of the chapel's priest. 'For tyme out of minde', they reported, 'he had been required to synge and say masse for the studyent gentilmen and felaws of the house of Gray's Inn'.

The chapel was enlarged, when rebuilding was necessitated after the war, in order to provide adequate accommodation for the Masters of the Bench and their ladies (who sit in opposite pews!) and other members. The east window, erected in

1895 and removed during the war years, commemorates members and preachers of Gray's Inn who became archbishops, namely Whitgift, Juxon, Wake, and Laud. The centre panel commemorates Thomas à Becket, whose image was to be seen in the chapel until 1539.

The maple wood of pews, lectern and pulpit was the gift of the Canadian Bar Association.

The chapel is open between the hours of 10 a.m. and 4 p.m. in winter and 6 p.m. in summer.

The chaplain appointed by the Inn is known as the Preacher. At dinner in Hall he has the right of sitting eighth among the Benchers, that he may bless them by name on his fingers.

GRAY'S INN SQUARE

Gray's Inn Square is a charming example of late seventeenth-century architecture, although seven of the fourteen houses are replicas of ones that were destroyed in the war. The south side is made up of the chapel, garnished with its little cupola and clock, and the sedate buttressed hall. There is an entrance gate on the east from Gray's Inn Road over the arch of which is the Pegasus, a gift from Inner Temple, in recognition of the ancient amity between the two Inns, another example of which is to be seen on the entrance gates to the Walks. Hereabouts was the original manor of the de Greys, The best preserved house in the Square is No. 1, and its interior contains fine wood panelling of 1684.

~ Urn in ~
Grays Inn Square

1707

VERULAM BUILDINGS

A passageway from the north of Gray's Inn Square leads to Verulam Buildings, a long terrace of five large houses parallel with Gray's Inn Road and overlooking the Walks on the other side. They were erected in 1803-11 and named after Francis Bacon (who was created Lord Verulam in 1618), and unfortunately they took the place of the flower garden he had laid out 200 years earlier. They scarcely have the warmth of the older parts of the Inn, but perhaps their inhabitants may take comfort from the words of him whose name they bear: 'Houses are built to live in, and not to look on: therefore let Use be preferred before Uniformity, except where both may be had.'

FIELD COURT AND GRAY'S INN PLACE

Leading west out of Gray's Inn Square, past the recently rebuilt common room, an archway gives access to Field Court which contains two handsome eighteen-century houses facing the fine iron railings bordering the Walks. Next to the houses a gateway leads the pedestrian into Fulwood Place and so back to High Holborn. The gateway carries stone griffins. Affixed to a wall hard by are two notices saying 'Ancient Light', signifying that the building had acquired a prescriptive right to light (and air) at that point and putting any prospective builder on notice that he would interfere with that right at his peril. Such notices used to be quite common but are now rarely seen, outside the Law Reports.

Field Court continues as Gray's Inn Place, which contains buildings remarkably different from each other. No. 1 is an exquisite, small three-storey house, early nineteenth century. There are Corinthian pillars to the door, which has a fan-light with a pattern in wrought-iron tracery. On the opposite side two charming little verandahs, painted light blue, also have delicately patterned wrought-iron tracery, bringing a feeling of Viennese Baroque to London. No. 3 is a graceless mid-nineteenth-century lump, while the biggest building of all, twenty years old, is uncompromisingly functional with plain red brickwork and large metal-framed windows, although it is quite out of proportion. Through it a passageway leads to Warwick Place and High Holborn and over the archway on the other side there may be seen, surrounding excellent coloured representations of the arms of the four Inns, the name of the building: Inns of Court School of Law.

This School is managed by the Council of Legal Education, set up by the Inns in 1852. Its policy is now controlled by the Senate of the Inns of Court and the Bar. Hardby, a plaque commemorates the warrior Sun Yat-Sen — his nom de guerre was Sun Wen (1866-1925), who organised the secret revolutionary societies at Canton which overthrew the Manchu dynasty in 1911. Chinese associations today survive and are preserved by another member, the respected Leader of the Hong Kong Bar, Charles Ching (Q.C.), who has befriended many an Englishman in the Orient.

RAYMOND BUILDINGS

From Gray's Inn Place a path leads north, past the only tennis court within the Inns of Court and a little wicket gate giving an exit to Bedford Row, to the five-house terrace of Raymond Buildings, which run up to Theobald's Road. Built in 1825, they form a precise juxtaposition to Verulam Buildings at the other side of the Walks, and are named after Sir Robert Raymond, who was Chief Justice of the Common Pleas in 1725. Their construction, alas, obliterated the 'mount' that was one of the features of Bacon's landscaping, on which had originally stood a Banqueting House thirty feet in height.

Winston Churchill's confidante and Private Secretary, Eddy Marsh, lived for many years at No. 4, and whose friends may never forget either his bushy eyebrows or the overhanging array of paintings which covered his garret chambers.

THE WALKS

Gray's Inn gardens are known as the Walks. They run from Field Court to the northern boundary of the Inn along Theobald's Road. It was Bacon, one of whose best-loved Essays is 'Of Gardens', who laid them out, but, alas, his design was mutilated when Raymond Buildings were erected on the site of his 'mount' and Verulam Buildings on his flower garden. Nevertheless what remains is a charming feature of the Inn, dear to its heart. The Bencher in charge of horticultural affairs in the Inn is known as Master of the Walks.

An early account of Bacon's handiwork is as follows:

> I next come to the Walks, which are very large and beautiful. Of these the first mention that I find is in 40 Eliz. Mr Bacon having upon his account made in 4 Jac. allowed the sum of £7 14s. to be laid out for planting elm trees in them, of which elms some died as it seems; for at a Pension held here 14 Nov. 41 Eliz. there was an order made for a present supply of more young elms in the places of such as were decayed; and that a new rail and quickset hedges should be set upon the upper long walk at the discretion of the same Mr Bacon and Mr Wilbraham: which being done, amounted to the charge of £10 6s. 8d. as by the said Mr Bacon's account, allowed 28 April 42 Eliz., appeareth.

The Walks are entered from Field Court through imposing wrought-iron gates bearing the date 1723. Golden letters show this to have been the year when the Treasurer (T) was one William (W) Gilbey (W). The great key is inscribed: 'Members are entitled; the public in summer lunch-hours; and dogs never'. The gate posts are surmounted by the Inn's fearsome griffins, though here they are seated and hold between their paws shields bearing the winged horse of Inner Temple (compare the archway leading from Gray's Inn Square to Gray's Inn Road).

The main feature is a broad, gravelled path between an avenue of mature plane trees behind which are ornamental trees and shrubs. It is tempting to think that the catalpas at the end, now bowed with age and supported by crutches, grew from slips brought back from America by Sir Walter Raleigh and planted by Bacon.

The Walks have always been a popular promenade and a lovely place for social gatherings in the summer. It is an old custom for the Treasurer of the Inn to hold a garden party beneath the rafters of the sunlit foliage.

Charles Lamb called them 'the best gardens in London' and Joseph Addison in referring to them remarked: 'To touch on nature's tresses is my blessing'. When Samuel Pepys visited the Walks it was, typically, not the horticultural beauty that caught his eye: 'Very well pleased with the sight of a fine lady that I have often seen walk in Gray's Inn Walks', he noted in his Diary on 17 August 1662.

One hundred years ago the Walks were renowned for their rookeries but in 1875 the gardener, through an inadvertent order, felled the trees containing them regardless of the fate of their inhabitants. A bird-lover wrote to the press: 'It is to be feared that the habitual users of the garden will soon hear with less sorrow when the same fate, as must happen in the natural course of events, overtakes the Benchers . . . So one barbarism engenders another'. His anger had muddled his grammar, but one knows how he might have felt.

Let Bacon, the begetter of the Walks, have the last word:

> God Almighty first planted a garden; and indeed it is the purest of human pleasures. It is the

greatest refreshment of the spirits of man, without which buildings and palaces are but gross handiworks.

GRAYS INN ~The Walks~

CHAPTER 11

HISTORICAL ASSOCIATIONS
OF TEMPLE BAR

This epilogue has been written to acquaint the reader with London's famous gateway, which it is hoped will be returned to the City before it falls down.

HISTORICAL ASSOCIATIONS OF TEMPLE BAR

HISTORICAL ASSOCIATIONS OF TEMPLE BAR

Still he that scorns and struggles
Sees, frightful and afar,
All they that leave of Rebels,
Rot high on Temple Bar.

(G. K. Chesterton).

Temple Bar was taken rudely down nearly a hundred years ago, and lay as rubble in a yard off Farringdon Road, despite the most significant historical associations which date back a millenium. To posterity's good account and fortune, the renowned brewer, Sir Henry Bruce Hedworth Meux, philanthropist, decided to accept Temple Bar into his safekeeping and removed it at his own cost, lock,

stock and barrel (as it were), to his seat at Cheshunt, Theobalds Park, where it was re-erected in 1880.

The literary, historical and royal associations with Temple Bar are numerous and fulfil an intimate record in the annals of the City of London.

The earliest reference to Temple Bar is in a patent roll, 'the Bar of the New Temple, London', in the year 1293, and it was again mentioned in 1301. In another patent roll of 1315 reference is made to a dangerous and muddy track which led from Westminster, through 'Charynge and St. Clement's' to Temple Bar 'the whole length' of which required repair.

The City had its western gates in Lud Gate and New Gate but trade moving along this rough riverside road needed further protection, and Henry III gave consent that posts and chains be set up, and these in turn – possibly in the early fourteenth century – became a more permanent structure. In 1351 William de Mourden made a bequest to 'prisoners in the prison of Temple barre', and seven years later one Adam de la Pole made a similar bequest. In those days gates of cities were often used for that practical purpose, being of sound construction.

In April 1357, the Black Prince, Edward, Prince of Wales, flushed with victory at Poitiers, rode through Temble Bar and into the City of London on a black pony leading his captive King, John of France, who was seated on a superb white horse. There he received a tumultuous welcome from his citizens. This was not the first historic event to be associated with the famous portal however. The gate was pillaged during the Peasant's Revolt in June 1381, and three days later — on Friday 15 June — an escort of some two hundred soldiers and courtiers under Richard II passed through Temple Bar from Westminster Abbey en route to Smithfield where the young King met the enraged peasants and their leader Wat Tyler. (At the latter venue, it will be recalled, the Lord Mayor of London, Sir William Walworth, rode forward and in front of the King, stabbed Tyler to death: Thus the City bears its dagger on its shield) some say.

It is intriguing to think of those lively characters, enshrined in English literature, who have passed through Temple Bar: Many pilgrims in the Middle Ages would have begun their travels at Temple Bar on their way to Canterbury or into the City itself to visit the places and buildings associated with the martyr, Thomas à Becket, had been born in London in the year of 1118, in a house at the corner of Ironmonger Lane, which after his death was commemorated as a chapel dedicated to St. Thomas of Acon. This title was taken from an Order instituted in the Holy Land as a branch of the Templars who had a house at Acre, and this chapel remained until the time of the dissolution by Henry VIII. A chapel dedicated to St. Thomas (who was canonised by Pope Alexander III in 1170) had also been established on London Bridge. Among those passing through Temple Bar in about April 1385 were the pilgrims, who joined with Geoffrey Chaucer at the Tabard Inn and set off together for Canterbury. Chaucer gathered together the conversations of the travellers and wrote the *Canterbury Tales* about the year 1393.

The next reference to a gateway is in 1502, the date of the Acclamation of the League between Henry VII and the King of the Romans. One year later the hearse containing the body of Henry VII's Queen, Elizabeth of York, halted at Temple Bar on its way to Westminster Abbey from the Tower of London, and the abbots of Bermondsey and Westminster blessed the body.

We are told the gate was 'newly painted and repaired' in 1533 (for the coronation of Anne Boleyn), at which 'stood diverse singing men and children', and it was again refurbished in 1574, and supplied with new battlements, for Edward VI coronation ... Edward was destined to reign only six years and, when in January 1553, His Majesty entered the last stage of illness, his Lord President of the Council, the Duke of Northumberland, wove a complex plot to secure a future position as England's regent. His Grace selected as a candidate for the throne, a devout Protestant, his own daugher-in-law Lady Jane Grey, and in June 1553 he persuaded the dying King to sign a will bequeathing her his crown. Edward VI duly died on 6 July and Queen Jane succeeded to the throne although she insisted that Mary Tudor was the rightful heir. Mary Tudor was a Catholic and Northumberland was fearful that she would overturn the Reformation and return England to Papacy. Further intrigue was occasioned before Mary Tudor was proclaimed Queen of England and on 19 July Lady Jane Grey — after a reign which had lasted only nine days — was arrested and placed in the Tower together with her husband Lord Guildford Dudley, and her father-in-law the Duke.

All were sentenced to death and Northumberland's, along with other heads, were executed in August. The fate of the others was sealed in January 1554 when Sir Thomas Wyatt raised the standard of revolt in Kent, and marched on London at the head of 4,000 men. Approaching the City from the west he forced Temple Bar but found Lud Gate secured against him, and being hemmed in by cavalry and as short of men as of arms, he surrendered at Temple Bar, which resulted in the execution of Lady Jane Grey, her wretched husband, and Sir Thomas.

Mary Tudor — 'Bloody' Mary — married Philip of Spain at Winchester Cathedral and was received at Temple Bar with, *inter alia,* a Latin oration. New gates were hung in the celebration, as the engraving by Wenceslaus Hollar displays.

England returned to a more peaceful era with the accession of Queen Elizabeth I. Queen Elizabeth passed regularly to and fro the gate during her reign of forty-five years and several occasions are worthy of mention. On 23 January 1570, attended by her retinue, she journeyed from her home at Somerset House (in the Strand) to the home of Sir Thomas Gresham in Bishopsgate Street and after dinner she visited the new Exchange he had built, where, 'finding it very much to her liking, commanded the herald to proclaim it the Royal Exchange'.

The defeat of the Spanish Armada gave rise to national rejoicing and celebrations were held at St.

Paul's Cathedral, including one on Sunday 8 September (1588), when eleven flags seized from the enemy were displayed from the lower battlements: this jubilant mood of the citizens culminated with the special service of thanksgiving at St. Paul's on 24 November 1588.

The Queen went to the cathedral in great splendour seated in a conveyance which resembled a triumphal chariot... Four pillars supported a canopy surmounted by an imperial crown, with a further two pillars on the front of the carriage supporting a lion and dragon with the arms of England; the vehicle was drawn by four white horses and presented a magnificent spectacle as it lurched through Temple Bar.

This event, it is believed, was the first occasion of the Lord Mayor presenting the sword and keys of the City to the Sovereign on entering The City. It is a ceremony which has been enacted at Temple Bar on every subsequent occasion that the Monarch has entered the City, and continues to this day. It is worth signifying this traditional custom: As time went by the idea of an Entrance to the City disguised itself in a pageantry of formal welcome of the monarch, and the idea crystallised into a ritual. The gates were shut against the Sovereign who asked leave to enter his own capital, but, once inside, was dutifully presented with the keys and sword in homage. Having touched them as a token of possession, they were then returned at once to the power behind the throne, in this peculiar case, the Right Worshipful the Lord Mayor.

Alas and alack that these scenes are forgotten, but the historic significance of Temple Bar survives as the site where London begins and Westminster, the Royal City, ends.

Shortly after Wren's design for Temple Bar had been executed, and within the next few years, the arch was to be decorated with effigies of a very different kind, for in 1684, in the words of Walter G. Bell, 'the Rye House Plot brought the first trophy to the Golgotha of Wren's Temple Bar'. This referred to the gruesome custom of exhibiting the heads or private quarters of those executed over the gates or entrances which served both as a warning to other citizens and as further degradation of the felon.

The first trophy proved was the forequarter of an unlikely candidate, Sir Thomas Armstrong, and 'his' was placed there after being boiled in pitch at Newgate. Meanwhile, Sir Thomas's head was placed over Westminster Hall and the rest of the body sent for exposure to Stafford, his constituency in Parliament. A job should always be done thoroughly.

On 10 April 1696 John Evelyn wrote, 'The quarters of Sir William Perkins and Sir John Friend, lately executed on the plot, were set up at Temple Bar, a Dismal Sight which many pitied. I think there never was such at Temple Bar till now except once in the time of Charles II, namely of Sir Thomas Armstrong'.

A dialogue between Johnson and Goldsmith concerned the heads on Temple Bar and is worth repeating here: they were together in Poet's Corner at Westminster Abbey when the doctor said to

Goldsmith: 'Perhaps some day our names may mingle with these' — which was very possible. Later their walk took them past Temple Bar where Goldsmith said to Johnson: 'Perhaps some day our names may mingle with THESE!' — and pointed to the heads (which were probably those of the Scottish Lords who were executed after the failure of the Second Jacobite Rebellion of 1745 after their defeat at the battle of Culloden on 16 April 1746).

It is said that when the head of the young Earl of Derwentwater was placed on the Bar in 1716, his young widow conspired to retrieve it. At dusk that day she was driven under the arch in a cart while her hired henchman threw her husband's head down to her from the parapet above. Some wives make good husbandmen.

At one time it was possible, according to Horace and Walpole, to hire for a halfpenny a telescope or spy-glass with which to see the heads more clearly. The English have always respected the dead.

Amongst the heads added to the Bar as a result of the Jacobite Rebellion were those of Colonel Townley and his fellow officer, one Fletcher. The head of Lord Fraser of Lovat — *the last person to be executed on the block in England* — was placed upon the Bar in 1747 and when taken down, it is said to have been kept for some years in the room above the gateway, which at the time was used by Child's Bank. The last head to be placed on the Bar fell down on 31 March 1772, and the spikes on which the heads and other gruesome remains were placed, were removed at the beginning of the nineteenth century. Until 1753 the gates were locked every night, but in that year the City Corporation ordered that the posterns for pedestrians be kept open all night.

In 1787 the Court of Common Council discussed a proposal for the removal of the gate on the grounds that it was causing congestion to the free flow of Fleet Street, but the proposition was happily lost by one vote and the gate was saved for another hundred years.

The funeral of Sir Joshua Reynolds was held in St. Paul's on Saturday 3 March 1792 and the Lord Mayor gave instructions that the gates to Temple Bar were to be closed and locked by 10 o'clock and that all traffic in the City should cease 'lest the service be disturbed'. An eye witness writing in the Gentleman's Magazine narrates how Sir Joshua Banks, President of the Royal Society, was unavoidably detained firstly by attendance at a Board of Longitude 'until late', and, after every effort to join the funeral of his old friend and colleague, he was still prevented from entering the City by reason of the Lord Mayor's order.

Some fourteen years later new gates were made and hung and Temple Bar was suitably draped in mourning for the State Funeral of Lord Nelson, on 9 January 1806, when the funeral car, fashioned at front and back to resemble the bows and stern of HMS 'Victory', proceeded through the arch en route to its resting place, St. Paul's.

In 1821 the funeral of Caroline, unfortunate Queen of George IV, passed through the arch on its way to the docks. The crowds in Fleet Street were most indignant of the royal treatment meted to their

Queen and it was feared at the time that they would show their disgust. Doors and windows were barricaded by the shopkeepers, but when news reached the crowd that the Guard had been called out to scatter an affray at Cumberland Gate, Hyde Park, and that three of the rioters were reported killed, this acted as a deterrent and the procession passed through Temple Bar with no more ado than booing from the populace.

During the late eighteenth and early nineteenth centuries a number of political riots caused the habitual closure of Temple Bar and the gates were locked. The John Wilkes mob on 10 May 1768 attempted to stop a procession of citizens on their way to St. James' with a petition asking for the Crown to put down sedition that was going on. The City Marshal and Sheriffs were even pelted with mud when they attempted to open the gate. In 1830 a riot ensued over the Reform Bill and the Gate was locked: To be followed in 1832 when the crowds rose up and chased their national hero, the Duke of Wellington himself, through the Temple Bar and up Chancery Lane. Temple Bar was closed during the Gordon Riots because it was feared that the Bank of England would be attacked. From that time and until its demolition, sentries from a detachment of Foot Guards would march through Temple Bar every night to take post at the Bank.

Queen Victoria passed under Temple Bar on 9 November 1837 to attend the first Lord Mayor's Day of her reign at the Guildhall.

On 14 September 1852 the Duke of Wellington,

Lord Warden of the Cinque Ports, died at his official residence Walmer Castle, in Kent. After a preliminary lying-in-state at the castle, the body was brought to London to lie in state in the great hall of Wren's Royal Hospital, Chelsea. For most of his life this great soldier and statesman had dominated the public scene and in doing so had earned the highest respect from the people of this country and abroad. Queen Victoria summed this up in her speech at the Opening of Parliament on 11 November 1852 when she spoke of 'that illustrious man whose great achievements have exalted the name of England'. Few people could remember an England uninfluenced by Wellington and they now held a deep sense of personal loss.

The day before the funeral the body of the 'Iron Duke' was moved to the Horse Guards. On 18 November 1852, the procession passed through the arch of Temple Bar on its way to the service at St. Paul's Cathedral. In splendour it was the greatest state funeral ever given to a subject of the realm, exceeding those given to our other great heroes, Admiral Viscount Nelson (1806), Field-Marshal Lord Roberts (1914) and even that of Sir Winston Churchill (1965) all of whom passed by the site of Temple Bar on their way to St. Paul's.

The funeral car of the Iron Duke was specially designed by Gottfried Semper and built of English oak clad with the gun-metal melted down from cannon recovered from the battlefield of Waterloo (1815). Both metal and wood were richly worked with figures, in relief, mouldings and battle honours, and adorned with displays of Corps and Regimental

292

Colours, weapons and accoutrements and the kettle drums of the regiment of the Household Cavalry. The vehicle weighed 18 tons and although it is said to have been manufactured at Woolwich Arsenal in 18 days by 100 men it is obvious that a lot of work must have been done in the preparation of moulds for casting and so on. The funeral car was drawn by twelve horses sporting large black plumes, and the entire car, fittings and horses were black. It was undoubtedly the largest, heaviest and in its own sombre way, the most magnificent vehicle ever to pass under the historic arch.

Fortunately this vehicle can still be seen, and stands at the west end of the Crypt in St. Paul's Cathedral. However it has been 'rifled' over the years by souvenir hunters to the dismay and astonishment of the Dean and Chapter. The canopy was later removed to the Crypt.

When a campaign was started by the newspapers in 1853 asking for the removal of Temple Bar, it had little effect on the public and the gate remained in virgo intacta. Temple Bar was magnificently decorated in 1863 when London welcomed Princess Alexandra, Consort of the future Edward VII, and, in February 1872 Temple Bar was (for the very last time) washed, cleaned and decorated on the occasion that Queen Victoria and the Prince of Wales passed at the Thanksgiving Service at St. Paul's held on 27 February for the recovery of the Prince from Typhoid fever.

After the buildings on its north side were demolished on 22 March 1868 a verdict on Temple

Bar came in a report that it was unsafe. It was finally taken down in January 1878 with the building of the new Law Courts. For long it lay in pieces in a yard off Farringdon Road before Sir Henry Bruce Meux, the well-known London brewer, paid the expense of its removal to his estate at Theobalds Park near Waltham Cross in Hertfordshire, where it was re-erected in 1880 and presently stands.

Theobalds Park was for many years the home of the Cecil family while the Tudor Dynasty owned nearby Hatfield House. As was his wont, James I took a liking to Theobalds Park, and 'made' an agreement with Robert Cecil to exchange their properties, which was confirmed in an Act of Parliament of 1607, and it was at Theobalds Park that James died on 27 March 1625. It may have been by design or just a coincidence that some 250 years after his death, His Majesty returned to Theobalds in the form of one of the four effigies on Temple Bar.

Links with the Lord Mayors of London were not yet passed and on the 22 September 1935 the Lord Mayor then in Office, Sir Stephen Killik, passed through the ancient portals of Temple Bar as the guest of Alderman Sir George and Lady Collins who were then the owners of Theobalds Park, and of course the historic gate itself, Sir Stephen became the first Lord Mayor in office — and possibly the only one — to have passed under the gateway since its removal from London.

From the outset there were many people

who, although understanding the need for its removal from a busy thoroughfare, nevertheless regretted that, being so interwoven with the traditions and history of the City, it was not possible to find a closer home for Temple Bar, in either the City itself or at the very least in central London.

Several moves have been made since to have this famous relic of old London returned to a suitable site within the capital. In 1960 Lord Mottistone, when Surveyor to the Fabric of St. Paul's Cathedral, produced a drawing, in concert with Lord Holford, showing it against the north elevation of the North-west Tower of the Cathedral and forming the entrance arch through which the public could walk into St. Paul's Churchyard on the north side. This would undoubtedly be a fine site for it, nestled beside Wren's great masterpiece.

The Trustees of the Meux Estate, the present owners, have offered this national monument to the City of London since 1948. They are delighted at the positive proposal now being carried out (which may coincide with the anniversary of H.M. the Queen's Silver Jubilee) to save Temple Bar for the nation.*

The author is involved in the project to save Temple Bar and wishes to draw attention to the great assistance being given by innumerable dignitaries of the City, members of government departments, and others, to the scheme.

Today more than ever before Temple Bar reflects neglect. The drive leading to the house over which this gate sat has been diverted elsewhere, and this historic gate through whose portals have passed the Crowned heads of state, their families, the great Citizens of the Common Wealth, and this National monument which has shared with the people of England, of joys and sorrow, ceremonies, pomp and pageantry, which stood for two hundred years as the symbol of the old independence of the City of London, Temple Bar now stands roofless and derelict yet, ever proud, behind an enclosing fence of concrete, beer bottles and barbed wire. The gate may yet be saved and restored to its former glory — its masonry repaired, and its statuary made good — but time is of the essence. All this must be done while those sculptors and stone masons capable of undertaking this class of work are still active, and these artists, who served their apprenticeship with Wren's architecture after the last war, will not be able to bequeath their wealth of knowledge beyond their lifetime.

In the meantime, the old gate waits peacefully, in the solitude of the park, and in the stillness of dusk and echoes still to the sounds and footsteps of yesteryear who frequented Temple Bar, the mascot of Legal London and the City.

Her time is nigh.

CHAPTER 12

ANGLO-AMERICAN ESSAYS

by Professor John M. Crawford

THE AMERICAN CONNECTION

> There is no such thing as a successful system of education in a vacuum, that is to say, a system which is divorced from immediate contact with the existing intellectual atmosphere. Education which is not modern shares the fate of all organic things which are kept too long.[1]

It may be a temptation for a legal thinker to suppose that legal facts, propositions, sentences, and all of the machinery of justice exists in some pure and simple form which is removed from the ethos of everyday life. One may yield to this temptation and begin to believe that the conceptual life of the law is led in a state of sheltered and historical purity. It is an easy step from there to begin to believe that one can produce, without a need to attend to historical differences, a symmetrical and wholesome comparison between the 'parts' of one system and another system. One might even attempt to show how one system evolved from the other. We seem to enjoy creating our own myths.

I doubt if one must, of necessity, yield to this temptation. Judicious thinkers have not.[2]

299

In this chapter I wish to talk somewhat about legal education in England at the Inns of Court, and how that education differed from education for the law in the United States of America. When the reforming spirit in legal education began to move through the Inns of Court in the early nineteenth century, already in America law schools had been established and legal education would develop there in its own way. It is true that the renaissance in American legal education did not begin until the latter part of the nineteenth century when writers like Holmes or Brandeis or Wharton had begun to write and be felt in the legal community.

The two countries, England and America, certainly had a common law. The decisions in one country would be used in the other country, more English decisions moving to influence early American notions of torts or contracts. In constitutional law the American tradition would rather much be unto itself, and there the Supreme Court of the land would introduce fresh notions into its case law, albeit showing respect to the English authors and decisions.[3] 'It was well in the 1800s before court systems with appellate courts were generally established. A new country differing in nearly every respect from England called for law suited to its own conditions.'[4] A distinction could be made between substance of the law and ritual in the law. There may have been transferences of substance, one case in an English jurisdiction influencing decisions in a state jurisdiction in the United States, while the ritual of the English law (as when a judge enters the court carrying a bouquet of posies to symbolise and remind us that the flowers were thought to be able to ward off the plague during the period of the Black Death) would not be carried over into American courts and manners.

No legal system can be transported like a package from one country to another. When the House of Lords decided *D.P.P. v. Smith* [1961] A.C. 290 the law which it developed, or announced, in regard to the law of homicide was promptly renounced by the High Court in Australia when, in *Parker v. The Queen* (1963) 111 C.L.R. 610, it said that the decision of the House of Lords should not be considered binding in law in Australia. What is done in one common law jurisdiction does not imply that the same will be done in some other jurisdiction. When the Criminal Law Revision Committee[5] recommended,

> 28. We propose to restrict greatly the so-called 'right of silence' enjoyed by suspects when interrogated by the police or by anyone charged with the duty of investigating offences or charging offenders. By the right of silence in this connection we mean the rule that, if the suspect, when being interrogated, omits to mention some fact which would exculpate him, but keeps this back till trial, the court or jury may not infer that his evidence on this issue at the trial is untrue. Under our proposal it will be permissible to draw this inference if the circumstances justify it. The suspect will still have the 'right of silence' in the sense that it is no offence to refuse to answer questions or tell his story when

301

interrogated; but if he chooses to exercise this right, he will risk having an adverse inference drawn against him at his trial.

the Committee certainly did not have before its eyes the opinion of Mr. Justice Sutherland in *Powell v. Alabama* 287 U.S. 45, 53 S. Ct. 55, 77 L. Ed. 158 (1932), who stated that an intelligent layman, let alone an unlettered person, is often not his own best judge of what to say or not to say when charged in a criminal case, and that the unskilled, however honest, might make admissions damaging to themselves when the case went for trial. Later Supreme Court decisions have affirmed this. In other matters the American Supreme Court did not think that it should be bound to follow itself[6] absolutely, and would reverse itself when needed; this doctrine came late to the House of Lords.[7] In a recent case in the Court of Appeal[8] Lord Denning, M.R. remarked,

4 Conclusion

In my opinion, therefore, *Remmington v. Larchin* (1921) 3 KB 404, (1921) All ER Rep 298 is no authority on the 1968 Act (i.e. Rent Act 1968, various sections discussed in the case); and *Zimmerman v. Grossman* (1971) 1 All ER 363, (1972) 1 QB 167 was wrongly decided. So much so that I do not think it is binding on us. *I have often said that I do not think this court should be absolutely bound by its previous decisions, any more than the House of Lords.* (italics mine) I know it is said that when this court is satisfied that a previous decision of its own was wrong, it should not overrule it but

302

should apply it in this court and leave it to the House of Lords to overrule it. Just think what this means in this case. These ladies do not qualify for legal aid. They must go to the expense themselves of an appeal to the House of Lords to get the decision revoked. The expense may deter them and thus an injustice will be perpetrated. In any case I do not think it right to compel them to do this when the result is a foregone conclusion. I would let them save their money and reverse it here and now.

I would allow the appeal, accordingly.

The other two justices, Lord Justice Lawton and Lord Justice Scarman commiserated with Lord Denning, M.R., but did not allow the appeal. Lord Justice Scarman could say 'I happen to think that a wrong turning was taken by the Court of Appeal in 1921 *(Remmington)*. But only the legislature, or the House of Lords in its judicial capacity, can put the courts on what I believe to be the right road.'[9] And Lord Justice Lawton, joining Scarman, L.J., in disallowing the appeal could say,

As did *Zimmerman v. Grossman,* This appeal has revealed a gap which Parliament has left (whether wittingly or unwittingly I know not) in its attempts to prevent the exploitation of those in need of houses or flats. Many would think that this gap should be closed as quickly as possible. I certainly do. *I would close it at once if I could;* (italics mine) but, in my opinion, I could only do so by stretching the law. Adapting Shakespeare's words, I might be doing a great

303

> right but I would be doing a little wrong and as
> Portia said [Merchant of Venice, IV.i.220]:
> 'Twill be recorded for a precedent, And many an
> error by the same example will rush into the
> state. It cannot be.'
>
> I would dismiss the appeal.[10]

Judicial restraint is seldom so modestly defended and advanced, especially in paraphrase of a speech itself highly ironic!

It is easy for one to forget, or simply to be unaware of, that the past is not just an older picture of what we see now in the present. Legal education in America was not a transplant from England, and the Inns of Court, however homey in this year of independence it might seem to suggest. Americans did travel abroad to become members of one of the four Inns of Court.[11] Godwin states that

> ... between 1750 and 1755 large numbers of
> students from the colonies were admitted to the
> Middle Temple. About half a century later there
> were no less than two hundred and thirty-six
> American-born barristers on the Inns of Court,
> one hundred and forty-six being Middle
> Templars.[12]

Americans travelled to the Inns and apprenticed themselves there and then returned again to the colonies, as did Edward Rutledge, a signer of the Declaration of Independence. But legal education at the Inns had fallen into decay,

> The decay of the Inns of Court seems not to
> have excited, for two hundred and fifty years,
> any adverse comment. But towards the middle

304

of this reforming century many influential
lawyers were impressed with the need of a better
preparation for admission to the Bar.[13]

Professor Ames had made these observations in 1901
when he spoke at the dedication of a new building at
the law school of the University of Pennsylvania.
When the revolution did arrive, and when normal
colonial life was disrupted, the influence of English
legal writers still made its impression upon American
minds in spite of a war.[14] James Kent, in a letter to a
friend, dated 6 October 1828, from New York says of
a period of his youth during the time of the
revolution,

> ... When the College was broken up and
> dispersed in July 1779 by the British, I retired
> to a country village and finding Blackstone's
> com. I read the 4th volume, parts of the work
> struck my taste, and the work inspired me at the
> age of 16 with awe, and I fondly determined to
> be a lawyer.[15]

Maitland observed that twenty-five hundred copies of
Blackstone's *Commentaries* reached the colonies, as
well as mentioning Kent's awe of Blackstone
(although he gives Kent's age as fifteen), and he said
that John Marshall read a copy which was his
father's.[16]

Education in good part reflects temperament, and
to judge the temperament of the times may be more
of an aesthetic impression than it would a factual
assessment.[17] The United States seemed to be a more
fertile soil for legal teaching, but, I fear, that
comment must be carefully qualified. It could easily

305

be misunderstood. The habit of the English legal mind, as seen in and through the Inns of Court, has been towards a social conservatism. There have been great scholars who came out of the Inns of Court, and who lived there, but their scholarship never impressed large numbers at the Bar, or on the Bench. English lawyers tend to think that law is a practical art, and that if one wishes to be jurisprudential or theoretical in one's approach to the study of law, then it would be best for one to take oneself off to the academy where purer realms of thought are to be found. Certainly this is a rum view of university life, but it does permeate the English Bar, and it is not without its pitfalls. If the academy is viewed as ivory-towered, then the exchanges between the Bench and the university can be tinged with acrimony, each, in some way, distrusting the other. In his chapter concerning judicial appointments (coming as they do only from the Bar and not from the university), Mr. Justice Megarry gives an accurate picture of the differences in English legal life which are not to be found, for the most part, in American legal life:

> But in the end I would not be unduly astonished if what seems to be the predominant view at the Bar were proved to be right. I would also harbour the suspicion that the academic mind, accustomed to contemplating the great verities of the law, might recoil from the great bulk of the humdrum work, devoid of academic interest and ranging over territory little honoured in the academic world, which forms the daily fare of even appellate courts.[18]

306

The effects of this division can, as I suggested earlier ago, show how fierce the differences of opinion can be on common matters between the Bench and the University. When he came to deliver his Lionel Cohen lectures some years ago (and which he had intended not to have printed) Professor Glanville Williams, Q.C., of Jesus College, Cambridge, said in his preface:

> ... the continuing lack of agreement upon basic concepts appears to make it essential to continue the task of discussing what might at first sight be the kindergarten part of the criminal law.[19]

It was an abrupt and precise rebuttal of the legal opinions which Lord Denning, Master of the Rolls, had espoused in his own Lionel Cohen lecture for 1961, entitled *Responsibility before the Law.* The academic opinions of Lord Denning's lecture seemed to suggest that his theories about the nature of the criminal law were not responsible theories, and much critical ink flowed in the English law journals to suggest that the academics, and not the Bench, saw the true light.[20] The century earlier, when John Austin, a barrister of Inner Temple, gave his lectures on jurisprudence in 1832, as brilliant as they were, they were rather much a failure if the measure of success meant that one had attracted a large audience of barristers and judges, and then changed their minds noticeably. The *Preface* by Sarah Austin, John Austin's wife, to his *Lectures on Jurisprudence* tell us that however brilliant were his lectures on the subject, nevertheless, '... as jurisprudence formed no part of the necessary or ordinary studies of a barrister, his professorship became nearly an empty title.'[21] For the Inns themselves, living relics of mediaeval sociability and of mediaeval ritual and role where one prepared himself to be a gentleman, what need would there be for formal and abstract lectures on jurisprudence when law was viewed purely as a practical and non-academic life? That the Bar, from the early part of the nineteenth century, was moved to change, in some way, by forces within it would have been hard to predict. The changes were not embraced openly, as testimony shows.[22]

One of the more curious of answers given during the course of the inquiry on whether legal education ought to have been reformed was that proffered by Lord Brougham. His reply deserves our attention:

> *Question:* 3801. It is proposed to have a public examination previously to admission to the Bar?
> *Reply:* None of the Inns of Court have gone the length of saying that there must be a public examination to qualify. They consider that a very difficult and delicate matter. They doubt whether without the help of the Legislature they would have the right to do it. A person, as the law now stands, upon being entered at one of the Inns of Court, has an inchoate right to be called to the bar; and if the Inns of Court were to prescribe, as a condition precedent of obtaining the exercise of that right, the attending any class, or much more, answering questions satisfactorily at any examination, we conceive that we should be immediately at-

tacked in a court of law, because it would be said that we have no right to close the doors.[23]

One may wish to reform and to introduce standards, but what reason would one have to reform a living institution which functioned properly? To ask that it function *well* is to commit oneself to a serious category mistake; namely, to confuse the category of 'ritual' with the category of 'manufacture'. One does not ask the Archbishop if he conducted the services in the cathedral efficiently; on the other hand one may ask after the automobile workers at British Leyland if they work efficiently.

By turning to a notion in sacramental theology one may consider one of its Latin maxims: *ex opere operato,* a translation of which means 'from the work it is effected (*or* worked)'. The force of this expression is to suggest that a ritual, i.e. the doing of it, or the working of it, justifies itself; the effectiveness of the ritual is to be revealed through its performance, and the performance, the very doing itself, is connected to the forces of the culture in which the ritual is exercised. One need not measure the ritual itself by an appeal to a third party, an alien standard or an arbiter, since the excellence rests within the ritual itself revealed in its performance by the actor. The ritual is accepted, and it is a force of the culture, expressing cultural forms and acceptances and life. The soul of a culture and its organic embodiments are present in ritual workings.

If the Latin maxim is varied slightly (as it was during sacramental controversies in the past) to read, *ex opere operantis,* 'form the work of the worker' we are led to consider the efforts themselves which the worker effects; it is the doer of the ritual who and which is important, and not simply the ritual itself which is important. Ritual now has brought into its basic conceptual components not only the simple notion of 'to do' but it is overshadowed by other components. Worth, or efficiency, or the performer *qua* performer (his own personal qualities, his excellence, his character), are categories against which the ritual, the doing, is to be measured. The ritual is to be checked against other than itself. The doer of the ritual now brings along with himself a measure of the success, or − often forgotten − a capacity to fail and not to achieve. He may win, or he may lose; he may himself do the ritual, or he may be invigilated while doing the ritual, and judged by other than himself.

The degree to which one can participate in a ritual shows if the ritual is living or is dead. If the roots of the ritual be lost, if the ritual is no longer rooted within the workings of its culture, then what the ritual expresses is not a substance but only a form. *Ex opere operantis* either may import a dependence upon eligibility, as when one would say that a person may be eligible for admission to practice at the Bar *because* he is a member of an Inn of Court (as Lord Brougham was wont to suggest), or it may mean, in addition to this aspect, that eligibility to do (this or that) arises because a candidate has met some external standard, has proved himself able to do. Simple 'eligibility' is conjoined to 'utility'. A confusion which possibly may arise develops when one

310

considers that the concept 'eligibility' must necessarily include, or be conjoined to, the concept 'utility'. It may, and it may not. How is one to provide a clear rule to decide what should or should not be the case? Lord Brougham wanted 'utility', as a category of measure, to be excluded from eligibility. If one introduces some other conceptual feature, and suggests that the feature may or may not be a necessary feature upon a prior feature, that 'eligibility' must be linked to 'utility', then one begins to undermine the force of a ritual in itself; the ritual does not work itself by simply being performed, and, likewise, it does not justify itself by simply being worked by the worker. *Ex opere operato* falls to the heretical side of the pack. One may attempt to make a compromise (a medieval rite may be changed from being performed in Latin, from which it sprung, and may be put into English, which is alien to its ritual forms) but a compromise tends to reveal that the ritual is no longer connected to the living forces and substance of its culture. To be maintained henceforth it must be preserved or embalmed. Judges will walk into court holding bouquets of posies not because they believe resolutely that the bouquet will ward off the plague, but because it was once done, and now, in ritual mumification, is preserved.

I do not think what I have discussed is that strange to us today, although the particular way in developing the notion by appeal to notions from sacramental theology may, at first sight, be strange for one's eyes. Modern comparisons readily come to mind. The increase of malpractice suits throughout

311

the United States of America show that the 'common man' is asking, in the most forceful of civilised ways to put a question by use of a court, 'How do I know that this doctor, or lawyer, or dentist, or academic, or contractor, or pharmaceutical firm, or other professional body, is to be relied upon?' The soaring cost of malpractice insurance premiums show that question, when answered in a court of law, is bothersome and expensive. In England,* at the Bar, the ritual compromise at least protects a barrister against malpractice suits. He may not be sued for lack of professional competence, and, in that way, *ex opere operato* does still work in the life of the Bar. Some, however, suggest that such a privilege exists because of judicial arbitrariness, and has little justification in the course of normal life. By way of a token *quid pro quo* a barrister may not sue for fees owing to him by a solicitor, for, in theory, no contractual fees owe. A barrister receives an honorarium: namely, a voluntary token from another to him in recognition of his merit and worth.

Lord Brougham did believe that the forces of the market place would adequately judge the worth or unworth of a barrister's ability, just as a congregation need not to have attended the services of a cleric which it disliked, whatever the true reasons. When a further question was put to Lord Brougham he said,
    Question: 3802. Could it not be made con-

---

* Followed recently in New Zealand in *Rees v. Sinclair* [1974] 1 NZLR 180, which held that a barrister who was conducting a law case is not liable for an action for professional negligence against him because of his conduct of the case. *Rondel v. Worsley* [1969] 1 AC 191 was applied.

ditional upon entering the Inns of Court, that
the student should bind himself to submit to
such examination?

Reply: It might be made so; but all the subjects
of the King have a right to enter at the Inns of
Court, and that inchoate right would be inter-
fered with. It would be just removing the
difficulty a step farther, and bringing it on at an
earlier stage. It would be preventing a person
from becoming a member of any of the Inns of
Court; and I have grave doubt whether the Inns
of Court have the power of imposing any such
condition; indeed I have very little doubt that
they have not. It is to be observed, that an unfit
person acquires no benefit from his call to the
bar; he only becomes capable of practising, if he
can obtain clients.[24]

Continuing, he went on to state that if entrance
examinations and legal examinations were to be
desired, then it would be a better form to attract
candidates and aspirants to the Bar by appealing to
their sense of honour rather than to resort to the
force of legislation in order to reach a state of
approbation. If one did distinguish himself in an
examination, the taking of which would be
honourary, then the merits of success could be turned
to profit, and, most likely, clients would seek out
counsel who had elevated themselves through voluntary efforts at self-improvement. But compulsory
examinations in themselves, he believed, ought not to
form any part of life at the Bar. We can see, can we
not, how part of his sentiment has found its way into

313

the American legal profession when law firms give preferential consideration to an applicant who has distinguished himself by membership of a law review?

Times change. Slowly the Inns began to establish conditions for entrance, but the conditions were mild ones. The testimony given the next day of the hearing, 14 August 1846, tells one of the eventual signs of the times. Lord Campbell, distinguished for his lives of the chancellors, disagreed with the sentiments expressed by Lord Brougham, and is reported to have said, in the record of the investigation,

> 3852. The Inns of Court would be very much to blame, and would be liable to the censure of Parliament, if they were to lay down any capricious or unreasonable conditions — but if they were to say, 'You are not to be called to the bar till you have attended such and such lectures, and gone through such and such examinations,' I think no one would have any right to complain.[25]

The outcome of it all was a compromise, urged, rather much, by Richard Bethell, a Bencher of Middle Temple, and later to have been elevated to the peerage as Lord Westbury. One may read through the archives of Middle Temple, for the period, to see how he himself moved others from amongst the other Inns, and in his own Inn, from 1845 onwards during various parliamentary meetings in the Inns with their Benchers to consider seriously that the reform of legal education ought to be conjointly undertaken by the four Inns of Court. The formal learning of the law

314

during that period he, and others, saw to be abysmal.[26] When the *Report* of 1846 appeared with its voluminous testimony by Benchers, Treasurers, and visiting scholars, the ferment and dissatisfaction with what had been the case and optimism caused the four Inns of Court to come together (and that was and is no mean feat) and, by means of a joint resolution, to empowered and found the Council of Legal Education. The Council began in 1852, Bethell having been appointed its first Chairman. The modern period had begun for the Inns, but they would never undertake to enter it with vigour. When, during the 1960s of our century, the Inns did undertake to reform how they educated students for the Bar (because the students had protested so loudly) the education would still be modest, certainly by standards present in American and Canadian law schools, and what was offered through the Council of Legal Education (an entity of the Senate of the four Inns of Court) for legal education would never escape severe criticism by its own English critics.[27]

The practice of law in the two countries, America and England, though moved by the method of the common law, developed in different ways. The American practice and example has been to permit easy movement in and out of the profession. A man may have a flourishing commercial practice, and then he may decide to teach law formally at a law school, or he may move to advise government (as did Professor Archibald Cox, who moved from his distinguished post at Harvard, to become Solicitor-General [and then Dean Erwin Griswold after him], then

315

back to Harvard to teach, then again to Special
Prosecutor, and then — alas — back again to Harvard)
or after all of this, be promoted to the Federal Bench,
or elected to the State judiciary. There seems not to
be a dislike and distrust of academic pursuits within
the course of a career in law in the United States; in
England, to the contrary, this easy movement, nor
the desire for such an easy movement in the
profession, is not to be witnessed. If a man is
appointed to the Bench, there he stays. One could
not retire, as one might in the United States, to
resume the practice of law. If one enters into his Inn,
and seeks chambers there, one remains as a practising
barrister. If one 'dabbles' in academic life too, one
has a good chance of damaging his career at the Bar.
One is *either* an academic; *or* a barrister in chambers.
One cannot be like Wittgenstein's 'duck-rabbit' in his
Philosophical Investigations: looked at one way the
image is that of a rabbit, whilst looked at in another
way the image appears to be that of a duck. No, at
the Bar, one cannot be an 'academic-lawyer'. Some
have felt that this rigid caste distinction, a strong
vestige of unreason in the social life of the Bar, harms
it, and tends to make it insular and parochial, and
conservative in the perjorative sense of that word.
The English Bar, in this regard, could certainly learn
much of value from the American Bar and the sense
of personal freedom which is present at the American
Bar.[28]

The Council of Legal Education continued to
develop, but it, and the Inns, were subjected to
criticism in the nineteenth century. For example, on

18 March 1862, Sir George Bowyer, joined by others, presented a private members bill in Parliament '... for the better government of the Inns of Court, and for Discipline of the Bar.'[29] Some years later (for time did not move all that fast in legal life of the Inns) saw the 1875-76 session of Parliament post the introduction of the INNS OF COURT BILL which, in effect, was another attempt to desacrilise the power and control which the Inns exercised over the life and education and government not only of its students, but over all of its members.[30] One does not have to be under attack for long to initiate a self-defence, and such was undertaken by the then Treasurer of the Honourable Society of the Middle Temple, George Loch, Esq., who prepared a reply, part of which I quote from his notes:[31]

> That your Petitioners have for a considerable period been engaged, in concert with the other Inns of Court, in establishing a system of Legal Education, of which the results, so far as ascertained, are satisfactory, and afford promise of being so hereafter in an increasing degree.
>
> That this system, intended as it is for the Legal instruction of Students for the Bar, is deemed, by those who have made themselves acquainted with its arrangements, to be well adapted for that subject.

Loch may sound like an educational sociologist to us now, but he was not. He was making a few simple debating defence points, chief of which he did not want Parliament, or any committee of it, to have control over the Inns. It is a fear to this day of many in the Inns of Court that Parliament might cause to be done to the Inns what it did to the medical profession after the Second World War; namely, nationalise it, and make it a composition of medical 'workers' paid for by the state. Loch could in no way have sensed the fears of today that such could happen. His claims were modest. He believed that the new scheme of legal education, in the hands of the Inns once again as it had been during Elizabethan and Stuart times, demonstrated in a satisfactory way that the Inns were their own best governors, and what was best for the Inns of Court would, on the whole, be best for legal England too. It would take the better part of a future hundred years, the forces of decaying industrial capitalism, and the pressures of a declining England after 1945 to intimate to some that the times were a-changing, and that the Bar would not be spared the forces of change, however carefully it tried to deny that those forces were present.

J. M. B. Crawford, A.B., M.A., Middle Temple.
May 1976

REFERENCES

[1] *The Organisation of Thought,* by A. N. Whitehead (LONDON, Williams and Norgate, 1917) at page 70.

[2] For the growth and development of English law, and how its cases influenced American law, one may see: *An Introduction to Legal Reasoning* by Edward H. Levi (Chicago, 1949); *Foundations of Legal Liability* by T. A. Street (1906, New York, in three volumes); 'Foreseeability in Negligence Law' by Leon Green, COLUMBIA LAW REVIEW, Vol. LXI, No. 8, December, 1961; *The Common Law,* by Oliver Wendell Holmes, esp. chapters II-IX (BOSTON, Little, Brown, and Company, 1881).

[3] cf. Marshall, C. J., showing how the English authorities were 'unsatisfactory' to understand what 'levying war' meant in *United States v. Aaron Burr* [4 Cranch's Reports, Appendix, 470]. cf. 'The Development of the Doctrine of Stare Decisis and the Extent to Which It Should Be Applied' by Leon Green, ILLINOIS LAW REVIEW, Vol. XL, No. 3, Jan-Feb., 1946, at pages 312-318 to show how American and English doctrines differed regarding *stare decisis* in colonial America.

[4] ibid., Green, page 312. Also cf. 'Case Law in England and America' which comprises Chapter III of *Essays in Jurisprudence and the Common Law* by Professor A. L. Goodhard (CAMBRIDGE, At the University Press, 1931) at pages 50-74.

[5] ELEVENTH REPORT, Evidence (General), Cmnd. 4991 (*London*, Her Majesty's Stationery Office, June, 1972), page 16.

[6] 'In *Washington v. Dawson and Co.* 264 U.S. 219, 238; 44 Sup. Ct. 302, 309 [1924], Mr. Justice Brandeis cites twelve instances in which the Supreme Court has reversed itself' as cited in Goodhart, page 58, 'Case Law in England and America'.

[7] H.L. [1966] 3 A11 ER 77, statement of the Lord Chancellor to the effect that the House of Lords had the freedom to depart from their previous decisions where it was right to do so.

'Before judgments were given in the House of Lords on July 26, 1966, LORD GARDINER, L.C., made the following statement on behalf of himself and the Lords of Appeal in Ordinary:

Their lordships regard the use of precedent (1) as an indispensable foundation upon which to decide what is the law and its application to individual cases. It provides at least some degree of certainty upon which individuals can rely in the conduct of their affairs, as well as a basis for orderly development of legal rules.

Their lordships nevertheless recognise that too rigid adherence to precedent may lead to injustice in a particular case and also unduly restrict the proper development of the law. They propose therefore to modify their present practice and, while treating former decisions of this House as normally binding, to depart from a previous decision when it appears right to do so.

In this connexion they will bear in mind the danger of disturbing retrospectively the basis on which contracts, settlements of property and fiscal arrangements have been entered into and also the especial need for certainty as to the criminal law.

This announcement is not intended to affect the use of precedent elsewhere than in this House.'

Also cf. 10 HALSBURY'S LAWS OF ENGLAND, 4 ed., Vol. 10, pages 341-342, parag. *745-*

[8] *Farrell v. Alexander* [1976] 1 A11 ER 129 at 137 e-g.

[9] ibid., page 147 e.

[10] ibid., page 143 e-g.

[11] cf. *The Middle Temple* by George Godwin (LONDON, Staples Press Limited, 1954), chapter XV, 'American Templars', pages 144-151.

[12] ibid., at page 146.

[13] 'The Vocation of the Law Professor' in *Lectures on Legal History,* by James Barr Ames (Harvard University Press, 1913) at page 355.

[14] cf. *Law and Lawyers in the United States,* by Dean Erwin N. Griswold (LONDON, Stevens & Sons, 1964) who showed how the traditions from England were transformed by Americans after the revolution of 1776.

[15] Volume one, page 838, in *Select Essays in Anglo-American Legal History* (LONDON, Wildy & Sons, 1968), 'An American Law Student of a Hundred Years Ago'.

[16] *English Law and the Renaissance* by Frederic William Maitland (CAMBRIDGE, At the University Press, 1901) at page 32.

[17] cf., Chapter IV, 'Harvard College (1854-1858)' in *The Education of Henry Adams,* An Autobiography (BOSTON and NEW YORK, Houghton Mifflin Company, September, 1918) pages 54-69.

[18] *Lawyer and Litigant in England,* by R. E. Megarry, Q.C. (as he then was at the time of writing the book), (LONDON, Stevens & Sons Ltd., 1962) at pages 121-122.

[19] *The Mental Element in Crime,* by Glanville Williams, LL.D., F.B.A. (JERUSALEM, The Hebrew University, 1965) at page 5.

[20] cf., the review of J. E. Hall Williams of *Responsibility before the Law* in THE MODERN LAW REVIEW, Vol. 25, Nov. 1962, pages 754-755, 'Even if Dr. Williams' attack on *D.P.P. v. Smith* went a little too far in its criticism of Viscount Kilmuir's speech, one fears that Lord Denning's lecture must be regarded as a rather unconvincing attempt to defend the indefensible. It might have been better to have dissented at the time rather than to have regrets afterwards.' at page 755.

[21] *Lectures on Jurisprudence* (2 vols.) by John Austin, as edited and revised by Robert Campbell (LONDON, John Murray, 3rd edition, 1869) page 9, volume one.

[22] cf., Parliamentary Papers, volume 473 (Middle Temple Library) for the period 1827-1846, REPORT FROM THE SELECT COMMITTEE ON LEGAL EDUCATION, House of Commons, 25th of August, 1846.

[23] ibid., page 285.

[24] ibid.

[25] ibid., page 293.

[26] If one reads through the *Syllabus or the Heads of Lectures publicly delivered in the University of Cambridge, 1797,* as arranged by Edward Christian, A.M. (who himself edited Blackstone), one will see that the law syllabus and lectures were little more than commonplace notes, with the topics under legal headings running seriatum, and

pages bound into the book on which a student could copy down lecture notes to expand upon the topical headings already printed in the book. The work was more of a simple legal catechism for a student than being a detailed book of law.

[27] cf. esp. 'Legal Education' by Jeremy Smith, Barrister, in the *Haldane Society Bulletin,* January 1974 (LONDON), pages 12-16; *What's Wrong With The Law?* edited by Michael Zander (published by the British Broadcasting Corporation, 1970), cf. 'Tomorrow's lawyers' pages 98-126: 'The Mid-Nineteenth Century Debate Concerning Legal Education' (part two) by Gillian Hawtin, pages 24-31, in Volume 3, Summer 1973, *Bulletin of the Haldane Society* (Lincoln's Inn, London, W.C.2.); 'Lawyers at the bar' *The Economist,* 21 February 1976, pages 15-16.

[28] One notices, too, how the Federal Bureau of Prisons of the Department of Justice in the United States has learned how to promote from within its ranks. Most wardens of penitentiaries in the Federal system have first been prison guards in the institutions prior to entering the administrative side of penal life. England, as a direct counter-example, does not appoint governors of H.M. Prisons from the ranks of the guards. The policy is rather much to keep separate and always distinct enlisted men from the officers. The American practice is much to be admired and imitated.

[29] Middle Temple Archives: INNS OF COURT GOVERNMENT BILL, House of Commons, 18th of March 1862 (Bill 43), as sponsored by Sir George Bowyer, Mr. W. Ewart, and a Mr. Hennessy.

[30] Middle Temple Archives: 'A Bill entitled: An Act to constitute a Council of the Four Inns of Court, Settled by Joint Committee, 5th of February 1876 (printed by: F. Cartwright, 57 Chancery Lane).

[31] Middle Temple Archives: the handwritten draught of a 'Petition Against the Bill of 1876 by George Loch, Esq., Treasurer of Middle Temple' pages two and three thereof.

COMMON FAITH AND COMMON LAW*

Conservatives and Reformers should alike welcome the revival of Moots in Gray's Inn, for it has been both a reform and a restoration. The only thing that surprises me is that the example should not have been followed elsewhere in the Inns of Court. In American law schools, the practice of argument in moot courts is treated not as a luxury or diversion, but as an obviously necessary part of legal education. But in our law schools, such as they are, it seems impossible at present to shake off the superstition that paper examinations are all-sufficient. When we have all become wiser, it will be remembered with gratitude that Gray's Inn showed the way to better things.

F. Pollock

November, 1896.[1]

O n Monday, 23 November 1896, Gray's Inn reinstated the ancient practice of holding moots

---

* I wish to thank Professor John Quinn, of the University of Dayton, in Dayton, Ohio, for his helpful, kind, and encouraging discussions on the matter of this chapter.

within the charming great hall of their Inn. Sir Frederick Pollock, Bart., presided.[2] The high period for accomplishment for the Inns *qua* Inns (when they were centres of instruction and initiation) from the middle sixteenth to the middle seventeenth centuries had passed, and from then onwards they had declined in spirit and vigour, which, like most declines into an unwelcome old age and state of desuetude, causes one to have a sense of sorrow for the beauty of what once was and is now no more. There had once been a thriving literary life in the Inns, Shakespeare and Jonson knowing it well, as well as lesser poets and dramatists.[3] Life then was not only lived within the walls of the Inns; it was to be found there in full power. One learned his law in the Inn then, he heard moots and readings on law and statutes, and he saw what a barrister and serjeant at law was as a public figure who had distinguished himself in the profession of the law.

One may choose from many examples. Robert Holborne, Esq., gave a reading in 'Lincolnes-Inne, Feb. 28, 1641. Vpon the STAT. of 25.E.3.cap 2, Being the Statute of TREASONS'. An eager student would hope to obtain a copy of the reading, either from notes he, or some other, would take during the reading, or obtain a printed copy of the reading, if it were printed. In this case Leonard Lichfield, from Oxford, issued Master Holborne's reading in 1642 in an offprint sixteen pages long. In the reading the definition of Treason is set forth, and historical annotations appear alongside the paragraphs of the text. A student, reading such, would be able to read

324

more on the matter by returning to the cited references. Then two separate cases are set out and discussed by Holborne, whence the lecture is completed by the third part, a lecture, on what constitutes petty treason: '. . . petty treason do very little differ from felonies, for by the pardon of all felonies, all petty treasons are pardoned'. More examples are then offered, case law and legal writers are cited, and his reading is concluded. The English practice still survives at university. When a professor is elected to a Chair he gives his inaugural lecture, and then it is published. This practice, however, seems not to have been adopted by American universities generally.

Have we made much improvement upon the teaching of law now? Before one attempts to answer the question it may be wise to ask if such a question can be answered at all; or is it as a question a psuedo-question because it masks some flaw by its grammatical form? The question, like the first trace of cancer, may have deeper roots than what is at first revealed in its public form, and to answer it at all one may have to ask about the nature of 'law' itself, and how that is related to the society in which it occurs, as well as what that society expects of its law. We seem to need to set off in order to return. We may need to look at how others thought law should be learned. In his inaugural lecture at Cambridge, Professor Stein remarked on how three major English legal thinkers learned about their law. It is a fine summary, and I quote it fully:[4]

> Bracton got his Roman law from the Glossators, Hale from the Humanists and Austin from the

325

Pandectists. In each case the English writer was affected by the form and tendency of his source. Bracton found a legal grammar with which he was able to build up a picture of English law in substantive rather than in procedural terms. Hale found an account of the parallel development of law and society from a primitive sophisticated system. Austin found the categories and tools of analysis with which to test the scientific quality of the law against an external standard. In each case their study of Roman law gave them more perspective and objectivity in facing the theoretical problems raised by the English law of their times. They could more easily see how far the problems could arise in any legal system and how far they were peculiar to English law.

But one may be asking two distinct questions and be not aware that distinctions are present within the asking. On the one hand one may be asking about the nature of law itself, 'What is law?' and then seek to frame an answer by turning to investigate various systems of law (which Stein suggested that his three authors did, to their own profit), or one may be asking a specific set of questions about one's own national body of law (what are the customs of the nation, its statutes, its judicial decisions, its various administrative instruments or tribunals, etc.), and then the question is transformed into, 'How ought one to learn the law of the land?' This subdivision in no way exhausts what elements could be present in the question. One may be asking a strictly juris-prudential question, 'What are the elements of a

system which makes it a legal system?' We may be
asking what kind of student ought to study law
(though a question of this type comes dangerously
close to being a species of 'legal phrenology', and one
is in danger of having candidates chosen by examinations made by professional examiners or by com-
puters programmed to select a type of undif-
ferentiated mass average)? and this leads one into
considering how humane the study of law ought to
be.[5 & 5a]

If one is asking how the law should be studied, we
have a rather clear and humble statement given by
Edmund Plowden in the preface to his *Commentaries,*
the preface being addressed '. . . to the Students of
the Common Law of England, and especially to his
Companions of the Middle-Temple . . .' whom he '. . .
wisheth encrease of Learning'.

> When I first entered upon the Study of Law,
> (which was in the twentieth Year of my Age,
> and in the thirtieth Year of the Reign of the late
> King Henry the Eight of famous Memory) I
> resolved upon two Things, which I then pur-
> posed earnestly to pursue. The first was, to be
> present at, and to give diligent Attention to, the
> Debates of Questions of Law, and particularly to
> the Arguments of those who were Men of the
> greatest Note and Reputation for Learning. The
> second way, to commit to Writing what I heard,
> and the Judgement thereupon, which seemed to
> me to be much better than to rely upon
> treacherous Memory which often deceives its
> Master. These two Resolutions I pursued ef-

fectually by a constant Attendance at Moots and Lectures, and at all Places in Court and Chancery, to which I might have Access, where Matters of Law were argued and debated. And finding that I reaped much Profit and Instruction by this Practice, I became at last disposed to report the Arguments and Judgements made and given in the King's Courts upon Demurrers in Law, as abounding more copiously with Matter of Improvement, and being more capable of perfecting the Judgement, than Arguments on other Occasions. Upon this I undertook first one Case and then another, by which Means I at last collected a good Volume. And this Work I originally entered upon with a View to my own private Instruction only, without the least Thought or Intention of letting it appear in Print. . . But these Reports were made and collected by no other than by myself alone, a Man of simple Understanding, and of weak Memory to retain Things uttered, and therefore I thought it more proper to keep them up in my own private Study (with which Design I at first collected them) than to make them public in the World. . . And at last, upon these and other Motives, and hoping that it might be of some Benefit to Students of the Law, I resolved (as you see I have done) to put it in Print.[6]

The date of his preface was 20 October 1578. Save for the quaintness of the language, could one read a clearer exposition of what it means (and meant) to study the law and to master what one has studied? If we take the time from Plowden to Matthew Hale, Chief Justice of the Court of King's Bench, who died in 1676 on Christmas Day, one could safely assert that he had the full measure of what the study of law might mean. If that is the case — my belief could be quite mistaken — have we learned much from our past from the Inns? Have we 'improved upon' Plowden or Hale, given as we are to a belief in progress, the fruits thereof?

To answer such a question, in whatever form it be put, 'How ought the law to be taught' needs us to locate ourselves in our own times. I said that the past is just not an older picture book of our present. As the past is different so is the present in which we live different. One is talking not only about a theory (how to teach) but one is giving an aesthetic preference (it is important to teach in this particular way). and then one looks to the familiar past (which Plowden and Hale embody for our own experience in common law countries) to see what was, and what is different from what was. Difference in itself does not imply that quality will result from what changes (if any) we introduce in our scheme of teaching. But we should at least be able to ask ourselves, 'Is what we are now doing different in any important way from what once was done?' It is not to be desired to entrap oneself into making comparisons of the wrong kind, 'wrong' being rather much understood by an appeal to our practical reason and experience.

Let me give several instances of what I am suggesting. Should a student, when a course continues on over one academic year (of three terms, or two semesters), be subjected to an annual comprehensive examination in the subject(s)? The concept and practice (in this day and age) of the annual examination seems, to me, to be a barbarous practice, and one which has a suspect rational justification, if at all. It is not a rational justification to assert that such a practice is done; that is to make an appeal to custom, and to assume that the custom is intellectually self-evident and self-justifying. It is not a justification (for the practice) to state that law professors do not like to give fortnightly examinations; that is to appeal to whimsy, or power, or to the status quo, or to the 'conventional wisdom'. If one aspect of the life of the law is its reason, then one would have thought that tribal rituals of the gruelling sort would long ago have been extinguished, and would have been replaced by more humane and sensible practices. During the infancy of the Council of Legal Education Sir Peter Edlin, Q.C., occupying then the chair for a meeting of the Board of Examiners for the Council, 10 January 1896, was able to state,

> 7. That there shall be an examination on paper in all cases, and a *viva voce* examination at the discretion of the Examiners.[7]

Our concept of what it means to examine will tell us something about how we see what we are doing. If we view our subject as one being practical and humane, then we ought to avoid using mechanical methods for testing, and we ought to employ methods which are more within the natural rhythm of time. If we are obsessed by mechanical time, then, no doubt, everything is made to fit into our pre-ordained schedule, and we do not trouble ourselves to question why we have pre-ordained the world in the way we have.

England and America have a great deal to share with one another about the law (as they do about many other matters). In England, if one reads law at a university, one enters his college at age seventeen or eighteen, and attends law lectures and tutorials for three years, thereupon graduating from university with his degree in law. He may stay on for one more year to convert his B.A. into an LL.B. But it is sufficient for him to take his degree in three years, attending college in three terms, each term approximately eight weeks in duration. He will have come down from his public school (or have finished his high school years by the American equivalent), and then will proceed straight on to the study of law. Lectures are given in each subject.[8] In England the student does not learn law by means of the 'case-book' or 'hornbook' method. Here he is given lectures on leading cases, the principles to be explained by the lecturer as well as his reason for citing the case and its importance to English law. A student may, if he so wishes, read in a casebook, but such reading it not necessary for his professional examinations, and most students do not spend a great deal of time reading additional and superfluous law cases. One distinguished teacher at Cambridge told me that he tried to introduce the American method of teaching into the law faculty, and that it met with polite non-acceptance. He returned, some years later, to lecturing, pure and simple, about law.

If the student here wishes to come to the Bar it is

not necessary for him to possess a law degree from a college. All that is necessary is for him to pass his bar examinations, parts one and two, and if successful in those parts, he then enters for one academic year at the Inns of Court School of Law (which is a function of the Council of Legal Education) to study, what are called in England, his 'practicals'. When he completes his academic year (beginning in late October, a vacation at Christmas and then at Easter, with term ending in April or early May) he then sits his final bar examination. Generally areas of criminal and civil law will be covered during the course of the examinations; some practical procedure will be covered, as well as family law, trusts, equity, and tax law. It is a modest examination by most standards for the American Bar. When he succeeds in this final of his three previous examinations (generally one year awaits the taking of each examination, although the Council will permit one to sit the first part of the tripos in June, and then in September for the second part, and then one year later, after attendance at classes, the final part in May) he will be called to the Bar by his own Inn, and then, for the next year he will remain in 'pupillage' to a barrister, accompanying his 'master' to court in order to learn more about the practical aspects of the law.

It is not an unreasonable course of study if one remembers that there is no necessity for a candidate to have spent four or more years first in the pursuit of an academic degree unrelated to law, as one is required to do in the United States. With some college tuitions in the United States reaching to the

332

$5,000.00 to $6,000.00 mark, plus the cost of living expenses (books, food, lodging, clothing, leisure expenses), a young man in England (or an older person for that matter who wishes to enter the Bar later on in life after having pursued some other profession) is saved the cost of anywhere from $40,000.00 to $60,000.00 (or the family, most likely, of the son or daughter are saved that pressing amount).[9]

At this point an English critic (if I may be permitted to construct one) looks at American college education and states that it is costly, and is needlessly so. It is to be admired that the British government will pay most of the cost of college education of a student by means of a student grant (tuition to a college plus monthly living expenses), and a parent will only be called upon to contribute to the expenses *if* the family can afford to do so. Some local authorities (who would be like county or parish districts in the United States) will give educational grants to those who do not wish to attend college but who do wish to prepare for the Bar. It is highly sensible and equitable. From this side of the Atlantic one finds it hard to understand (and it must be part of a national temperament just as to be phlegmatic is part of the English temperament) that a country as inventive as the United States is in so many ways, cannot yet perceive the contradiction that it is able to fund a department of defence in 1976 with a defence budget in excess of $111 billion dollars, but is not able to remove a true hardship from the shoulders of American families by extending college grants to families. Even land-grant universities which are supported by means of state taxes are expensive if one has to board at them; furthermore, they tend to have a surfeit of applicants.[10]

When an American student enters an American law school he generally is possessed of a first college degree (which was expensive to obtain) and even a second degree, and then he prepares to begin a three or four year study of law, itself expensive. He has to take entrance examinations, the worth of them which a number of critics have questioned, some holding that entrance examinations after one is possessed of a college degree is either a holdover from the conservative and dubious corporation practices from the middle '50s to have men 'tested' at every rung of the corporate ladder; or it is some mass sorting method to 'select' but not to require a law school to be responsible for whom it admits. One can always fault the pre-selection test for not selecting well. On the other hand the pre-selection tests may simply admit those who do well in pre-selection tests, and the value of that accomplishment may be as if we admitted only doers of *The Times* crossword puzzles to the Bar!

The casebook method never did fare well in England, as I said earlier; but it did not fare well because it did not command respect. I can recall, a number of years ago, listening to an English judge lecture to an American law faculty during a seminar. He openly blasted their assumptions, and exuded legal charm from every pore. He asked his American hosts why they wasted all of that time discussing, in a

334

non-directed way, law cases with callow, even if intelligent, youths? When he had finished firing at casebooks (which he seemed to think served little purpose save to reveal the workings of pedestrian minds — he could say this because he had authored the leading books in his field of the law in England) he then proceeded to take aim at the 'silly' courses in American law schools, i.e. 'lawyer and client relations' or 'legal negotiations with insurance adjusters'. At the end of his lecture — or blitzkrieg, depending upon what side of the fence one sat — a very chastened faculty began to ask questions. They were bothered, annoyed, irritated, affronted, and, strangely, perplexed into thinking about much of their legal style and manner. To one questioner, who espoused the terribly expensive method of requiring candidates to have a first college degree before they could undertake the study of law, he seemed to suggest that American education must be a terribly expensive waste and baby-sitting service if it could not, as was done in England, prepare a man for mature study by the time he was seventeen or eighteen, and then he concluded by giving his impression of what a young lawyer ought to be, 'We are not concerned at the Bar about how brilliant a young man is. We are concerned that he learns the law, takes his time, represents his client adequately, and takes his place in line until he takes silk, and we judge that this process takes upwards of fifteen years'. It was a devastating criticism to make to a faculty member who had assumed that law review had prepared one for an early Supreme Court

335

practice, and it was heresy even; but it made us all think; I daresay, even seriously.

The English ideal is rather much to call a student to the Bar at an early age, to give him a moderate preparation in law, and then to let the Bar itself educate him. This is a wholly sensible view, especially of a society which views law as a practical subject. If one who is called to the Bar wants to know more about his subject he is free to join other honourable societies, for example, the Selden Society, which publishes ancient renaissance and Elizabethan law texts, and in this way he may come to acquire a lasting historical knowledge about common law. But to do so in order to be called to the Bar so that he can practice is not needed, and would be looked upon as unpractical, and not the least as an expense which it would be hard to justify. The Bar, being older than the United States, and certainly as old if not older than most religious communities, can speak with the wisdom of age and lasting survival. If its way of life had been so foolish or impractical or tenuous over these centuries then one would have expected to find a great deal of foolish legal writing from the Bench, and, for the most part, this has not been found or produced.

It may be fashionable to criticise for it is often said that the critic produces nothing. Criticism of this kind ought to be avoided. What might be done, a wedding of the best of both worlds at law, would be to attempt this when teaching students law. One would lecture once or twice a week during a term on the principles and leading cases (say) of criminal law, and one would explain to his students why these cases are of importance to them. No doubt, in a long span of time they could discover why, but that seems to fly in the face of reasonable expectations. One could, perhaps, re-discover how a light bulb were made, but why? At the end of a fortnight one would take that matter upon which he had been lecturing, and over which tutorials had been held, and prepare a short examination, on a Friday, perhaps, so that one could correct his scripts over the weekend. On the following Monday one would discuss the tests, showing why some succeeded and then explaining why others had missed the mark. A teacher would by the simple method gain an impression both of what his students were acquiring, and how he was succeeding. The tutorials could be used to encourage research papers in broad areas, and one could have two or three of those done each term.

The fortnightly examination serves a wise teaching purpose. Most who fail examinations, apart from sheer inability, fail because they do not know what is to be expected from them. As students they are possessed of bits and facts of information, but they are not possessed of patterns and shapes. They have not written books of any type (a novel, a play, a critical study) and they have not that kind of knowledge which comes from having created a work which is whole and entire. The fortnightly examination may be an easy remedy for an obvious illness. It provides a picture, and it prevents self-deception on both sides. The student comes to see whether he is grasping legal principles or not, and comes to know

337

this in a short space of time; the teacher comes to see how clear are his lectures, and tutorials, by reading how they are reflected in test questions which a student submits. In England, for most major examinations (annual examinations), external readers* are called upon to read the scripts. We do this because we believe that it stops testing from becoming too private or whimsical an art. The standard of success is what the scholarly community judges it to be; while in the United States, at a law school, the standard is what the teacher of the course sets it to be. When one makes clear to his students what it is he expects, and, by extension, what the discipline itself expects, then learning and understanding may occur. Not to voyage into psychological predictions, nevertheless I am impressed at what an examination is supposed to do to a student. From a piece of behaviour, his answers to the questions, he is taught to reinforce his own character by internalising the grade or mark or stigma he receives. I am judging this to be an 'A' or 'B' script, and there it should stop. But it does not. He then internalises this mark and becomes the 'A' or 'B' student, as if to become a predestined soul in society. The model for testing in this situation is punishment, the higher the grade the lesser the punishment. On the other side I am suggesting that we should advance curative and medical models. We should help the student come to understand, and we should guide him by showing how to express what he understands.

The ideal to which a teacher ought to aspire is twin

---

* From other universities.

complimentary concepts, that of 'to understand' with 'to learn'. One who succeeds in producing a unity from a division (giving the pattern of the law from its millions of particular case incidents) is more the artist than he is a person guided by some rule or command. There is no easy rule to guide practical reasoning, as there may be a rule for addition, or subtraction, or logical entailment. One wants a student, who is a novice to legal reasoning (and a novice to living), to come to understand what legal reasoning is, in its various modes, and one also wants a student to learn how to use examples in case law in much the same way that an artist will use colours from his palette, not to put splotches of paint on to the canvas, but to put the paint on to the canvas in forms. I have often thought that it is unfortunate that criminal law, torts, and contracts are taught in the early years of law school; they should be taught in the last year when one has been able to draw upon some legal past he has so as to appreciate how rich those subjects are.

When we get older we seem to suffer from selective inattention to the obvious. If one observes how small children will play with puzzles we can learn a great deal, simply, about learning. If the puzzle, or toy, is something which has many parts to it and which requires much muscular co-ordination to put together, the child will at first try, and then, afterwards, grow cross that he is not succeeding. He is cross because he does not like to fail (he has succeeded with his other puzzles, so why should he enjoy now failing with this one?). A simple colour puzzle, as a collection of cardboard animals that can be easily assembled by associating one general colour with an animal (the hippo will be green while the tiger will be yellow), will send a child happily on his way, and from it he learns. His curiosity is aroused, he wants to show you and tell about his puzzle, and he will even 'teach' you how to construct animals from the pieces. But give the same child a terribly complicated assembly kit, one of those plastic piece sets from which cars, trains, planes, or just 'assembled things' can be made, and he may become upset. He notices, for instance, that the toy easily breaks, or that it is hard to assemble. The little slots are difficult to push together, or what he assembles is not clear to him (it has no name other than 'thing'), or he is stymied by what he is supposed to do (since he has no fund of knowledge or vast experience to draw upon), and soon he is angry and frustrated and crying. With little knowledge or experience he cannot confer new names upon his objects because he cannot even see what is before him as an object which should receive a name. He may confer a name, this is 'gloobla', but the name signifies little more than the immediate pattern; it does not convey the pattern.

How many law teachers see themselves as 'professionals' not wanting to take time to teach? The model seems to be that their duty is only to transmit sets of facts, as they themselves had been subjected to such transmissions when they were students. But that is just one step away from the 'teaching machine'. If, on the other hand, the model for the law is to understand, then one is not after a machine; one is seeking after reasoned understanding, a form of seeing into what is the case, and what could be the case. To use the machine model of learning is not to appreciate legal experience as one knows it to be in a court. The whole of the appellate process is to reveal how a problem is seen and then solved. Can one imagine that a student during a final examination would be able to give a satisfactory answer to the *Quinlan* case?* The conclusion may be simple to state in a tautological form: either she will live or die. But the concept of 'to be permitted to live or die' alters the tautological form. What does one mean by 'to permit'. Into what conceptual hierarchy of legal and jurisprudential notions is that concept to be understood? One court said one thing, whilst another court says another. If the appellate process is one of discovery and of seeing, why then should legal learning be less than that? What would prepare the first year student, either in criminal law or in criminal

---

* *In the Matter of Karen Quinlan,* Supreme Court of New Jersey, A-116, September Term, 1975, argued 26 January 1976, and decided on 31 March 1976, on appeal from Superior Court, Chancery Division, 137 N.S. Super. 227 [1975]. It was argued that Karen Quinlan was an alleged incompetent, and the issue before the State Supreme Court of New Jersey was a difficult issue. The Court itself, speaking through Hughes, C.J., said (page 2), 'The central figure in this tragic case is Karen Ann Quinlan, a New Jersey resident. At the age of 22, she lies in a debilitated and allegedly moribund state at Saint Clare's Hospital in Denville, New Jersey. The litigation has to do, in final analysis, with her life – its continuance or cessation – and the responsibilities, right and duties, with regard to any fateful decision concerning it, of her family, her guardian, her doctors, the hospital, the State through its law enforcement authorities, and finally the courts of justice.' (My own discussion of this case is forthcoming in Vol. 51, 1976, of LAW & JUSTICE [published by the Plowden Trust, 51 The High Street, Hampton, Middlesex, England], and will appear under the title of 'PRIMUM NON NOCERE').

procedure, to discuss that case adequately during a final examination? The opinion of the New Jersey Supreme Court extends to fifty-nine pages, and was a reserved judgment (it was heard in January, and then decided in March). Or, upon matter as complicated, how would the beginning student, in his final examination, be expected to answer the *Edelin* case?†

The division between the learning of the law and the practice of the law may be akin to the conflict which types of reasoning present us. There are some who can reason only by an appeal to distinctions, and they produce a wealth of distinctions, almost mathematical-like in precision. But there is another form of reasoning which seemed to have included itself in our common law traditions, and it is the reasoning which attends to the particular. A distinction which the Reverend Georg Florovsky once produced in a lecture (1961) on orthodox religious thinkers was to assert, and it may have been his artistic impression of history, that what separated the West from the Orthodox thinkers of the Eastern religious tradition was that the West began with the abstract concept of God and of the Trinity, and then decended to talk about Christ, while the East began with the fact of Christ's existence, and then proceeded to talk about the Trinity and God. In much the same way if we return to the Middle Ages we see that the common law method developed during a time when case to case

---

† *Commonwealth v. Kenneth Edelin,* Commonwealth of Massachusetts, Supreme Judicial Court for the Commonwealth, Suffolk County, December Sitting, 1975, No. 393, will be argued in the latter part of 1976. The brief for the defendant is one hundred and sixty-five pages long.

reasoning was not popular. The various marriage rotas* found it necessary to fit the particular into pre-existing theological formulas. The facts were to fit into a distinction. But this is not case law (however much of this method, sadly, does find its way into modern family law). Case law is concerned about the particular *qua* particular, and the particular is not merely an instance of an enfleshed universal. There is something about a set of particulars which is more than a string of predicates (as we would produce in a proposition which deals with universals). The teacher tries to show his student how to see, and he also shows him that there is something to see. But this seeing ought to be placed within appellate practice. If the courts do not give answers (if they did, then why need we have review procedures) primarily why then must the student be told that he is to give an answer primarily? He may advise, he may form judgments (as do courts), but all of this comes after developing an ability to see and to perceive. [11] The annual examination may present good examination problems; but good examination problems may not make good lawyers simply because the process of the law does not work on the answer model. In English courts the process of law is an audile model: one reads to a judge, one tries to present a cogent

---

* cf. *Compendium totius tractatus de s. matrimonii sacramento* by Thoma Sanchez (Coloniae Agrippinae, 1624), or *De sancto matrimonii sacramento disputationum tomi tres,* same author (in three volumes, Lugduni, 1690).

Also cf., Diaz de Luco (Juan Bernard), *Practica Criminalis Canonica* (Lugduni, Apud Theobaldum Paganum, M.D.XLIII), as well as Galdericus Galinus, *Compendium . . . verae practicae Criminalis* (MILAN, Apud Iacobum Lantonum, 1621).

verbal argument, one tries to enable the other to 'see' in this way, one engages in discussion, and one tries to press home some model he has of what the particular is, and how it ought to be seen as *this* particular within the body of the law. One does this day in and day out; one does not do it but once a year for a few hours during the heat of a final examination, as if from a scene in *The Paper Chase*. One can see how a moot may thrive on the examination problem, but there, even, one is hearing various sides of the issue, one is listening to advocates try to create their side, one is observing a judge (or judges) ask questions of counsel, and one sees that an 'answer' is not easily forthcoming. If it is, then the question is trivial.

I have dwelt at length on law teaching. I do not think it employs good models, and I think it has not learned much from its past. One guest from an American university who was installed on the Cambridge law faculty for a year, told me that his colleagues did not favour departing from the standard examination models. They were not wont, generally, to substitute research papers for examinations. If there be a problem it may be a simple one: the life of an institution which is removed from the law, as are schools of law, may generate models of what law is which, in practice, are models of what the law is not.

Our common faith in the common law may be to hope that it can continue to solve human problems. We may also be asking too much of common law processes.[12] If the normal processes in a society begin to faulter, then the law is called upon to do

344

more than it reasonably should do. One need only review the pressure under which the Supreme Court was put when it was called upon to decide against (then) President Richard M. Nixon in *U.S. v. Nixon.* It is easy for us to turn the process of the legal arbitration, finding a rule under the law (or, in restricted cases, filling in the legal blanks left by the legislature), into the process by which we replace normal law-making procedures. The legislature begins to leave larger and larger blanks, and the courts then have to fill them in more and more.

What we need at the present time is to return to the roots of the common law and try to make a system available to more equitably so. The cost of litigation is crippling now for most persons (corporations may not find it so) and this should not be so. The cost of a legal education is now entering into the sphere of the wealthy only, and this serves to defeat what our democratic experiment was about. What we need to try for again is simplification, and for us this may be difficult to do. We spring from a culture which is taught to consume and taught to replicate and taught to waste and taught to be vulgarly ornate; why should we assume that such methods of consumption and such ways of waste will not infect our institutions? State institutions tend to view themselves as private institutions differing only in that they gain their support from the state. Most large state law schools refuse to adapt to the needs of their communities (such as by opening night law schools, or making creatively flexible programmes of study) and are offended, if I may personalise an institution, that they are asked to do 'less than the best'. They never spell out what the best is, and oftentimes they have a very false model of what it ought to be.[13] We do not follow the careers of law graduates that closely to relate what they did fifteen years ago in Federal Procedure actually was of help to them later in this particular case at the United States District Court. But yet we talk as if it did, while in fact we are only believing it did. A belief *may* be knowledge, but then again it may not be knowledge in any way.

We may have found it hard to come into this century. We have video cassettes, and we seldom use them. Most of the lectures of finer law professors have been lost to the wings, rather than having been preserved on tape for a student (and teacher too) to use. We seem to believe in face-to-face contact with lectures, why then not preserve what they have had to say, and use it? Why can we not make our appellate courts centres of learning, putting them in ampitheatre shape so that students could listen to cases for one or more terms, in the same way that surgeons learn how to operate by watching surgeons in the ampitheatre, or from closed TV circuits? We could set up centres where law lectures were given, and we could advise students to use bar libraries which are in most city centres (the Inns of Court libraries are working bar libraries; they are not research facilities for graduate study). How much time must a student spend at a library? Would that not depend upon what kind of study and work we should think it would be best for him to do? Do we want him to read endless lists of cases, or do we want

346

him to begin to learn at an early age in his career how to prepare legal briefs and research documents? I do not mean legal writing, pure and simple. I mean legal research. Can what he is doing now be of help to him when he prepares to enter a court? or give an advisory opinion? We do not need to build costly large law schools with costly re-duplicated law libraries. For whom are those monuments built? Librarians may like to see large libraries, but how necessary are they for the beginning student? Do we expect him to be an encyclopaedia of the law? Once while at dinner in my Inn I asked a Law Lord, who visited our table after dinner, if many had appeared before him in the House of Lords who held a legal rank of less than a Q.C., Queen's Counsel? He said that he remembered one occasion when a non-Q.C. had appeared before them, but he was a very senior junior. If we set our models lower, assuming that a beginning lawyer will first appear in the lower courts and will deal with simpler problems, we might be able to graduate more law students. Yes, there will always be the unusual occasion when a young lawyer might appear in a High Court, or at the State Supreme Court, but the chances of this happening are more like wins from the Irish Sweepstakes than like the regularity that night follows day. In England one's law clerk would be most careful not to let a young barrister fly higher than he should; if he failed, his failure would harm him and his client. Why create casualties?

The American legal scene has come under considerable criticism, but I think much of the criticism has been too wide of the mark, and I realise that this is only a personal judgement on my part.[14] I think what both critics fail to understand is that the difficulties of the American legal system spring rather much from the costliness of the system, and from its inordinate desire for perfection. If the schools which teach law would make their entrance requirements much simpler (exclude a first college degree as a ticket for admission), and if simpler law schools were set up on the English model (like the Council of Legal Education in London of the four Inns of Court), one might find that the costliness of litigation might be halved because there would be more lawyers to handle litigation. But if the aim is to create a false restriction by having unreal standards of perfection then the American legal experience will always be one of costliness and scarcity, and that is good capitalist economics. But justice ought not to buttress an economic system, even though Marxists would advance the notion.

I may have been indulging the reader in an exercise of my own aesthetic preferences in this chapter, and my own aesthetic beliefs as to what I think are problems both in the teaching of law and the problems which the law faces now. (One does know that our common law system is facing grave difficulties, and one need not belabour the point.) I have found the solution to be in a return to simplicity, something which often I believed was fundamental to the ninth Amendment of the Constitution. One takes one side or the other; he believes that a work (of any kind) is organic, and that it has a certain natural unity, or he believes that the work is composed of a

348

series of unrelated complexities which can only be resolved *deus ex machina,* where, from on high, a deity, or avenging angel, or power moves in to lift up the hero from the complexities he himself does not understand. A student during his early period of law school may see the case law in just that way, and he may then leave law school and see legal problems in just the same way, in the end only to be solved by the Supreme Court flying down to save its people by imposing a decision from on high.* Or, like a Greek tragedy, one may believe that a solution will arise from out of the complexities in the case because the complexities are a reflection of the organic unity inherent in the actor or events he generates or encounters. The wisdom of the common law is that it worked well within the limits of the human condition. Simplicity does not preclude or exclude perfection; it tempers perfection to make it human, and thus humane. The genius of the English experience is that it works well with little. We do not demand that our students, in order to prepare themselves for living, spend endless years in graduate schools, all so costly, to certify themselves fit for life. The *Wizard of Oz* proclaimed a marvellous truth when it lampooned the need for 'certificates' when the Wizard conferred them upon the Tin Man, and the Cowardly Lion, and the Scarecrow. He was wise as a wizard to recognise that what they wanted

---

* *Roe v. Wade,* 410 US 113 and *Doe v. Bolton* 410 US 179 certainly have to them the ring of *deus ex machina* however popularly approved those decisions are. cf. *The New Law Journal,* 11 March and 18 March 1976, 'Abortion: A Logical Oddity'.

had always been within them; he could not give them courage, or a heart, or a brain. We might have more mature men and women in our culture if we gave them the chance to be mature at a younger age, and did not, as we do, subject them to endless years of school and endless hurdles until we set them free to be adults. John Marshall, who attended law lectures in 1779 which Chancellor Wythe gave at William and Mary, was then licensed to practice in 1780. He did not fare badly as a young advocate! Many of our judges and barristers in England never read law, or even studied it formally, but the common law was and is none the worst for it. It may be time now, if we wish to be true to the spirit of the common law, to leave the model of the Germanic school where we stuff our students full of information like a farmer stuffs a Strasbourg goose. We may need to return to simplicity and to eschew extravagance. Simplicity has always been present in the workings of our common law whether we knew it or not. What then could be more revolutionary?

J. M. B. Crawford, A.B., M.A., Middle Temple.
May 1976

REFERENCES

[1] *The Gray's Inn Moots* (LONDON). Printed by Walbrook and Co., 14 Whitefriars Street, 1896. The preface.

[2] The moot is appended to the close of this chapter.

[3] cf. *John Marston of Middle Temple* by P. J. Finkelpearl (Harvard University Press, 1969), esp. Part 1, chapters I-VI.

[4] *Roman Law and English Jurisprudence Yesterday and Today.* An inaugural lecture by Peter Stain (Cambridge University Press, 1969), pages 12-13.

[5] cf. 'Law in the Liberal Arts' by R. D. Abbott, *Canadian Legal Studies/Les Etudes Juridiques Au Canada*, Vol. 1, No. 3, May/Mai, 1966, published by BUTTERWORTHS, Toronto.

[5a] On jurisprudential matters, cf. *The Concept of Law* by H. L. A. Hart (Oxford, 1961) and *Concept of a Legal System* by Joseph Raz (Oxford, 1970). For a fundamentally legal approach, cf. *The Elements of Law* by Thomas E. Davitt, S.J. (Little, Brown and Company, Boston), in the Law School Textbook Series. Also cf. Davitt's *The Nature of Law* (St. Louis and London, 1951) for a Thomistic approach to legal theory.

[6] *The Commentaries, or Reports, of Edmund Plowden, of Middle Temple, Esq.*, in two volumes, LONDON, printed by S. Brooke, Paternoster Row, 1816, from the preface, volume one, pages iii-vi.

[7] Middle Temple Archives on the Inns of Court School of Law. Pollock, of course, wryly criticised 'paper examinations' as I indicated at the opening of this chapter.

[8] cf. *Report of the Committee on Legal Education*, Cmnd. 4595 (LONDON, Her Majesty's Stationery Office, March, 1971) as chaired by (then) the Honourable Mr. Justice Ormrod, esp. the *Appendices*, pages 100-243, for a picture of courses given by the various institutions for preparation in law, as well as a comparison with other non-legal professional qualifying requirements. Also cf. 'The Graduate School of Law, Soochow University, Republic of China' by Robert E. Tindall, appearing in THE INTERNATIONAL LAWYER, Vol. 7, No. 3, July 1973, to see how the more expensive American system of study travelled to China when the university was established at Soochow in 1900. I say 'more expensive' because the student needed to be possessed of a first college degree which was most likely not related to law at all. Why is this needed?

[9] *International Herald Tribune*, Paris edition, 8 April 1796, 'Major Rise in Tuition, Charges Set at U.S. Colleges This Fall' by Gene I. Maeroff, at page 3.

[10] One wonders if *DeFunis v. Odegaard*, 40 L Ed 2d 164 [1974] would have reached the United States Supreme Court if the state university system of Washington had not been over-taxed?

[11] cf. Chapter 4, 'Precedent', pages 56-83 in *The Judicial Decision* by Richard A. Wasserstrom (Stanford University Press, Stanford, California, 1961).

[12] TRB (*The New Republic*, 10 April 1976, Washington, D.C.) observes that *Hills v. Gautreaux* (then pending before the U.S.S.C.) and *Milliken v. Bradley* (July 1974, decided 5-4 by the Court) may be examples of problems which the law cannot solve, but should have solved: namely, complicated racial problems. Also cf. *Dockers' Labour Club and Institute Ltd. v. Race Relations Board* [1974], 3 A11 ER 592, where the House of Lords overturned the Court of

Appeal (Lord Denning, M.R., Stamp and Scarman, L.J.J.) and held that a dockers' club (of which there are many in England) could limit as guests whom it would, even if a large class of individuals would not be admitted as guests. The members, associates, and guests who attended the club were not a 'section of the public' within s. 2(1) of the 1968 *Race Relations Act*. The decision was a classic 'damned if you do; damned if you don't' case. Also cf. *New Law Journal*, 17 July 1975, address to *Justice* by the then American Ambassador, Hon. Elliot Richardson, who suggested in his annual address to the Society at Lincoln's Inn, that the aims of the individual and the aims of the society as a whole seem to be putting marked pressures upon the legal system to resolve the conflicts which these competing aims can generate, and that recognising this is now a present duty of the common law.

[13] cf. *The Price of Perfect Justice* by Macklin Fleming, Justice of the Court of Appeal of California (Basic Books, Inc., New York, 1974) who demonstrates rather effectively in his book what harmful consequences are generated by the mistaken notion of 'perfection' at all costs in the administration of the law, and how such a notion makes the common law administration imperfect. It is an interesting paradox.

[14] cf. *Judicial Administration: The American Experience* by Delmar Karlen (LONDON, Butterworths, 1970). Also see 'The Special Skills of Advocacy' by Warren E. Burger, Chief Justice of the United States (The Fourth John F. Sonnett Memorial Lecture, Fordham University Law School, November, 1973).

---

23 November 1896,
Gray's Inn Moot Society

Question:

Several of the leading tradesmen in a country town form an association for the protection of their common interests. It is agreed among other things that any member may be excluded by a majority of the members. It is understood, but not formally agreed, that no member will employ a clerk or shopman who has been discharged by another member within a year. A, a member of the association, discharges one of his clerks, Z. Shortly afterwards Z applies to P, another member, who takes him into his employment. A, after consulting the other members, and with their consent, informs P that if he does not forthwith discharge Z the association will exclude P from membership.

P protests, being of opinion that A's reasons for discharging Z were not well founded, but, finding that the other members persist in their intention, discharges Z with due notice.

Has Z any right of action against A and the members of the association other than P?

ARGUED BEFORE SIR FREDERICK POLLOCK, Bart.

LEGAL L

A Map showing the INNS of
those LEARNED in the LAW · Wi
The CHURCHES · COLLEGES & I
HOTELS · TAVERNS · & other pl
the ROYAL COURT.